Star Trek's Philosophy of Peace and Justice

T0244273

Star Trek's Philosophy of Peace and Justice

A Global, Anti-Racist Approach

José-Antonio Orosco

BLOOMSBURY ACADEMIC
LONDON • NEW YORK • OXFORD • NEW DELHI • SYDNEY

BLOOMSBURY ACADEMIC
Bloomsbury Publishing Plc
50 Bedford Square, London, WC1B 3DP, UK
1385 Broadway, New York, NY 10018, USA
29 Earlsfort Terrace, Dublin 2, Ireland

BLOOMSBURY, BLOOMSBURY ACADEMIC and the Diana logo are trademarks
of Bloomsbury Publishing Plc
First published in Great Britain 2022

Cover design by Ben Anslow
Cover image: Starship Enterprise, "Star Trek-The Motion Picture", 1979
(© Glasshouse Images / Alamy Stock Photo)

A catalogue record for this book is available from the British Library.

A catalog record for this book is available from the Library of Congress.

ISBN: HB: 9781-3502-3679-0
PB: 9781-3502-3680-6
ePDF: 9781-3502-3681-3
eBook: 9781-3502-3682-0

Typeset by Deanta Global Publishing Services, Chennai, India
Printed and bound in Great Britain

To find out more about our authors and books visit www.bloomsbury.com and
sign up for our newsletters.

Contents

Illustrations

Acknowledgments

Sunday nights were always special when I was growing up because it was time for *Star Trek*. My mother and I would watch the local newscast on Channel 4 and then prepare for a rerun of *ST: The Original Series*. For the next hour, I was transported into a magical world that would come to shape my imagination for the rest of my life. Those stories, I now recognize, gave me a thirst for philosophical reflection about the nature of humanity and our possibilities for building a better society. My mother nourished this fascination by buying me *Star Trek* books, comics, and toys and encouraging me in all forms of science fiction. I owe my enchantment with *Star Trek* to her, and I am sorry she is not around to appreciate this book.

My academic interest in *Star Trek* began after I started using it to teach ethical issues. I am grateful to wonderful colleagues and mentors, such as Terry MacMullan, Kevin Decker, Randy Millstein, Chryss Allaback, Walidah Imarisha, Andy Fiala, Greg Moses, and Tony Vogt, whose work stimulates my understanding of how science fiction can be a crucial tool for thinking about how to solve the world's problems. I also want to thank my student assistants over the years, Robyn Morris, Brianne La Bauve, and Mohammed Shakibnia, who have helped me to bring *Star Trek* and its lessons to my classes. I also want to thank audiences at meetings of the Concerned Philosophers for Peace, as well as at Rose City Comic Con, Wizard World Comic Con, and Oregon State University for important feedback on ideas and, most importantly, encouragement to write about peace and justice in the Star Trek Universe. Thanks also to my editor at Bloomsbury, Jade Grogan, for all her insight and assistance, as well as the anonymous reviewers who provided excellent feedback. Any errors or shortcomings in the work remain entirely my own.

Much of this book was written during the first year of the Covid-19 pandemic. This moment of enormous human suffering was also punctuated by the eruption of demonstrations around the world protesting the murder of George Floyd by police. These events, along with crises of unprecedented wild fires across the Western United States, and political violence and insurrection in the United States, preoccupied much of my thinking while I worked out these ideas on the future. They reinforced my belief that the kind of social transformations we need to confront all these problems has to be grounded in hope, imagination, and solidarity with one another. I want to thank my lifelong friends—Alan Bahm, Paul Bustamante, and Phillip Giarratano—who were all important for conversations, care, and fun during this time. Finally, I am ever grateful for the support of my family—Sophie, Marta, James, but especially my wife, Theresa, who reads everything with a critical, yet encouraging, eye. Her ability as a writer inspires me to be better. Best of all, she tolerates me when I tell her I've bought one more *Star Trek* uniform for my collection.

Introduction

Star Trek and the Philosophy of Peace

"We come in peace . . . isn't that the whole idea of Starfleet?" Michael Burnham asks her commanding officer, Captain Philippa Georgiou, in the series premiere of *Star Trek: Discovery*.[1] The conversation between Burnham and Georgiou, which opens the episode, encapsulates the utopian ideal of a human civilization committed to peace and justice that has long been the hallmark of the *Star Trek* Universe (STU).[2] For more than fifty years, the STU has distinguished itself among popular science fiction franchises by presenting an idealistic vision of a future in which human beings have overcome war, poverty, hunger, and greed, and set off as explorers, rather than conquerors, of the galaxy. Peace has always been central to the mission of Starfleet and the stories that *Star Trek* has to tell.

Star Trek's unique portrayal of humanity is the focus of much popular and scholarly study. Along with numerous *Star Trek* fan websites, conventions, podcasts, holiday cruises, and university classes, there are dozens of books investigating the physics, metaphysics, biology, ethics, political theory, economics, and religious themes within *Star Trek*.[3] This book seeks to join the tradition of scholarly examination of the STU. My starting point is the view that *Star Trek* "embeds complex scholarly arguments within images and stories that are widely accessible."[4] Many of its episodes are moral fables that grapple with complex real-life ethical concepts and debates. I agree, at a minimum, with philosopher Judith Barad that we can develop better understandings of some of these ideas, and of our own moral principles, by studying how *Star Trek* stories frame and resolve these moral dilemmas.[5] However, I argue in this book that the STU articulates a unique and powerful philosophical perspective on the ideals of peace and justice, one that tackles some of our most entrenched social problems and offers sophisticated guidance for the progress of humanity into the future.

In the following chapters, I analyze how *Star Trek* episodes illuminate the meaning of certain concepts, theories, and controversies within the field of peace studies. This is an academic discipline dedicated to understanding the meaning of concepts such as peace, war, violence, and justice. Its theoretical frameworks attempt to identify the social, political, and economic obstacles to these ideals while also imagining the social action and policies required to realize them in practice. So, on the one hand, this book can be used to familiarize students with issues and theories within peace studies, since it discusses how *Star Trek* episodes illustrate the significance of various debates within the field as it currently stands. But, on the other hand, I actually think the moral fables in the STU call on us to do more than just study how peace and justice are discussed in the world today.

I maintain that *Star Trek* urges us to be more critical about contemporary society by presenting a vision of humanity, and of a more just and humane future, that compels us to achieve it. The STU vision of the future is one that puts a radical anti-racist, egalitarian, post-colonial, and environmentalist message at its core. In order to achieve something like the world of the Federation, we will need to foster a philosophy of peace and justice that supports political action to dismantle structural racism, and to envision new forms of power and collective decision making that confront social, political, and economic inequality today. *Star Trek* is not necessarily a blueprint for a utopian future, but it can highlight aspects of the horizon to which we can aspire, highlighting new values and inspiring new ways of relating to one another and to the natural world. Thus, *Star Trek* episodes demonstrate important concepts within peace studies, but the STU articulates a particular image of what it will take to build a more just future for humanity that robustly challenges the field to take on radical positions about social transformation.

Let me first begin with an account of the history of the discipline of peace studies and how its utopian aspirations run parallel to the vision of humanity presented in the STU. I will then analyze why in this particular historical moment utopian ideals are markedly relevant. Millions of people across the globe are currently experiencing frustration with their political, social, and economic institutions. Many are seeking ways to understand their feelings through books and films that have a particular dystopian edge to them. I believe that science fiction, and especially the stories embedded in the STU, can be valuable tools to nourish the imagination of people seeking change. These tales can help us to think carefully and critically about the efforts needed to build a more just and humane future for all human beings.

What Is Peace and Justice Studies?

ST: DISC begins with the story of a self-appointed Klingon messiah named T'Kuvma. For years, T'Kuvma witnessed the disintegration of the mighty Klingon Empire into squabbling factions. At the same time, the multispecies Federation continued to grow and start to encroach on Klingon borders. In the first season episode, "The Battle of the Binary Stars," T'Kuvma gathers the great houses of the Klingon High Council and warns them that a violent confrontation with the Federation is morally required according to their codes of honor. The Federation, he cautions, will mouth the phrase "We come in peace," but what it really wants to do is eradicate Klingon culture by assimilating it "into the muck, where Humans, Vulcans, Tellerites, and filthy Andorians mix." For T'Kuvma, the Federation's dedication to peace is just cover for galactic imperialism by other means, and he convinces the great houses to initiate a devastating war against the Federation.

T'Kuvma's mission is driven mostly by his xenophobia and egoism, but he does embody a common misperception in our own society today. This is the view that says that peace is what weak nations talk about when they want to appease more powerful and aggressive nations into not attacking them. Peace, in other words, is for cowards, or for fools who do not understand the realities of power. T'Kuvma is willing to gamble that the Federation's talk of peace is ultimately a sign of its weakness in the face of a united Klingon force. He is almost correct in his assessment. In the span of a few months after his war begins, Starfleet loses almost a third of its fleet, and the Federation home worlds are on the verge of destruction. In desperation, the Federation engages a plan that will result in the genocide of the Klingon race. However, Commander Michael Burnham and the crew of the *Discovery* rebel at the idea in the episode "Will You Take My Hand." They force the Starfleet leaders to realize that a victory at such a cost is morally abhorrent and contrary to their whole mission. The Klingon-Federation war concludes when the Federation finds its way to really live up to its principles and not just give lip service to the ideals of peace and justice. As Burnham says at a Starfleet ceremony marking the end of the war:

> No, we will not take shortcuts on the path to righteousness. No, we will not break the rules that protect us from our basest instincts. No, we will not allow desperation to destroy moral authority. . . . We have to be the torchbearers, casting the light so we may see our path to lasting peace. . . . Yes, that is the United Federation of Planets. Yes, that is Starfleet.

ST: DISC, then, is one of the latest *Star Trek* installments that illustrates how the STU is deeply devoted to the view that humanity flourishes when it pursues the ideals of peace and justice. *Star Trek's* utopian vision about peace is one that resonates deeply with the aspirations of human communities from time immemorial. As literary theorists Gregory Claeys and Lyman Sargent point out, utopianism—or what they call "the various ways of imagining, creating or theorizing about alternative and often dramatically different ways of life"—is contained in some of humanity's oldest written records and myths.[6] Many of these stories explicitly connect alternative societies to the expectation of peace and the cessation of war and violence.[7] More recent important theorists in peace studies, such as Nobel Prize winner Jane Addams and Mohandas Gandhi, have also tied their understandings of peace to notions of social progress, believing, like *Star Trek's* creator, Gene Roddenberry, that as humanity evolves war will come to be seen as a regressive trait.[8]

Without a doubt, the narrative DNA of the STU also aligns with the value commitments of the academic discipline called peace studies. This field is broadly interested in two aims: (1) understanding the meaning of peace, justice, and the causes of war and conflict; and (2) finding ways to transform social, political, and economic structures that will reduce, if not eliminate, most forms of war and violence, and create the foundation for justice and human rights.[9] In that sense, peace studies is not an academic field that is content merely to theorize about the nature of peace and conflict in the world today. It is not interested in knowledge merely for knowledge's sake. It also aspires to be an activist practice that uses its research and findings to bring about a more peaceful and just world through institutional change.[10]

The academic examination of these utopian peace ideals and their impact on political, social, and economic policy is something that arose in the early twentieth century. In the aftermath of the First World War, political scientist Quincy Wright began the Study of War Project in 1926 at the University of Chicago in an attempt to provide an interdisciplinary understanding of war and how to prevent it.[11] Yet, it was the Second World War—one of the single most destructive conflicts in human history—that really generated interest in the formal study of peace. Many colleges and universities housed courses on peace and war in their political science or international relations departments at this time. But the first undergraduate academic program devoted specifically to peace studies was developed in Manchester College in Indiana in 1948.[12] Peace and justice programs continued to crop up, especially after the Vietnam War and in response to the Cold War in the 1970s and 1980s. In 2008, there were over four hundred international programs offering degrees in peace studies.[13] The Peace and Justice Studies Association lists close to three hundred peace studies programs in the United States alone, offering a range of degrees from two-year associates to PhDs.[14]

It seems significant that the field of peace studies is born in the aftermath of the Second World War—a conflict generated by the rise of vicious fascism and that ended with the display of awe-inspiring military technology in the form of atomic weaponry. The exhaustion with political terror, and the fear of the possible extinction of the human race, compelled the great consolidation of what historian Kent D. Shifferd calls the "global peace system"—an interlocking network of international organizations, technological advances, and cultural changes—that advanced an ideal of world peace and security for the future.[15] An important foundation of that peace network was the adoption of the United Nations Universal Declaration of Human Rights (UDHR) in 1948.[16] This document—consisting of thirty articles spelling out the civil, political, economic, and social rights of all human beings—represented an effort by a global consortium of scholars to define the value principles by which the United Nations could "maintain the peace of mankind and, as it maintains peace, to make ever more full the lives of men and women everywhere."[17] While the UDHR is not legally binding on the member states of the United Nations, it serves as an important intellectual touchstone about the importance of protecting the civil and political rights of individuals and guaranteeing socially just economic and cultural provisions. Many of its articles have been built into national constitutions and a variety of covenants, conventions, initiatives, and treaties, including, most notably, the Convention on the Prevention and Punishment of the Crime of Genocide (1948), the International Convention on the Elimination of All Forms of Racial Discrimination (1965), and the International Criminal Court (2002).[18]

Peace studies, then, comes about at a historical moment in which there was great international fervor about constructing a global order in which the diversity of humanity can be united around common value commitments of peace, freedom, equality, and the dignity of each human being. While thinkers from Dante in the 1300s to Kant in the eighteenth century had all long dreamed of world government putting an end to war, the twentieth century actually had in place the international institutions that could begin to make it happen.[19] It's not surprising then to notice how much that the flag of the United Federation of Planets—the multicultural union of space faring species in the STU—is so closely modeled on the flag of the United Nations. Both institutions represent the human aspiration for living in a world of peace, cooperation, and justice (Figures 1 and 2).

Figure 1 Flag of the United Nations. *Source:* Wikipedia commons.

Figure 2 Flag of the United Federation of Planets.

Even though war, oppression, and human rights violations persist today, some seventy years after the creation of the United Nations, this impulse for global cooperation continues to inspire utopian social dreaming in politicians, peace theorists, and activists. For instance, former dissident and then Czech Republic president Vaclav Havel, writing in the aftermath of the genocidal Balkan Civil Wars in the 1990s, reaffirms his hope that humanity can rise to the challenge of "understanding itself as a multicultural and multipolar civilization, whose meaning lies not in undermining the individuality of different spheres of culture and civilization, but in allowing them to be more completely themselves."[20] Human rights historian Richard Falk encourages us to endure on a quest for what he calls "humane governance," a normative project that posits "an imagined community for the whole of humanity" in which "difference and uniformities across space and through time are subsumed beneath an overall commitment to world order values in the provisional shape of peace, economic well-being, social and political justice, and environmental sustainability."[21] Peace theorist Elise Boulding urges us to use our imagination to envision a future that builds upon the past accomplishments in peace work: "The challenge is to draw on the best of the hopes and the best of the learning skills, and the relationship building, networking, and coalition forming skills that have developed in this past century, so that that long term future may yet birth new cultures of peace."[22]

Yet, perhaps the most significant example of utopianism influencing peace and justice activism in the twentieth century comes from the Civil Rights Movement in the United States. Many Trekkies are familiar with actor Nichelle Nichols's story about how she found out that Dr. Martin Luther King, Jr., was a fan of *Star Trek*.[23] It was one of the few shows he allowed his children to watch on network television. He told Nichols, who portrayed Communications Officer Uhura on *ST: The Original Series*, that he greatly admired the way the show represented a racially diverse future in which prejudice and discrimination on the basis of skin color and heritage were things of a distant past. But the utopian hopes embodied in the STU had long sedimented in King's philosophical formation, even before he saw the show.

In 1952, a young Coretta Scott gave a 23-year-old Martin Luther King, Jr.—the young man who was courting her—a copy of Edward Bellamy's book *Looking Backward 2000-1887*. Bellamy's book is a work of speculative fiction, depicting a socialist United States in which peace and economic and racial justice prevail. King told Scott that he was deeply impacted by the possibilities portrayed in the novel. He wanted to devote his life's work to such a vision:

> Let us continue to hope, and pray that in the future we will live to see a warless world, a better distribution of wealth, and a brotherhood that transcends race or color. This is the gospel that I will preach to the world. At this point, I must thank you a million times for introducing me to such a stimulating book.[24]

Moreover, Reverend James M. Lawson—one of the people credited with teaching Martin Luther King, Jr., about the theory of nonviolence—confirms that these utopian hopes were more than just incidental to this struggle for racial justice in the United States. He says that at the core of that fight for Civil Rights Movement was the ideal of each African American activist as a "citizen of a country that does not exist" but that could be brought into existence through community organizing.[25] It is no coincidence, then, that King was such a massive fan of *Star Trek*. His life's work inspired some of the most significant forms of collective political action in the twentieth century all around the world, and it was clearly nourished by visions from speculative literature. Such a background gives King's most famous public speech a new resonance. In his "I Have a Dream Speech" from 1963, King exhorted the nation to imagine along with him a more just society. He understood that working toward racial justice in the United States required more than political statements and mobilization. It required political imagination nourished on utopian dreams. As legal scholar Drew Hansen puts it: "Political argument against segregation was valuable, but it was only a beginning. Imagination, as well as reason, needed to be renewed. By telling the audience about his vision of a nation healed of the sins of racial discrimination King began the process of bringing that new nation to life—if only, at first, in the minds of his listeners."[26]

Peace in a Polarized World

We also live at a time in which there is a craving all over the globe for reflection and speculation on social values and utopian thinking. Since 2016, there has been an enormous increase in the popularity of dystopian and alternative history literature in the United States— the kind of stories that ask readers to imagine worlds characterized by rampant oppression, alienation, and despotism.[27] Yet, the United States is not alone in this growing fascination. There is evidence of growing popularity of dystopian/speculative literature in China, Latin America, and Africa.[28] The Covid-19 pandemic has only fueled interest in gloomy films about societal collapse because of a disease outbreak.[29] Part of the reason for this fascination in alternative futures might stem from a need to daydream away from a not-so-happy reality. Yet, I think that something else might be going on than mere escapism.

Dystopias are often keen and sophisticated reflections on the social, political, and psychological developments of modern society. The key to most of them is that they focus on the failures and frustrations involved in attempting to achieve social perfection.[30] Think of a classic such as George Orwell's *Nineteen Eighty-Four*, which attempts to show the limits of bureaucratic communism, or more recently, the television series *Black Mirror*, which demonstrates how technology that is thought to make our lives easier can quickly turn them into nightmares. This does not mean that dystopias are inherently nihilistic or intended to erase all hope for the future. As intellectual historian Gregory Claeys argues, the major point of dystopian works is to help educate our imaginations about the range of our possible futures so that we then might create better alternatives than the ones portrayed in dystopia.[31] In other words, our fascination with dystopias is ultimately an indication that we desire to picture and build better utopias—worlds in which our social, political, and economic institutions function much better to care for people's well-being, and for human flourishing, in general.[32]

Research on the political attitudes of young people in the United States demonstrates a yearning for this kind of education of the imagination. Not only is dystopian literature popular among young adults today but they also tend to be much more politically aware and engaged than previous generations. US Americans[33] between the ages of 18 and 25—often known as Generation Z—show an unprecedented willingness to engage in electoral politics, voting in record numbers in the 2016 and 2020 US elections.[34] But interestingly enough, they are not particularly interested in joining traditional political parties, such as the Democrats and the Republicans.[35] In fact, many of them believe these parties are controlled by elites who do not really respond to the interests of voters. Instead, young people are doers—they are more likely to join organizations that advocate around particular issues, such as gun control, climate justice, or reproductive justice, than they are to join a political party organization. Research in the European Union, Latin America, and Africa indicates similar patterns of young people withdrawing from formal political parties into more issue-oriented, or grassroots, organizations or to social media activism.[36]

Young people are also somewhat idealistic in that they are drawn to talk about wholesale reform or transformation of traditional political and economic institutions. The majority of Generation Z and Millennials (ages 25 to about 35) in the United States are willing to entertain ideas of abolishing market capitalism and building alternative economic institutions in a way that previous generations would never consider.[37] Young people in Latin America and Africa are also interested in increasing participation in politics, particularly of indigenous peoples and women, through new forms of technology and creating more transparent deliberation practices to root out endemic corruption.[38] It is clear that young people today would like to build a better world by imagining new values and forms of politics. However, it is also the case that young people are quite frustrated with the political status quo. Many in the United States feel there is something fundamentally broken about US American democratic institutions and social values.[39] Large pluralities of them do not feel that life in the United States will improve within a decade. Yet, they have hope that the political life of the nation will get better sometime in the future—they are pessimistic about their immediate present but hopeful about the future.[40] They join millions of peoples worldwide who increasingly feel committed to democratic principles and values but believe their current political institutions and leaders are failing them.[41]

In her book *How to Start a Revolution: Young People and the Future of American Politics*, Lauren Duca confirms many of these findings in the United States. As a columnist for *Teen Vogue*, Duca travels and talks to many young people about their interests and political aspirations. She notes that the election of Donald Trump to the US Presidency in 2016 awakened many young people to realize that national politics were not distant phenomena that had no bearing on their lives but processes of decision making that directly impact their everyday existence. However, she finds that many of these bright young people flounder as "activists without the activism": people with a lot of political passion but unaware of how to turn that energy into civic engagement.[42] Duca recounts a 2018 meeting of young people at the Granger Leadership Academy—an organizing institute put together by the Harry Potter Alliance (HPA), an international organization that uses the magical universe of the Harry Potter world to inspire political activism—in which she got a glimpse of their imaginative creativity and yearning to find guidance for their own lives. These fans found inspiration for their own political activism in the hero journeys of characters in the Harry Potter universe. This made Duca realize how her own journey to political agency was influenced by her father reading *The Hobbit* to her as a young girl. She learned not to settle for the status quo in politics and to understand that political gatekeepers are not the only ones who wield ultimate power.[43]

I believe that Duca's encounter with the HPA encapsulates the craving of young people all around the world today to have some kind of imaginative guidance for their aspirations. They are eager for change and are willing to upend political and economic institutions that seemed untouchable just a few generations ago. But they are not sure with what to replace these structures or how to map out the steps to make these alternatives a reality. They seek future utopias to draw them out of their dystopian present.

Science Fiction, Political Imagination, and Social Activism

So why might science fiction, in particular, be helpful for nurturing our imagination to picture radical possibilities? First, it's important to get clear about what science fiction is, especially compared to other related art forms already mentioned, such as fantasy. There are numerous definitions of science fiction, but literary theorist Darko Suvin offers a popular one: "A literary genre whose necessary and sufficient conditions are the presence and interaction of estrangement and cognition, and whose main formal device is an imaginative framework alternative to the author's empirical environment."[44] The notion of "cognitive estrangement" is important to capturing the idea of imaginative space opened up by science fiction. Suvin believes science fiction intentionally immerses us in a world that appears strange in order to make us feel out of place, and to jar our usual associations and beliefs about how the world works. The feeling of alienation and distance from the present moment, then, is key for the genre.[45]

Yet, this sentiment is not quite enough to distinguish science fiction from other forms of speculative literature, such as fantasy or horror, which also evoke cognitive estrangement. Theorists Fred Miller, Jr., and Nicholas Smith specify that science fiction usually presents the world as a setting that is primarily knowable through reason and the use of the scientific method, rather than through magic or divination. Whereas fantasy often takes place in worlds far removed from ours (J. R. R. Tolkein's Middle Earth or George R. Martin's Westeros) or in secret worlds hidden just below our reality (J. K. Rowlings's Hogwarts), science fiction usually assumes a universe with the same basic foundational structures of reality as our own. Stories can then create cognitive estrangement by extrapolating from current scientific, technological, or cultural trends into a future world, or by speculating about how the world might look different through the intervention of some significant scientific, technological, or cultural events that radically transform the present. In *Star Trek*, for instance, science and the rules of physics work basically the same as they do for us, but technological development has allowed for faster than light space travel and limitless food and resource production, creating a world with very different possibilities than our present reality.

According to some literary theorists, the sense of alienation embedded in science fiction stories allows them to accomplish aims that other literary genres cannot. For instance, Brooks Landon thinks that science fiction has an inherent agenda: "Science fiction is not just a literature of ideas or of 'thought experiments' but also somehow points to or promotes better thinking."[46] Esther Jones adds that "the critical thinking and agile habits of mind prompted by this type of literature may actually produce resilience and creativity that everyday life and reality typically do not."[47] Ericka Hoagland and Reema Sarwal clarify that this agenda is a philosophical one: science fiction traditionally encourages examinations of the human condition that are driven by "an overwhelming desire to understand who, and what, we are."[48] In other words, by encouraging cognitive estrangement, science fiction encourages us to reflect about what is actually real, valuable, and important in comparison to the speculative world. Understood in this way, science fiction shares intellectual goals with philosophy, in that both aim to inspire critical self-examination that can hopefully lead to better lives and social relationships. As the science fiction writer Ursula K. Le Guin reflects: "Our thoughts and our dreams, the good ones and the bad ones . . . it seems to me that when science fiction is really doing its job that's what it's dealing with. Not the 'future.'"[49]

Philosophy has long privileged logic and reason as tools, but as philosopher David Kyle Johnson points out, imagination is also a capacity on which philosophers rely.[50] From Plato's Allegory of the Cave to more recent inventions such as John Rawls's Original Position, Robert Nozick's "experience machine," and Phillipa Foot's Trolley Problem, philosophers have often relied on narrative mechanisms called "thought experiments" that use fictional settings to test our intuitions and principles for ethical decision making. For some philosophers, such as David Hume or Immanuel Kant, imagination is integral to ethical thinking; the capacity to be a moral agent for them depends on the ability of a person to imagine and interpret the emotions of another or to envision a complete world in which one's own desires and yearnings form its rational structure. Indeed, some contemporary philosophers such as Mark Johnson argue that ethical thinking is just a kind of imaginative contemplation of the metaphors that frame our lives.[51] Mary

Warnock concurs about the importance of imagination for philosophical work, holding that imagination is that capacity "which enables us to see the world, whether present or absent as significant, and also to present this vision to others, for them to share or reject."[52]

While philosophy instructors often use science fiction stories simply as teaching devices to illustrate certain moral perspectives for students, it is also possible to talk about science fiction as a kind of philosophical discourse.[53] That is, science fiction can also help define concepts, put forth claims about what ought to be important or valuable in our lives, and present images of possible worlds that activate and educate our imaginative capacity—a capacity that is a key ingredient in being able to think about the requirements of an ethical life and developing resilience in the face of oppression and crisis.[54] Again, Le Guin ruminates on this power of science fiction, explicitly mentioning *Star Trek* as an example of the kind of storytelling she admires:

> The imaginative fiction I admire presents alternatives to the status quo which not only question the ubiquity and necessity of extant institutions, but enlarge the field of social possibility and moral understanding. This may be done in as naively hopeful a tone as the first three *Star Trek* television series, or through such complex, sophisticated, and ambiguous constructions of thought and technique as the novels of Phillip K. Dick . . .; but the movement is recognizably the same—the impulse to make changes imaginable.[55]

Indeed, I think imaginative fiction can even do more than nurture our imagination, train us in critical ethical thinking, and build resilient attitudes (as important as all those things are). There is evidence that it has the power to inspire the building of social movements and to affect ideas about proper forms of political activism. For instance, Shelly Streeby points out that Rachel Carson's *Silent Spring*—the book that almost singlehandedly generated the modern environmentalism movement— begins with a piece of speculative fiction that asks readers to imagine a world devastated by some kind of unseen blight. Inspired by *Silent Spring*, numerous scientists went on to organize and to begin a series of lawsuits that eventually lead to the formation of the Environmental Protection Agency in 1970.[56] More recently, protestors from Ferguson, Missouri, as well as from Hong Kong and Thailand have all incorporated slogans and symbolism from *The Hunger Games* films to express anger at authorities and indicate solidarity with one another.[57]

In addition, political scientists Calvert Jones and Celia Paris have conducted several studies to investigate whether dystopian stories impact people's ideas about social change. They find that exposure to dystopian fiction can make people feel that violence and revolutionary upheaval are justified in the face of oppression. This effect is more pronounced than even showing test subjects violent, fast-paced but nonpolitical movies or exposing them to news footage of actual protests against injustice.[58] Jones and Paris caution that the dystopian fiction craze might motivate us to guard against forms of injustice today, but it also could encourage violent extremism as a solution to complex problems.[59] They recommend that we need take fictional narratives very seriously in the shaping of contemporary political ethics and imagination.

Why Is *Star Trek* Important Now?

So many people today, particularly young people around the world, seem to be hungry for stories that speak to their hopes for a better world and they are turning to speculative fiction to nourish their imaginations. But why turn to *Star Trek*, in particular, to find the visions that reimagine systems of governance and new paradigms of social relationships which young people crave? After all, as writer Brianna Rennix points out, *Star Trek* is renowned, even by some of its fans, for being, at worst, "campy," "sugary and insubstantial," "preachy," or at best, a collection of tales suitable for children but not to be taken as seriously as the modern dystopias that seem to speak to specific elements of our gritty times.[60]

Political theorist George Gonzalez, on the other hand, maintains that the STU deserves serious political consideration. In his view, the STU is made up of science fiction stories that, for the most part, present a coherent philosophical position on the conditions of justice.[61] While I do not necessarily hold Gonzalez's philosophical assumptions about the STU, I agree that *Star Trek* episodes present matters of peace, violence, war, and justice that enable us to understand the complexity of these issues in our world better. More importantly, they help us to think about what it will take to construct a more just and humane future.

That is because the tales of STU, while presenting a utopian future, are really stories about surviving the apocalypse. The STU's setting in the 23rd and 24th centuries does indeed depict a post-scarcity world in which there is no money, no commodities, and no forced hierarchies of class, race, gender, and so on that prevent people from pursuing self-realization.[62] But it is a world that is achieved after much hardship, collective struggle, and the near extinction of the human race. The STU, then, comprehends the anxieties of our current era, but it does not rely on the kinds of easy solutions to problems that concern scholars of dystopian fiction.

How is *Star Trek* dystopian? The 20th and 21st centuries in the STU are depicted as times in which the world is devastated by authoritarianism, global wealth inequality, nuclear war, and genocide. In the *ST: TOS* episode "Space Seed," for instance, we learn that unfettered genetic technology in the late 20th century led to the creation of a group of enhanced human beings called the Augments. This group went on to take political power all across the globe and to subordinate most of humanity to their capricious wills. After a destructive rebellion, in which some 30 million people died, the Augments were overthrown and exiled into space. The instability created after this Eugenics War exacerbated global wealth inequality. Protests and violent riots wrecked governments in Europe and North America, as seen in *ST: DS9* episodes "Past Tense: Parts I and II." Global insecurity and legitimation crises then contributed to a nuclear confrontation, World War III, in the mid-21st century, killing some 6 million human beings. To make things worse, a military leader, Colonel Phillip Green, arose to commit a genocidal purge of people with radiation poisoning, murdering some 37 million people (*ST: TOS* "The Savage Curtain and *ST: ENT* "In a Mirror Darkly, Part II"). The film *Star Trek: First Contact* (1996) shows us that the end of the "post atomic horror" period only came about because Zephram Cochrane, an eccentric engineer and scientist, invented warp drive technology in 2063, allowing us to travel in space faster than light. His invention attracted the attention of an alien race, the Vulcans. They established diplomatic relationships with humanity, ushering in the beginning of the *Star Trek* utopia as we now know it.

For *Star Trek*'s creator, Gene Roddenberry, a menacing future as the backdrop to *Star Trek* was important because such a setting allowed for stories in which humanity activates some of its most important traits.

Roddenberry often mused that humanity is a "childish" race lacking maturity, but we have an amazing ability to learn from our mistakes and grow wiser as a species.[63] Human history contains numerous eras of scientific and technological development, but human history for Roddenberry is really the story of human *moral* progress. George Gonzales attempts to illustrate this idea by reconstructing the historical time line depicted in the STU leading to the formation of the Federation. Various *Star Trek* episodes mention the American Revolution, the US Civil War, and the fight against fascism in the Second World War as central world historical events. Gonzales then continues the time line to include *Star Trek* dystopian events, such as the Eugenics War, the Bell Riots against inequality, and World War III. In this way, we see that the STU is the story of the progressive maturation of humanity as it deals with, and resolves, social, political, and economic crises.[64] Along this journey, Roddenberry believed humanity would learn how to value diversity in different forms of life and to hone our capacity for what he called our sense of "basic human decency"—the resistance to harming others and the need to nurture and care for one another—into a more sophisticated ethical attitude that would permeate all our major social institutions.[65] Indeed, in one of the most famous *ST: TOS* episodes, "The City on the Edge of Forever," Captain James T. Kirk points out that one of the most influential novelist of the 21st century will promote this ideal strongly and influence the ideals of the Federation: "'Let me help.' A hundred years or so from now, I believe, a famous novelist will write a classic using that theme. He'll recommend those three words, even over 'I love you.'"[66]

Thus, I think *Star Trek* is important for us today as we search for narratives to build our imaginations not simply because it paints a hopeful future to which we can aspire but because it illustrates an ethical path toward it, navigating through a not particularly hopeful near future that is just a few decades away. The STU is about human beings learning to become fully committed to tolerance, openness, curiosity, equality, and peace. Most importantly, it says this is a real possibility because we have already accomplished some of the historical steps on this evolutionary journey. *Star Trek* is like other science fiction in that it is about the wondrous possibilities within technology and scientific knowledge to change human life. Yet, I think what makes *Star Trek* unique and important is that it projects a possible future based on our ethical potential. Our utopian future is grounded in the moral accomplishments in resisting tyranny, building democratic forms of life, and fighting racial caste slavery and fascist authoritarianism that we have already made up to this point. Our world today is not the utopia of Starfleet and the United Federation Planets, but Roddenberry wanted us to believe we have, within our ethical repertoire as human beings, the ability to overcome the worst dystopias imaginable. Author David Garrold, who was responsible for writing one of *ST: TOS's* most memorable episodes "The Trouble with Tribbles," described this idealism this way:

> It was as simple as this: men and women who cared looked around at the ruins of Europe and Asian, the disaster that WWII had inflicted on the world, and had slowly, painfully come to the realization: "We have to do better than this. We have to be better than this." Star Trek wasn't the only expression of this idea . . . but Star Trek was the most accessible and the most popular expression of the idea that the future can be a better place.[67]

Plan of the Book

In the chapters that follow, I analyze different *Star Trek* episodes and films, spanning over fifty years of television and movie history, in order to show how they help us to better understand the concepts, theories, and controversies within the field of peace studies. More importantly, I want to demonstrate how *Star Trek* provokes us to imagine the work we need to do in order to build the more just, peaceful, and humane future it exemplifies.

In Chapter 1, I begin with the commonly held opinion that human beings are prone to war and violence because human nature is fundamentally aggressive and competitive. Such "realism" about human beings is often taken to support the idea that working for peace is an idealistic endeavor at best, or perilous at worst, since such efforts fail to comprehend the dangers inherent in our very natures. After all, if aggression and violence are essentially all we are capable of as a species, then why bother trying to work for peace? I consider several *Star Trek* episodes that seem to support this realist position that I call the Enemy Within Ideal. These episodes suggest that aggression is an important part of human nature and that this component of our psychological drives is a necessary and integral part of good leadership and well-being.

Yet, I maintain that the Enemy Within Ideal overstates the role of aggression in human nature. I contrast it with a second perspective that I draw from other *Star Trek* episodes, which I call the Situational Ideal. This view says that violence in human beings is less a matter of some inherent drive but a reaction to stressful environments. The work of social psychologists, such as Stanley Milgram and Phillip Zimbardo, suggests that ordinary people can be driven to engage in immoral action if they are placed in highly regimented circumstances, such as prisons, that constrain their choices and emphasize hierarchy and violence as a means of social control. Moreover, the recent work of archaeologists and anthropologists suggests that warfare, or organized group violence, is a rather recent occurrence in human civilization. Even if aggression and competition are inherent parts of human nature, the Situational Ideal demonstrates that war is not something that has always been part of the human story, and it does not have to be so in the future.

In Chapter 2, I examine the view that the best way to define violence is as physical harm, intentionally inflicted on a person by another person. This is undoubtedly one kind of harm, but the STU encourages us to complicate this understanding of violence in order to be able to prevent more violence in the world. *Star Trek* suggests that a better way to grasp the complex nature of violence is with something like the lens of the "pyramid of violence." This is a notion developed by one of the founders of peace studies, the Norwegian sociologist Johan Galtung. He distinguishes between three distinct forms of violence: personal, structural, and cultural. According to Galtung, violence is often thought to be a case of one individual intentionally harming another. But in many cases, that kind of "personal violence" is really the result of other underlying kinds of violence. Personal choices to be violent are often conditioned by how social-political-economic systems are structured (structural violence) or by the way cultural norms and traditions justify the harm inflicted on some groups (cultural violence). In other worlds, personal violence is often a momentary surface occurrence that erupts at the top of the pyramid as a result of underlying structural and cultural violence that simmers in the foundations of society for a long time.

Thinking of violence in the world in this way, I argue, aligns with the views of major theorists of nonviolence, namely Martin Luther King, Jr., and Cesar Chavez. Both these philosopher-activists point out that this framework enables us to understand much better a form of social disruption that is common today in our dystopian present, namely social unrest and riots. These events are rarely just a matter of scattered individuals trying to cause property destruction, or harm to each other, because of criminal intent. That opinion ignores, more often than not, that riots are circumstances that explode because of unjust social/economic arrangements and cultural narratives that allow grievances to be ignored and oppression to be continued. *Star Trek* story lines testify to the fact that comprehending violence only in terms of personal violence makes developing solutions for the prevention of war, violence, and oppression much harder.

If we agree that war, violence, and aggression are features of the world we want to either eliminate or at least reduce, then we need to learn how to work together to accomplish those goals. But is it possible to have no war and little violence in society and still not inhabit a world worth living? Dystopian novels, such as *Brave New World*, warn us about the possibility of a future full of pleasure, satisfaction, and no war or violence. But Huxley was adamant that such a world was one that we would not want to experience. What, then, does a really peaceful and just world look like?

In Chapter 3, I examine several episodes that help us to envision the contours of a truly peaceful and just world. I argue that the way to understand these different story lines is with US philosopher Jane Addams's distinction between negative and positive peace—a distinction which has become a core foundation of peace studies. Negative peace usually means a reduction or elimination in violence and war, while positive peace refers to a society with the presence of human rights, economic and political justice, and a commitment to sustainable relationships with the natural world. I suggest that one way to understand the meaning of this distinction is to use philosopher Martha Nussbaum's human capabilities approach to define the elements of positive peace. Her work helps us to articulate the different aspects of what we might want to call a full flourishing life for human beings.

This distinction raises a problem, however. The reduction, or elimination, of violence and war is important, but this can be pursued without a serious commitment to human rights, meaningful political participation, or a sustainable relationship to natural world. It is possible to imagine, for instance, a totalitarian regime accomplishing high levels of negative peace (by cracking down on dissidents, massive surveillance, and posting police everywhere, for instance) but not providing its inhabitants any say in their society or protecting their rights. Should we be compelled to intervene somehow or to aid people who find themselves in a society without positive peace? The answer to such a question has obvious implications for how we might respond to human rights violations in the international sphere today, including our understanding of policies such as humanitarian intervention and the United Nations' Responsibility to Protect doctrine.

Many of the world's conflicts stem from oppression or discrimination against social groups on the basis of different racial, cultural, or ethnic identities. This has led some theorists to think that the way to peace is to construct a world in which such identities no longer exist or are no longer salient. At the same time, some of the most important civil rights movements in the past hundred years have come from oppressed groups who strongly identify with, or want to protect and preserve, some racial or ethnic identity. In thinking about justice, should we seek a world in which people are blind to different social identities, or should we seek a world in which people hold onto, are proud of, and celebrate their social identities?

In Chapter 4, I examine this debate by considering three ideals about the role of race in modern democratic societies that are presented in the STU: the Colorblindness Ideal, the Multicultural Ideal, and the Critical Anti-Racist Ideal. I maintain that critical antiracism is the better position to take in this debate. This ideal is embodied by three characters in the STU: Captain Benjamin Sisko from *ST: DS*, Commander Chakotay from *ST: VOY*, and Cristobal Rios from *ST: PIC*. All these characters represent life in a multicultural future in which racial or ethnic background is a source of pride and celebration, as well as an important cultural resource for the betterment of society as a whole. The crucial question then becomes: How do we achieve a world in which people of historically marginalized identities can live in a world like the Federation? I argue that this multiculturalism is possible because the Earth of the Federation is an anti-racist and post-scarcity society with cooperative economics. It has eliminated conditions for resource competition that buttress racial hierarchies and group subjugation—the kind of world recommended by the work of Black critical race theorists such as W. E. B. DuBois, Keeanga Yamahatta-Taylor, and Ibram X. Kendi. If the discipline of peace studies is indeed motivated toward a future like that of the Federation, then it needs to incorporate this kind of anti-racist social, political, and economic critique into its core set of concepts, theories, and political aspirations.

As long as there has been violence, there have been attempts to design social remedies to repair the aftereffects. Some of the earliest conceptions of justice in human civilization are attempts to define appropriate retribution to harm, and to short-circuit cycles of retaliatory violence and feelings of vengeance. Yet, moral reformers such as Christ, the Prophet Muhammad, and more recently Gandhi and Martin Luther King, Jr., reveal that retributive punishment of wrongdoers, or those who commit harm to others, is not an adequate solution to solving the prevalence of violence either. What values, then, can we use to repair and heal from violence, war, and group oppression and make future societies more secure?

In Chapter 5, I examine three different responses to this question presented within episodes of STU: the ideals of mercy, grace, and forgiveness. I argue that the ideal of forgiveness is the most promising way to think about what might work to heal from the aftershocks of violence, war, and oppression. My view is that the work of Archbishop Desmond Tutu in South Africa provides an excellent example of how to institutionalize forgiveness. The example of Tutu's Truth and Reconciliation Commission has inspired numerous other societies that have been wracked by social conflict to find a process that allows people to heal, not by forgetting the injustices inflicted upon but by helping them to imagine and build a future without hatred, vengeance, and endless retaliation.

While peace studies usually focuses on understanding and preventing war and the violence inflicted by human beings upon one another, more and more peace theorists are responding to the urgent message from scientists that human harm to the natural world threatens our existence as a species on this planet. How can we imagine alternative arrangements of society that are more environmentally sustainable and less likely to build conditions for more violence? In Chapter 6, I examine three different ideals presented in the STU for envisioning a less ecologically damaged future: the Ecosystems Service Ideal, the Biotic Community Ideal, and the Earth Democracy Ideal. I argue that the Earth Democracy Ideal, developed from the work of Vandana Shiva, is the most promising one for offering an ethical and political framework that can offset the historical and economic processes generating our most pressing environmental challenges. The Earth Democracy Ideal maintains that human beings need to conceptualize animals, plants, and the earth not as resources for human use and consumption but as living organisms that are due moral respect and political recognition from social institutions. I believe that more recent series within the STU put forth the idea that the just and humane future of the Federation depends on engaging with something like the Earth Democracy Ideal for guidance about environmental justice.

I conclude by returning to the idea of utopia and how, for many, *Star Trek* stands out as a beacon of hope because it holds onto utopian ideals even when much popular culture tends toward dystopian tales. For several political theorists, such as Karl Popper, Hannah Arendt, and Isaiah Berlin, the utopian impulse is not a benign one. Utopian ideals, in their opinions, are responsible for some of the worst violence in the twentieth century, namely the rise of Nazism and Soviet authoritarianism. I argue that the STU, particularly in more recent series such as *ST: DISC* and *ST: PIC*, provides a more sophisticated understanding of the idea of utopia than this. In my view, *Star Trek* is more akin to what Tom Moylan calls a "critical utopia." Moylan understands that "utopia" is not about a particular place or future to achieve, a destination at which to arrive, but as the name for a struggle to build a better world. Such an understanding of utopia, I believe, is one that we need now as we contend with our dystopian reality and yearn for practical ways to build flourishing lives in a world of peace and justice.

Chapter 1

Violence and Human Nature

The Enemy Within

Star Trek Episodes

ST: TOS: "The Savage Curtain"; "The Enemy Within"; "Miri"; "City on the Edge of Forever"

ST: TNG: "Tapestry"

ST: DISC: "Die Trying"; "Terra Firma I"; "Terra Firma II"

In March 1964, Gene Roddenberry shopped around a proposal for a science fiction show to television network executives. He sketched out a variety of episode ideas dealing with a starship named the *USS Yorktown* that would explore the galaxy under the command of Captain Robert April. Among the stories for this new series was one that Roddenberry titled "Mr. Socrates." It was the tale of the *Yorktown* finding a planet in which historical figures are recreated and placed into gladiatorial combat with one another. This story line sat dormant for a few years until it was picked up once again by Roddenberry to fill in a script for the third and final season of *ST: TOS*. In the new story, the ancient Greek philosopher Socrates is reincarnated, along with US president Abraham Lincoln, and both of them are brought to the *Enterprise*. Captain Kirk, Mr. Spock, Socrates, and Lincoln are then transported to a planet surface by a mysterious alien race and forced to battle treacherous villains, including Adolf Hitler, Atila the Hun, and Mr. Green, a fictional dictator from late 20th-century earth.[1] Screenwriter Arthur Heineman worked with Roddenberry to produce a script that eventually became the foundation for the episode "The Savage Curtain." They removed the character of Socrates, but the final product did, nonetheless, contain at its core a fundamental philosophical question: What is the difference between good and evil?

The struggle between war and peace, good and evil, is depicted in "The Savage Curtain" as a fight between different groups of people. Yet, speculative fiction often treats this tension as something that lies deep in the heart of individuals. Robert Lois Stevenson's 1886 novel *The Strange Case of Dr. Jekyll and Mr. Hyde* sets the modern standard with a story of one man who can transform his identity with the use of a magical elixir that releases his most violent inner impulses. The serum does not turn Dr. Jekyll into a monster, it merely liberates the evil monster that lies dormant and repressed within him. The impact of Stevenson's novel on popular culture is undeniable. We often talk about people with "Jekyll and Hyde" personalities, for instance. And the novel's influence on the STU is also evident when we consider two other episodes that attempt to represent the nature of the conflict between good and evil within individuals: *ST: TOS* "The Enemy Within" and *ST: TNG* "Tapestry." Together, these episodes suggest that aggression is a dark and inescapable element of human nature. It can be harnessed as a necessary and integral component for good, but untrained, it can be malevolent and disastrous. I call this perspective the Enemy Within Ideal.

In this chapter, I examine how the Enemy Within Ideal is one that is articulated and advanced by several philosophers, such as Thomas Hobbes and William James, as well as in the psychological theories of Sigmund Freud. It has more recent versions that focus on human genetics, concentrating on the markers within our DNA that lead to inborn tendencies toward domination and hostility. Yet, I believe that the Enemy Within Ideal overstates the primacy of aggression in human nature. This emphasis matters because the Enemy Within Ideal is often used to support the claim that war and violence is a feature of human life that is simply inevitable.

Peace studies, under this outlook, is a naïve endeavor because it fails to comprehend that we are simply hardwired for conflict and hostility.

I contrast then Enemy Within Ideal with what I call a Situational Ideal that holds that violence among human beings is less an inescapable result of some inherent drive but more a reaction to stressful environments. I find this message pronounced in the ST: TOS episode "Miri," It is a moral supported by the work of philosophers, such as Peter Kropotkin, and various social psychologists, such as Stanley Milgram and Phillip Zimbardo, who hold that ordinary people can be driven to engage in violent and even immoral behavior if they are placed in highly regimented circumstances—such as prisons—that constrain their choices and emphasize hierarchy and violence as a means of social control. Moreover, the more recent work of archaeologists and anthropologists suggests that warfare, or organized group-on-group violence, is not a universal feature of human cultures nor something that has always been part of our species' history. Thus, even if aggression is an aspect of human nature, the Situational Ideal gives us hope that war is not an inescapable horizon for our future since it has not always been a feature of our past. Violence can be avoided and should not be conceived as an impulse that merely waits, like the wild urges of Mr. Hyde, in the recesses of our soul to be let loose.

Star Trek Episodes: "The Enemy Within," "Tapestry," and "Miri"

In the episode "The Enemy Within," Captain Kirk is divided, because of a transporter malfunction, into two physically identical halves. One Kirk is paranoid and aggressive, drinking Saurian brandy openly in the hallways and violently attacking crewmembers, including his own yeoman, Janice Rand, whom he sexually assaults. The other Kirk is intelligent and compassionate, but also passive and undecisive. He lacks willpower and the ability to focus on tasks. Without Evil Kirk's antagonism, Good Kirk is not able to be an effective leader. The *Enterprise* crew is able to discover the transporter procedure to reunify the two Kirks at the end of the episode. Reflecting on his experience, the whole Captain Kirk remarks: "I've seen a part of myself no man should ever see."[2]

An opportunity to tell a similar story about the essential nature of humanity appears in the *ST: TNG* episode "Tapestry." Captain Jean-Luc Picard suffers a near-death experience because of an accident that affects his mechanical heart. He is miraculously prevented from dying because of a visit from his old nemesis, the super being Q. Picard is given the chance to travel back in time to his first days as a Starfleet officer when he was a rash and impulsive young man. He is allowed to alter his future by avoiding the bar fight that ended with him being stabbed and needing to have his organic heart replaced by a mechanical one. Picard, thus, restarts his career with the wisdom and forethought of his older self.

Q then flashes forward several years in the time line to show Picard what this less competitive and impulsive version of himself had accomplished. Instead of commanding the Federation flagship *USS Enterprise-D*, the more measured Picard remained a lowly science officer. After a frank conversation with Commander William Riker and Counselor Deanna Troi in this new time line, Picard learns that his superiors believe he has little chance of moving up the ranks. Q forces Picard to realize that his leadership ability evolved from his youthful aggression, much in the same way that Good Kirk understood he could not make command decisions without Evil Kirk's ambition. Picard is allowed to go back in time to the bar fight and get stabbed through the heart again, resetting the normal time line. He ends up with his life as a captain, now with the knowledge that he owes his good fortune, in part, to his wild and aggressive youth.

Both these episodes affirm what I term the "Enemy Within Ideal." According to this perspective, human nature contains two elemental impulses in a dynamic tension with one another. One of these impulses is an aggressive, competitive drive and another is a more rational, caring, and compassionate tendency. Put in the proper balance, these drives offer an individual the opportunity to fashion an exciting, heroic, and creative life. When Dr. McCoy realizes the existence of the two Kirks and their dependence on one another, he tells the Good Kirk:

> We all have our darker side, we need it . . . men, women, all of us need both halves . . . it's half our humanity . . . it's not really ugly, it's human. . . . Without the negative half you wouldn't be the captain.

The strength of command is mostly in him. . . . The mental discipline to keep it under control, that he gets from you.[3]

The implication, however, is that without intelligent authority over the aggressive drive, violence and destruction will ensue.

Another story line from the STU appears, at first, to support this understanding of the Enemy Within Ideal. In the *ST: TOS* episode "Miri," the crew of the *USS Enterprise* encounter a planet that is a mirror image of Earth. Except on this planet, Earth Two, a pandemic wiped out all the adults during the 20th century, leaving only the children. Kirk, Spock, and Dr. McCoy learn that the scientists of Earth Two were experimenting with viruses in an attempt to extend human life spans and accidently unleashed one into the atmosphere. The disease delays aging in children but kills anyone once they begin puberty. The group of children they find on the planet surface are really hundreds of years old. At first, the episode presents these children as an ominous presence. They continually hide in the shadows from the *Enterprise* crew, but they often taunt them, or pelt them with stones, and then disappear into dark corners. As the crew eventually contracts the virus and gets severely ill, the children steal their communicators. Kirk seeks the children out to negotiate with them for the return of the equipment but they beat him with bats and lead pipes instead. The scene appears to be something straight out of the ending of William Golding's 1954 novel *Lord of the Flies,* and the message seems to be the same: children left outside of civilized society, and without adult authority to guide them, will become brutal and irrational, unleashing the Enemy Within in dramatic ways.

The Peace Studies Debate: Is Human Nature Inherently Aggressive and Violent?

The Enemy Within View

This kind of depiction of human nature is most associated with English philosopher Thomas Hobbes (1588–1679). In his book *Leviathan,*

Hobbes begins by imagining the natural condition of human beings before government and codified laws, which he calls the "state of nature." For Hobbes, such a state of nature would simply be a dystopian hellscape. This is because of the basic facts of human psychology. Our behavior, according to Hobbes, can roughly be described mechanistically as either attraction toward objects (desire) or repulsion from objects (aversion). Our moral vocabularies are simply conventional ways of labeling these impulses. We call something "good" because we are attracted to something and wish to acquire it; we call something "evil" because it repulses us and we wish to get it away from us. Human action, then, is about getting the goods what we want, and neutralizing, or destroying, the evils we fear and hate. If I think something is good, I'm going to want to acquire it, unless the attempt to get it will make me suffer more evil than the good is worth to me. In the state of nature, without an overarching authority to guide behavior through laws and fear of punishment, there will be nothing to stop me from attacking you to acquire your goods and resources. Likewise, there will be very little incentive to trust and cooperate with one another in the state of nature. If I want something, nothing prevents me from lying to you to get it, especially if I think I can get away with the deception. Even if you find out that I broke my promise to you, it will be up to you to overpower me to set things right. Hobbes says that in such a situation, "every man is enemy to every man" since no one can clearly trust anyone or effectively defend themselves from all corners. The natural state of human life, then, is one of self-interested agents acting in ways that inevitably lead to disagreement, conflict, and violence:

> In such condition, there is no place for industry; because the fruit thereof is uncertain; and consequently no culture of the earth; no navigation, nor use of the commodities that may be imported by sea; no commodious building; no instruments of moving, and removing; such things as require much force; no knowledge of the face of the earth; no account of time; no arts, no letters; no society; and which is worst of all, continual fear, and danger of violent death; and the life of man, solitary, poor, nasty, brutish, and short.[4]

Even if human beings are fundamentally individualistic and self-interested creatures who will tend toward war if left to our own devices,

Hobbes does not despair. He believes human beings also possess reason and will realize that living in the state of nature is ultimately not in our best interest. We will seek to establish political authority that can guide our individual desires toward cooperation out of a fear of state repression. The role of the state, then, is to wield coercive force over a group of individuals who have agreed to coexist with one another for mutual benefit and protection. Peace, meaning the absence of war and conflict, is possible as long as government leaders know how to administer just the right amount of fear and punishment to make lying, cheating, stealing, or killing not worthwhile.

A more recent version of Hobbes's account of human behavior comes from psychologist Sigmund Freud (1856–1939). In 1932, Albert Einstein, working under the auspices of the League of Nations, initiated a letter exchange with Freud by asking him: "Is there any way of delivering mankind from the menace of war?" Einstein believed that modern science had reached such a point that warfare was not just destructive but potentially a threat to the very existence of humanity (and this before the development of the atomic bomb!). He told Freud that he had hope in the idea of a global government that could settle disputes between member nations and curb the violent tendencies of national elites to use war to gain profit for themselves.[5]

Freud replied that he shared Einstein's pacifist aspirations and personally found war to be repulsive. However, he did not believe it would be possible to suppress aggressive tendencies that often erupt into warfare. Psychoanalysts, he argued, had categorized human instincts into roughly two types: (1) an "erotic" drive that focuses on conserving, caring, uniting with an attractive object; and (2) a "death instinct" that focuses on destroying, killing, or repulsing an object that elicits disgust.[6] These were not the same as moral concepts, such as good and evil, according to Freud, and were not even really opposite impulses. The erotic and the death instincts could be complementary, as in the drive for self-preservation—one's care for oneself might require learning how to repel or kill threating forces—or in the case of protecting one's children—the drive to care might require learning how to defend through violence. These impulses were inherent in the nature of humanity, Freud postulated, and while he recognized attempts to stifle aggression through social policy, he thought this was a hopelessly utopian project: "The Russian Communists, too, hope to be able to cause human aggressiveness to disappear by guaranteeing the satisfaction of all material needs and by establishing equality in other respects among all the members of the community. That, in my opinion is an illusion."[7]

Like Hobbes, Freud did not despair because of the resilience of aggressive impulses. Instead, he argued that the pacifist strategy might succeed if it could find ways to divert or sublimate the death instinct, rather than try to suppress it. For instance, people could be trained to expand their sense of affiliation and care broadly, to encompass wider circles than just tribe or nation and, therefore, give the death instinct less room to operate. Or people could also be educated to use their intellect to better understand the enormous costs and disastrous consequences of pursuing war. This might prevent some people from supporting militarism. Both of these options, Freud observed, were long-term solutions since they required changing cultural mores and social expectations:

> And how long shall we have to wait before the rest of mankind become pacifists too? There is no telling. But it may not be Utopian to hope that these two factors, the cultural attitude and the justified dread of the consequences of a future war, may result within a measurable time in putting an end to the waging of war. By what paths or by what side-tracks this will come about we cannot guess. But one thing we can say: whatever fosters the growth of civilization works at the same time against war.[8]

Just decades earlier, American philosopher William James (1842–1910) had come to the same conclusions as Hobbes and Freud: we can't change innate human drives, so if we want to eliminate war, we better learn how to channel them. In his 1910 essay "The Moral Equivalent of War," James argued that pacifists fail to win people to their political program of world peace because they do not appeal to the ethical and aesthetic needs of people to the same extent that the "war party" does. Pacifists do not understand that most individuals have inherent needs to build meaning in their lives through what James calls the "martial values": courage, ambition, dedication to a cause greater than oneself, and the submission to authority.[9] Up until now, the best place for the fullest expression of these tendencies has been the military and in warfare. For James, the task is to find the "moral equivalent of war," that is, the way to harness aggressive energy and put it to use building up human society rather than destroying it. He recommends that the martial virtues be routed from the battlefield "to coal and iron mines, to freight trains, to fishing fleets in December, to dishwashing, clotheswashing, and window washing, to road building and tunnel making, to foundries and stokeholes, and to the frames of skyscrapers" so that young people can experience hard work and sacrifice and "get their childishness knocked out of them and come back into society with healthier sympathies and soberer ideas."[10]

Yet, what if it is the case that it is not possible to reroute these basic human drives successfully in the manner suggested by Hobbes, James, and Freud? What if the death instinct is so specific that it can only be satisfied by violence or experiences of combat and not in any moral equivalent of war? This is a possibility explored in the Academy–award winning film *The Hurt Locker*. The 2008 film portrays the main character (ironically named William James) as a US soldier who becomes addicted to the adrenaline rushes from combat after his experience in Iraq and is unable to transition back to civilian life. Researchers suggest such experiences might, in fact, be real, constituting a form of post-traumatic stress which has been named "combat attachment."[11] Journalist Chris Hedges argues that war has an addictive allure not just for military personnel but for all members of society. War has a unique way of bringing meaning to our lives: "Most of us accept war as long as we fold it into a belief system that paints the ensuing suffering as necessary for a higher good; for human beings seek not only happiness but also meaning. And tragically, war is sometimes the most powerful way in human society to achieve meaning."[12] Here, Hedges suggests that the martial values cannot be satiated through a national public works program, or sublimated by education, because our culture is thoroughly infused with the reminder that it is the thrill of war itself which puts us in touch with our true humanity in a way that nothing else can:

> I learned early on that war forms its own culture. The rush of battle is a potent and often lethal addiction, for war is a drug, one I ingested for many years. It is peddled by mythmakers—historians, war correspondents, filmmakers, novelists, and the state—all of whom

endow it with qualities it often does possess: excitement, exoticism, power, chances to rise above our small stations in life, and a bizarre and fantastic universe that has a grotesque and dark beauty. . . . Fundamental questions about the meaning, or meaninglessness, of our place on the planet are laid bare when we watch those around us sink to the lowest depths. War exposes the capacity for evil that lurks just below the surface within us all.[13]

The psychological and cultural determinism of these views has also been supported by biological and genetic researchers. Biologist E. O. Wilson argues that all human behavior is a result of the evolutionary process of natural selection. Since aggression, competition, and self-interest are in evidence among human beings now, they must have been traits that provided for our species' survival in the past. We must accept, then, that we are hardwired with the qualities that give us a propensity for aggression, violence, war.[14] Similarly, biologist Richard Dawkins maintains that human beings simply mirror gene imperatives. Genes are inherently "selfish," meaning they seek only to perpetuate themselves and thus: "This gene selfishness will usually give rise to selfishness in human behavior. . . . Must as we might wish to believe otherwise, universal love and the welfare of the species as a whole are concepts that do not make evolutionary sense."[15] Wilson's more recent work continues to think of war as humanity's "hereditary curse" but believes intelligent action can be marshaled to contain the worst of its excesses.[16] His moderation has not deterred other genetic determinists, however, who in recent years have recommended research into very specific genes that they believe underlie aggressive responses to provocative stimuli. So rather than generalize about human life based on patterns of natural selection, these researchers are looking for distinctive "warrior genes" that might cause some individuals to have a propensity for violence.[17]

Gathered together, the philosophical, psychological, and scientific evidence from these fields appears to indicate that human beings are biologically programmed for aggressiveness, making conflict and war inescapable. The Enemy Within Ideal makes the struggle to achieve peace and justice in the world seem like a fool's errand from the very beginning.

The Situational Ideal

While most of the episode "Miri" seems to be a retelling of *The Lord of the Flies*, the ending veers off in a different direction, suggesting that the STU ultimately has a different message to impart about human nature than what is just found in "The Enemy Within" and "Tapestry." When Kirk goes to confront the children of Earth Two in order to retrieve the stolen communicators, he is beaten bloody by them while the ritualistic chant a nursery rhyme. He continues to plea with them, telling that they do not have long to live on the planet because they have eaten all the food stores. Yet, he assures them that he will help. They are not convinced and call for more violence.

Kirk then changes his line of argument and asks the children to realize what they have become. All their lives, he points out, they have feared the adults on Earth Two because the virus transforms them into monsters who prey upon them. Yet, by beating him, the children have become the ones with blood on their hands: "It's you hurting, yelling, maybe killing, just like the Grups [grown-ups] you remember and the creatures you're afraid of. You're acting like them and you're going to be just like them unless you let me help you. . . . Let me help you or there won't be anything left at all." Here Kirk is asking them to confront their deepest fears and to envision what they are likely to become if they continue to stay on their present course of action. The children realize they don't really want to be violent and they don't want to hurt anyone just for fun. Unlike the boys from *The Lord of the Flies*, the children of Earth Two stop their violence not when confronted by the mere symbol of social authority but when they are invited to reflect rationally on their emotions. Kirk implores them to use their moral imagination to picture a different world, with different kinds of lives that they would rather live. "Miri" treats aggression by individuals merely as one reaction to fearful or stressful situations, not as an essential or primary expression of human nature. This understanding of aggression and violence is what I term the "Situational Ideal."

In the mid-1980s, behavioral psychologist David Adams instigated a conversation among researchers about the theories of biological determinism, such as those of E. O. Wilson, that were gaining prominence. Adams was concerned that the popularity of these views was convincing people that human aggression is innate and, therefore, that war is inevitable. Even more worrisome were studies that indicated that such outlooks had the tendency to stifle people's interest in peace activism; if war is intrinsic to human nature, then why bother working for peace at all?[18] To counter these detrimental effects, Adams helped to gather an international group of scientists in Seville, Spain, in 1986. The researchers issued the "Seville Statement" that broadly contradicts the Enemy Within Ideal by maintaining that the capacity for aggression does not make war inevitable, and the emphasis on biological determinism ignores important the social and cultural factors that lead to war. The statement lays out five propositions:

1. It is scientifically incorrect to say that we have inherited a tendency to make war from our animal ancestors.

2. It is scientifically incorrect to say that war or any other violent behavior is genetically programmed into our human nature.

3. It is scientifically incorrect to say that in the course of human evolution there has been a selection for aggressive behavior more than for other kinds of behavior.

4. It is scientifically incorrect to say that humans have a "violent brain."

5. It is scientifically incorrect to say that war is caused by "instinct" or any single motivation.

The Seville Statement concludes: "We conclude that biology does not condemn humanity to war and that humanity can be freed from the bondage of biological pessimism . . . the same species who invented war is capable of inventing peace."[19] Several scholarly organizations within the United States endorsed the Seville Statement, including the American Psychological Association, the American Anthropological Association, the American Sociological Association, and the American Political Science Association.

Some twenty-five years later, in 2011, researchers gathered in Rome to reassess the Seville Statement in light of ongoing biological and genetic research on the relationship of the brain, aggression, and social factors. Once again, they reaffirmed that the basic findings of the Seville Statement were sound and that violence is not biologically determined but largely occasioned by social and cultural influences.[20] At the same time, new developments in neuroscience and in primatology are starting to indicate that there is as much evidence for hardwired empathic responses in human beings as there is for aggressive or competitive impulses.[21] If these conclusions are accurate, then it would seem that the philosopher who better understands human social life is not Hobbes but the Russian anarchist theorist Peter Kropotkin (1842–1921). In his 1902 essay *Mutual Aid: A Factor of Evolution*, Kropotkin argued that biologists were not wrong to identify tendencies toward aggression and competition in human beings, but they were misguided in making them primary.[22] Tendencies toward cooperation and sociability, what Kropotkin called "mutual aid," were just as much factors in the evolution of modern human beings: "We may safely say that mutual aid is as much a law of animal life as mutual struggle, but that, as a factor of evolution, it most probably has a far greater importance in as much as it favours the development of such habits and characters as insure the maintenance and further development of the species."[23] Historian Yuval Harari, more recently, stresses the importance of the capacity for robust forms of cooperation as perhaps the defining feature in the evolution of human beings:

> Ants and bees can also work together in large numbers, but they do so in a very rigid manner and only with close relatives. Wolves and chimpanzees cooperate far more flexibly than ants, but they can do so only with small numbers of other individuals that they know intimately. Sapiens can cooperate in extremely flexible ways with countless numbers of strangers. That's why Sapiens rule the world, whereas ants eat our leftovers and chimps are locked up in zoos and research laboratories.[24]

If aggression and self-interested competition are not necessarily the most basic or fundamental qualities of human beings but specific reactions that can be elicited by external social or cultural forces under certain circumstances, then it would seem crucial to identify which situations do that in order to prevent them. Here the work of social psychologist Phillip Zimbardo is instructive. Zimbardo is the notorious researcher who, in 1971, developed the infamous Stanford Prison Experiment. The project intended to investigate the psychological interactions between guards and prisoners in situations of incarceration. Young men, all Stanford undergraduates, volunteered for the study and were randomly assigned the roles of guard or prisoner and instructed to act accordingly. They were then placed in makeshift jail cells, with guards on patrol day and night. Within less than a week, the test subjects began to experience emotional turmoil because the guards started using mental and physical abuse to assert their authority.

In his book *The Lucifer Effect*, Zimbardo reflects on the experiment to answer the question: How could seemingly normal individuals suddenly turn aggressive and abusive toward other people?[25] His response is one that was suggested by earlier studies by Stanley Milgram who found that many test subjects were willing to inflict pain and suffering on other people if instructed by an authority figure. Human beings possess a strong disposition to "fit in" to their surrounding communities and this makes susceptible to the demands made by the figures and institutions they perceive as legitimate authorities. Milgram and Zimbardo

> showed how certain social contexts and cues (for example narratives about the justice and necessity of the cause and how individual acts could serve it narratives, about reverence to particular types of authority, narratives about the immorality of the enemy, etc.) can push individuals into taking actions, such as inflicting pain on others or accepting a higher risk to themselves that ordinarily they would not. The institutionalization and romanticization of war help establish the social contexts and cues that normalize and encourage participation in it.[26]

Freud, James, Hedges, of course, also maintain that social and cultural forces encourage people to be fascinated with violence and to support war. However, Zimbardo's work indicates that these external forces are not responsible for channeling some deep, innate, propensity for death and destruction out into the open. Instead, the innate impulse at work in the case of the Stanford prison is actually one of empathy and the need for connection that gets focused by authorities. Guards started to act abusively not because they were innate sadistic per se but, in large part, because they were doing what they believed what was required of them in the role they were playing in the system. Thus, according to the Situational

Ideal, the violent behavior of the guards did not so much "expose the capacity for evil lurking beneath of surface of us all" as Hedges puts it. A setting like a prison is a high stress situation that sometimes makes us desperate to do what we feel is necessary, even inflicting pain on others, in order to protect what we cherish and hold dear, even if it is our own understanding of ourselves as a part of the institution.

Another approach toward undermining the Enemy Within Ideal is to sever the connection between aggression and war. Even if aggressive impulses are hardwired into human beings this does not mean that war is unavoidable. Anthropologist Margaret Mead (1901–78) argued in her 1940 essay "War Is Only an Invention—Not a Biological Necessity" that war is not a universal human practice. There are some cultures, such as the Inuit of Alaska, that do not engage in it. They may have high levels of individual aggression and violence, but they do not have the traditions of, or even the words in their language to describe, organized group-on-group violence which we might recognize as war. War, then, is a cultural artifact that some cultures have developed to deal with conflicts in the same way that some cultures, but not all, have developed the traditions of dueling or the vendetta. Thus, some level of competition and conflict may be universal among all human communities, but only some have evolved the idea of war as a way to settle the struggles. Indeed, the recent work of anthropologist Douglas P. Fry gives us a way to distinguish the difference between warring and peaceful cultures. Fry maintains that some cultures have actually developed sophisticated "peace systems" rather than group violence as a way to settle conflicts and intergroup hostility. These communities, which include the Inuit of Greenland, the Iroquois Confederacy of North America, and some Aboriginal groups in Australia, have built networks of interdependence with their neighbors, rely on conflict-resolution practices that force participants to deliberate about their disagreements in public, and esteem heroes who are not warriors but peacemakers. Most importantly, peace societies are not limited to small-scale examples of indigenous communities. Fry includes the European Union as an ongoing continental experiment in building a multistate coalition of societies dedicated to peace and the promotion of human rights.[27]

While there is anthropological evidence suggesting that war is not a universal practice for settling conflict among all human communities, archaeological evidence is now also raising questions as to whether war has been something human beings have engaged in since our earliest days as a species. Anthropologist Raymond C. Kelly estimates the development of projectile weaponry at about 400,000 years ago, but argues that this technology was probably used mostly for hunting and not intergroup violence among hominids. Intergroup violence was most likely a rare occurrence because of low population density—hunting groups could simply avoid one another and move on rather than go to war with one another.[28] The earliest archaeological evidence of group-on-group violence among human beings, however, doesn't appear until about 10,000–12,000 BCE, at a site at Jebel Sahaba in Sudan. Before that, there is scant evidence in the fossil record of violent deaths due to group-on-group violence.[29] After that point, there are more skeletons, but they do not start to accumulate in greater numbers until almost five thousand years later, suggesting that warfare was sporadic and not a regular feature of human life until about 5000 BCE, when it became more widespread.[30] This period of 7000 to 5000 BCE roughly coincides with the growth of sedentary communities, particularly in Mesopotamia, that start to rely more on agriculture and domesticated animals for food and slavery for labor. It may be too much to argue that the development of the first states created the practice of war, but they certainly harnessed power in a way to make intergroup violence a necessary part of their existence in order to maintain trade routes and a captive labor force.[31]

Based on the best evidence we have now, then, we can say that even though modern human beings have been in existence for about 300,000 years, warfare has been a regular feature of our lives only in the last 10,000 years. That's only about 3 percent of our life span as a species. Indeed, the archaeological evidence indicates that we have been artists and craftspeople tens of thousands of years longer than we have been soldiers—our earliest cave paintings go back about 44,000 years, and one of the first example of art, the ivory figure of a lion-man creature found in Stadel Cave in Germany, is from 32,000 years ago.[32] All this tends to give support to a suggestion made by science fiction author Ursula K. Le Guin that it might be better to tell the story of civilization not as originating from spear-chucking hunters who develop more sophisticated weapons and war-making technology over time. Instead, it is more accurate to say that the story of humanity begins in the development and refinement of those objects, like slings, bags, gourds, and shells, that allow us to gather and carry the resources of sustenance back to our families and friends, so that we can live another day to imagine, tell stories, make art, and build community with one another.[33]

Let me end by suggesting a more recent *Star Trek* story line that really drives these lessons home. One of the many twists of the first season (2017) of *ST: DISC* is that one of the major characters, Captain Gabriel Lorca, is actually a refugee from the mirror universe—an alternative dimension that resembles our own prime universe except everyone is in reverse. Characters that are morally good in our universe are evil in the mirror universe and vice versa. For instance, the valiant and honorable Captain Phillipa Georgiou, who is killed in the Klingon-Federation war of the prime universe, is actually the supreme leader of the evil Terran Empire in the mirror universe. In season one of *ST: DISC*, Emperor Georgiou must flee the mirror universe after a rebellion and she then becomes a member of the *Discovery* crew in the prime.

In season three (2020), Emperor Georgiou accompanies *Discovery* into the 32nd century and she is immediately interrogated by the Federation officials. In the episode "Die Trying," Georgiou is questioned by holographic security personnel about her murderous tendencies in two universes. One of them tells her: "All Terrans are duplicitous by their biology." The other informs her: "You may not be aware, but in the past hundred years, we've discovered a chimeric strain on the subatomic level in the Terran stem cell." Georgiou shakes her head and responds: "Silly holo. You cannot rattle me by introducing a completely fabricated biological component to my nastiness and inherently bad behavior." Here we see Georgiou explicitly rejecting the Enemy Within Ideal, especially those more modern versions that seek a genetic component to aggression and violence.

But we see a more explicit endorsement of the Situational Ideal later in the season. It turns out Georgiou cannot remain in the 32nd century with the *Discovery*. She is not only from another universe but from an earlier time period and this causes her body to break down at the atomic level. In the episode "Terra Firma I," she finds a way to travel back in time to the 23rd century with an alien presence known as a Guardian of Forever (first introduced in the *ST:TOS* episode "City on the Edge of Forever"). However, the Guardian secretly wants to know if Georgiou deserves to be sent back, so it transports her back to the mirror universe a few months before the rebellion that deposed her.

Georgiou soon realizes that she can no longer exist in a world in which murder and backstabbing are cultural norms. Her time with the Starfleet crew has expanded her moral imagination and shown her the value of trust, cooperation, nonviolence, and toleration for other species. When she tries to rule her empire with these new values, she sparks another rebellion that leads to her death at the hands of mirror Michael Burnham. At that moment, the Guardian brings her back and lets her know that she has shown she is not the same murderous tyrant she was before. Because she had the experience of living in the prime universe, a new situation, she was able to expand her imagination about how people can live together and what institutions can accomplish when they are not based on oppression and imperialism. Her Terran heritage was not destiny, after all; instead we understand that her character, like all of ours, is transformable, given the proper circumstances and support. At the end of "Terra Firma II," as she departs to go back to the 23rd-century prime universe, Georgiou tells Burnham: "You have always been far greater than you could imagine, Michael." Burnham tearfully answers, "So have you, Philippa," and she gives her the Vulcan gesture of farewell.

Conclusion

Drawing on the narratives of two *Star Trek* episodes, "The Enemy Within" and "Tapestry," I have examined the prominent perspective which I have termed the "Enemy Within Ideal." This outlook maintains that human nature contains irradicable aggressive impulses which make communal life a continual story of competition, conflict, and war. I have tried to show how several philosophers, psychologists, and scientists have attempted to promote the Enemy Within Ideal as the best understanding of human life and of the possibilities for the future of humanity. However, I think that the *ST: TOS* episode "Miri" offers a compelling counterresponse to the Enemy Within Ideal, one that I term the "Situational Ideal." While it first it seems to retell the familiar account of humanity reverting to violence without the presence of strong authority, "Miri" actually ends by reinforcing the idea that human beings are not fundamentally savage and aggressive but that we also possess expansive capacities for empathy and moral imagination. Which of these capacities get activated largely depends on the social, political, economic, and cultural situations in which we find people. We can be competitive and violent as individuals, but the best biological, psychological, and anthropological evidence today points toward the idea that warfare is hardly a universal and ubiquitous practice among human beings. Moreover, it appears that war is a way of settling conflicts that grew in response to specific forms of sociocultural development. In other words, war is not something all human cultures engage in, and it is not something that has been with us since the dawn of time. That means that if we can recognize and check the situations that tend to provoke aggression and violent behavior, then war does not have to be an inescapable part of our future, either. In the next chapter, I look at the ways in which peace and justice studies investigates the phenomenon of violence in order to better understand the situations that provoke it.

Chapter 2

The Multiple Dimensions of Violence

Star Trek Episodes

ST: TOS: "The Cloud Minders"

ST: DS9: "Past Tense I"; "Past Tense II"

When they were given the go-ahead to develop a new *Star Trek* series in 1991, cocreators Rick Berman and Michael Piller struggled to find a way to distinguish *ST: Deep Space Nine* from the successful *ST: The Next Generation*. Both writers were guided by Gene Roddenberry's *Star Trek* philosophy for their worldbuilding, as Piller explained: "We had learned from him and from experience that stories that combine science fiction with philosophy with optimism, with a comment on social issues and an exploration of human values, are the stories that work for Star Trek."[1] Initially, Berman was told by studio executives to consider developing a story line inspired by old television Westerns. He did not like the idea: "And when I went back and discussed it with Michael, who I had asked to develop this with me, it didn't seem like the kind of thing we really wanted to do."[2]

Then the Los Angeles Riots took place. For several days in the spring of 1992, thousands of people took part in a civil uprising sparked by the acquittal of four police officers accused of using excessive force against an African American defendant, Rodney King. The LA Riots became the most destructive urban civil disturbance in modern US history: sixty-three people were killed, thousands injured and arrested, and property damage costs reached about 1 billion US dollars. Berman and Piller both knew immediately that they wanted the LA Riots to factor into the backdrop of this new series. *ST: DS9* became the story of Commander Benjamin Sisko, a Starfleet officer of African American ancestry, who takes control of a space station, Deep Space Nine, abandoned by the militaristic alien Cardassians. For some forty years, the Cardassians had used the station to invade and occupy the nearby planet of Bajor, all the while committing a variety of war crimes and atrocities upon its native population. As part of a treaty with the Federation, the Cardassians gave the station to Starfleet, but not before stripping and sabotaging it. Sisko, then, has the task of rebuilding it and trying to maintain order among the numerous alien groups that use its services. This story, Berman indicated, is the one they really wanted to tell in the aftermath of the LA Riots: "the idea of people rebuilding and of people living in an area that had been damaged and had been violated. And the spirit that goes into the rebuilding of it."[3] Piller explained the mood he was trying to capture much more explicitly:

> I was listening to the radio on the anniversary of Martin Luther King's birthday—a man who stood firm on the subject of violence—that violence is not the answer. . . . As I wrote Star Trek, there was no greater responsibility than to continue to tell that message in any way that I could. So when you see Captain Picard or Commander Sisko decide that logic, reason, and communication are the way to solve problems and not turn to violence, then we were telling something to our audience that needs to be said on a regular basis. It's very important.[4]

I think it is significant that the creators of *ST: DS9* were inspired by the worst riots in the twentieth century because one of the most important episodes of the series is about a fictional urban uprising that sets the foundation for the eventual development of the Federation and its philosophy of peace and justice. In this chapter, I want to explore the way this episode, *ST: DS9* "Past Tense" (Parts I and II), as well as the *ST: TOS* episode "The Cloud Minders" help us to understand the complex way that violence manifests itself in our world. Most people, when they think of violence, imagine some kind of physical harm intentionally inflicted by one person on another person. This is undoubtedly one form of violence, but the STU can help us to understand how this kind is often related to a complex network of other harmful social relationships. I unpack the idea of violence portrayed in these episodes using the "pyramid of violence" theory developed by one of the founders of peace and justice studies: Johan Galtung. His work helps us to see that the images of violence we often imagine are better thought of as momentary surface occurrences that erupt as a result of underlying structural and cultural problems. Finally, I connect the lessons from these episodes with the observations from two leaders of nonviolent social movements: Martin Luther King, Jr., and Cesar Chavez. Both of these activists bolster the view that the "pyramid of violence" perspective is the one best equipped to provide a clearer understanding of violent occurrences in our world today. More importantly, they argue that it is the morally appropriate perspective to take. If peace studies is concerned to assist and support socially just social movements that effect real change in society, then we need to learn how to comprehend the deep structures of oppression that condition individuals to respond violently.

Star Trek Episodes: "The Cloud Minders," "Past Tense, Parts I and II"

In "The Cloud Minders," the *USS Enterprise* is tasked with an emergency mission to travel to the planet Ardana and retrieve a supply of a mineral substance called "zenite" that is desperately needed on another planet to prevent a botanical catastrophe. Ardana is a deeply divided and unequal planet, populated by two groups. An upper-class elite group of artists and intellectuals live above the planet's surface in a cloud city named Stratos. They are supported by a workforce called Troglytes, who live on the planet surface and do the labor of farming and extracting zenite from the underground mines. The Stratosians believe that the

Troglytes are an aggressive, violent, and mentally inferior species which they rule over through intimidation and force.

When Captain Kirk and Mr. Spock arrive on Ardana, they are immediately attacked on the planet surface by a group of Troglytes. They are rescued by Plasus, the High Advisor of Stratos, and a team of city security officers. He informs the Starfleet officers that they were ambushed by a rogue faction of Troglytes. These Disrupters, as they are called in Stratos, are withholding zenite production until Stratos improves conditions in the mines. Kirk insists he needs the zenite right away. Plasus feels the pressure and assures Kirk he will get the shipment.

While on Stratos, Kirk and Spock experience the high art and culture of the city. But these moments of tranquility are interrupted with flashes of violence. A Troglyte is arrested for trespassing but rather than allow himself to be taken into custody he breaks free and plunges off a balcony to his death on the planet below. He would rather commit suicide than endure the interrogation by the Stratosians. Then, while he is resting in his quarters and awaiting Plasus's news, Kirk is attacked by a house servant, Vanna, who turns out to be one of the Troglytes that ambushed him on the planet. She is a leader among the Disrupters and Plasus proceeds to torture her for information. Disgusted by the violent interrogation, Kirk and Spock beam back to the *Enterprise* where they are informed by Dr. McCoy of a medical discovery. The raw form of zenite emits an invisible, odorless gas that has detrimental effects on the cognitive capacities of anyone who inhales it. He suspects that the diminished capacities and aggressive tendencies of the Troglytes are not due to any genetic defects but exposure to the gas as they work in the mines. The Stratosians are not inherently mentally superior to the surface dwellers, Kirk and Spock realize; they just do not have occasion to be around unrefined zenite that incapacitates the Troglytes.

Kirk hatches a plan to kidnap Plasus and take him and Vanna to the mines to show them the effects of the gas. However, the three of them end up trapped in a mine without breathing masks and, within a few hours, Kirk and Plasus are at each other's throats in violent confrontation. Upon seeing the effects of the gas firsthand, Vanna agrees to work with the *Enterprise* and releases the zenite shipment. The Federation agrees to provide respirator masks that will protect the Troglytes and reverse their brain damage. In the end, it is clear that the Stratosians and the Troglytes still have much to work on to heal hundreds of years of injustice, but the *Enterprise* has helped to level the playing field between the two groups.

A similarly complex story about violence is told in "Past Tense (Parts I and II)." Commander Benjamin Sisko, Dr. Julian Bashir, and Lt. Jadzia Dax suffer a transporter malfunction and are beamed down to Earth in the year 2024, some three hundred years in the past from their present in 2371. The 21st century is a time of extreme economic inequality around the world. One solution that has caught on in many cities in North America is concentrating the poor, homeless, and mentally ill into segregated areas called Sanctuary Districts. The inhabitants of the districts are supposed to receive state assistance to gain economic stability, but the programs are really nothing more than attempts to warehouse surplus populations away from the wealthy elites.

Sisko and Bashir are taken by city security officers to the Sanctuary District for San Francisco, and Sisko realizes they are there at a fateful moment in the time line. A series of events will soon unfold, sparked by a district resident Gabriel Bell, who had become fed up with the conditions. According to the history books, Bell led an armed uprising against the state forces that occasioned political changes in the use of the districts. However, one evening, Sisko and Bashir witness the murder of the real Gabriel Bell during a street brawl. Sisko recognizes the historic importance of the Bell Riots as paving the way for the moral attitudes that will serve as a foundation for the Federation. He knows that if the riots do not take place, then his own future time line will not be realized. Sisko steps in and takes the place of Bell, going on to coordinate the takeover of the district, including the kidnapping of district government workers

Meanwhile, Dax, who beamed down a few minutes after her companions, is rescued off the streets by a wealthy technology mogul, Chris Brynner. He owns a large media corporation that is a primary access point to the Net (the STU version of the internet in this time period). She convinces Brynner to help her find her friends who she eventually learns are imprisoned within the Sanctuary District. While Brynner is looking for Sisko and Bashir, Dax meets some of his associates at a cocktail party. In that scene, we get a glimpse of a multiracial, global elite ruling the world at the time. They are completely disconnected from the poverty in global cities and see the Sanctuary

Districts as important tools to keep the poor in their place while they vacation all around the world.

Dax is able to locate Sisko and Bashir and finds out that the tensions among the uprising leaders are increasing. She persuades Brynner to restore Net access to the district so that dozens of residents can broadcast the sorrowful stories of their neglect, exposing the nature of the concentration camps to the general public. The state governor, however, remains unmoved by the broadcast and, as in the case of Attica, orders police forces to take over the district. Gun battles blaze throughout the neighborhoods and many of the uprising leaders are killed. Bashir and Sisko are able to protect some of the kidnapped government workers from harm. In the aftermath of the police violence, the two Starfleet officers leave identification that indicate Gabriel Bell was a hero for standing up for the residents while also protecting civilians from the police bullets. The Bell Riots, Sisko tells Bashir, are "one of the watershed events of the 21st century" and that outrage over the violence during the police takeover completely changes the moral compass of the United States: "Outrage over [Bell's] death, and the death of other residents, will change public opinion about the Sanctuaries. They'll be torn down and the United States will finally begin correcting the social problems it has struggled with for over a hundred years."

Peace Studies Concepts: What Does Violence Look Like in the World?

Spectacular Violence

On May 28, 2020, US president Donald Trump created a firestorm on Twitter when he commented on the protests in Minneapolis, Minnesota, after the killing of an African American man, George Floyd, by police officers on May 25. For three nights, people engaged in rioting, vandalism, and looting. The end results left two dead, over six hundred people arrested, and property damage close to $500 million, making it one of most destructive urban uprising in modern US history after the 1992 LA

Riots. President Trump tweeted: "These THUGS are dishonoring the memory of George Floyd, and I won't let it happen. . . . Any difficulty and we will assume control, but when the looting starts, the shooting starts."[5] Commentators immediately criticized the president for inciting violent responses to the protests and for using words like "thugs" that some believe is a racially offensive slur for African Americans.[6]

However, President Trump is not alone among political authorities in striking this kind of tone to describe those involved in antipolice brutality protests. In response to the 1992 Los Angeles Riots, President George H. W. Bush remarked:

> What we saw last night and the night before in Los Angeles is not about civil rights. It's not about the great cause of equality that all Americans must uphold. It's not a message of protest. It's been the brutality of a mob, pure and simple. . . . The wanton destruction of life and property is not a legitimate expression of outrage with injustice. It is itself an injustice. And no rationalization, no matter how heartfelt, no matter how eloquent, can make it otherwise.[7]

And in 2015, President Obama also referred to individuals who engaged in looting during protests against the police killing of another African American man in custody, Freddie Grey, in Baltimore, Maryland, as "criminals and thugs."[8]

These three presidents were all attempting to distinguish what they considered legitimate protestors from those engaged in illegal activity. Yet, such language tends to focus attention on what philosopher Andrew Fiala terms "spectacular violence"—those acts of violence which "stand out against the background of ordinary life" just like "smoke from a fire billowing into the clear air."[9] Research shows that news media are much more likely to concentrate their coverage on spectacular violence during protests, especially those which are about anti-Black racism.[10] The effect of that kind of focus on vandalism, looting, and arson is that the public slowly becomes less interested in the underlying issues about racial inequalities or police brutality and thinks mostly of the spectacular responses by protestors. Indeed, one survey indicated that support for the Black Lives Matter protests dropped off after five months, with some respondents indicating that the spectacular violence in particular is what turned them against the movement.[11]

What I think is important about "Past Tense" and "The Cloud Minders" is that they both warn us against narrowing our attention on spectacular violence and, instead, guide us to scan for what Fiala calls "atmospheric violence"—the kind of unseen harm that "contaminates the atmosphere and changes our behavior, while also priming the conditions that can lead to direct and overt violence."[12] These two episodes are similar in presenting societies marred by social and economic inequality and facing upheaval from the long-suffering lower classes. They are both notable for not focusing on the spectacularly violent events perpetrated by the oppressed and directing the audience's attention to the inappropriate use of the force by authorities in response. Each of them also examines the way that violent outbursts are best understood as eruptions generated by complex forms of atmospheric violence—complicated webs of harmful social, economic, and cultural relationships that often remain festering in the background of everyday life. I maintain that the best way to understand the portrayals of these intricate networks of violence is to analyze them using ideas and concepts from peace and justice studies, most notably, the work of Johan Galtung. Let's begin by unpacking his categorizations of violence and then see how they help us to make sense of these moral lessons of the STU.

The Triangle of Violence: Direct, Structural, Cultural

It is fairly standard in much peace and justice studies literature today to rely on a distinction made by Galtung between direct and indirect violence, which correspond roughly to Fiala's metaphors of spectacular and atmospheric violence. Galtung thinks of direct violence in terms of "events," while indirect violence is usually a "process."[13] Both types of violence, more generally, are what Galtung defines as "avoidable insults to basic human needs, and more generally, to life."[14] Violence, whether as a spectacular event or an indirect process, involves an individual person or group inflicting harm on other people in a way that damages their capacity to live a fully humane life, or simply, to exist. Hitting, stabbing, and killing someone are all forms of violence, but so is poverty, racism, or gender discrimination in a society that could do otherwise. What is important to underscore in this definition is that violence is something that is avoidable. It is the result of people making deliberate choices, even though, as we shall see, not all violence is intentional. But violence is not a feature of human life that is inevitable or fated; different choices can be made in terms of how we want to relate to the basic needs and lives of other human beings. Galtung recognizes that direct and indirect violence manifest themselves in distinct forms, so it is important to analyze each more clearly in order to understand what kinds of alternative choices are possible.

The most familiar example of direct violence is the case of voluntary and intentional physical harm. One person hits or kicks another person's body on purpose, with the malicious intent to cause pain. This kind of example is distinct from an accident, in which someone, for example, clumsily bumps into someone else, involuntarily causing them pain. It is also distinct from the kind of pain inflicted by a doctor or health care provider in the course of medical treatment; in that case, the doctor's intention is not to damage the patient's capacity to live a humane life or to exist but to make the person healthier with a procedure that happens to be painful. This reveals an important aspect of direct violence in general; it is a form of "injury, damage, or offence—something done against our will, which violates our autonomy or sense of self and which harms us."[15]

Direct violence can also be inflicted psychologically or emotionally.[16] In such cases, a person voluntarily and intentionally subjects another to injury, even though the victim is not beaten, killed, or physically disabled in any bodily way:

> constant verbal abuse of someone, various instances of humiliation, betrayal and deception, strategies of terrorizing people into compliance, etc. all can be understood as involving greater or lesser degrees of psychological injury even if, it is said, "not a hand is laid on" any of the recipients. In these cases, someone is hurt by someone else and the hurt can be more or less debilitating.[17]

Indeed, more and more states are beginning to recognize this form of violence as quite pervasive in society and are finding ways to combat it. The UK, for instance, was one of the first countries to criminalize "coercive control" in intimate partner relationships which involves various forms of psychological and emotional intimidation designed to strip someone of their sense of autonomy and self-worth.[18]

The processes of indirect violence, for Galtung, also appear in two manners. The first is structural violence or institutional violence. Huston Wood defines this as a situation in which the "systematic, unequal distribution of resources [leads] to harm to people without access to the goods and services enjoyed by others."[19] Structural violence, then, refers to the conditions in which legal systems and social, political, and economic institutions arrange hierarchal societies so that those groups of people with less access to power, status, and resources are more likely to experience diminished capacity to meet their basic human needs or to suffer more direct violence because of their relative lack of social protection and power.[20] Galtung thinks the prime example of structural violence is economic exploitation. In this case, the laws and institutions around the exchange of goods and services in a society allow one group to prosper materially from the unfairly compensated labor power of another group, who are then susceptible to malnutrition, disease, and psychological misery.[21] Philosopher Iris Young's classic theory of the different "faces of oppression" allows us then to see that structural violence includes processes such as labor exploitation, as well as social marginalization (treating certain groups as inferior, different, or in need of segregation from a dominant group), cultural imperialism (treating certain groups as being in need of acculturation to mainstream cultural values and mores in order to be considered equal), and imposed powerlessness.[22]

The second form of indirect violence is cultural violence. For Galtung, this refers to "aspects of culture . . . that can be used to justify or legitimize direct or structural violence."[23] Huston Woods again explains that "Any ethnic, ideological, political or religious belief that excuses or normalizes structural inequalities supports cultural violence," and it is maintained "through stories told by families, friends, written histories, literature, the media, religions, and schools, in short, by any means of transmitting a culture's attitudes and beliefs."[24] Examples of cultural violence include the stories, literature, folktales, religious teachings, pseudo-scientific studies, and so on about the inherent intellectual inferiority of women, or nonwhite peoples, that perpetuate gender discrimination and racism, and justify acts of direct violence, such as spousal abuse or lynching. Or stories that say that certain groups of people are poor because they are lazy or wicked can justify maintaining systems of economic inequality rather than encourage programs of wealth or income redistribution.

Structural and cultural violence are unlike direct violence in two ways. First, whereas direct violence is typically harm inflicted by a distinct individual, or group of individuals, on another individual or group, indirect violence is not necessarily caused by any one particular individual or group of individuals. Second, whereas direct violence typically involves some agent intentionally harming another, indirect violence is often not intended as harm of anyone. We can see how this might happen in the case of labor exploitation. Such a form of structural harm is kept in place because there are a variety of laws on the exchange of goods and services, many different economic institutions with their internal organizational processes and arrangements for meeting market expectations, and numerous individual and collective agents like workers, consumers, managers, corporations, and government agencies all going about their ordinary business. It would be peculiar to say that a complex economic and political system like that operates with single purpose and intention in the same way an individual does when they commit direct violence. Nonetheless, such a system, with its normal functioning, creates conditions in which many people's capacity to meet basic human needs, or even to exist, is compromised. This is not to say that complex organizations with many members cannot directly injure people. Yet, there is a difference between the case of labor exploitation in a capitalist society and that, say, of corporate executives deliberately choosing to manufacture products they know are likely to result in injury to workers or consumers. In such a case as this, a group of powerful people make a voluntary and intentional collective decision to value profit over the protection of other people's safety and lives. Those executives might even be held criminally responsible for such action. However, what is insidious about indirect violence is precisely that way in which the concept "expands the range of moral accountability, and allows us to identify as perpetrators of at least indirect violence all members of a particular stratified society who actively support the economic, political/legal or cultural status quo."[25] As Galtung puts it, structural and cultural violence creates circumstances in which even normal, peaceful, and nonviolent people going about their everyday lives often participate in "settings within which individuals may do enormous amounts of harm to other human beings without ever intending to do so just performing their regular duties as a job defined in the structure."[26] Here, Galtung is referencing a phenomena made famous by philosopher Hannah Arendt with her concept of the "banality of evil"—the way in which every day Nazi party members did atrocious acts simply by following orders and going to work each day and not because they especially had any ideological commitment to Aryan supremacy or anti-Semitic hatred of Jewish people.

Perhaps what is most important about Galtung's categories of violence is how he explains their causal relationship with one another. He uses the metaphor of a triangle, placing direct violence at the top and structural and cultural violence at the two lower bases.

Direct violence, as we have seen, are those spectacular events that erupt against the background of ordinary life. Yet, now we can see that they do so largely because they are the momentary releases of long-standing harmful processes underneath that mostly go unnoticed since they are often just taken as "the way things are." Using the triangle of violence, we can understand the events of Los Angeles 1992, Ferguson 2014, Baltimore 2015, or Minneapolis 2020 this way: the spectacular beating, or killing, of an African American man by police officers sets off a reaction of rioting, which draws in the attention of the media and political authorities. The public discussions are mostly about the criminal intentions of the people engaging in direct violence. Less attention and analysis go toward the structural problems of poverty, de facto racial segregation and redlining, and unemployment that prime city residents to feel angry and desperate enough to loot or vandalize property. Even less is said about long-standing cultural narratives about Black male criminality or propensities to violence that justify strong and swift police reaction and often lead to acquittal of police officers accused of excessive force. Yet, violence at the top of the triangle would not burn so fiercely if not invigorated by the violence at the base that lays around and accumulates like fuel for the fire.

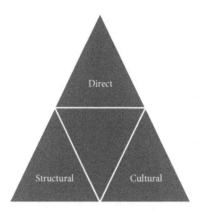

Figure 3 Galtung's Pyramid of Violence.

Star Trek Lessons: What Is the Morally Responsible Response to Violence?

"The Cloud Minders" is unique among *ST: TOS* episodes because it contains one of the only occurrences of a Science Office Log by Mr. Spock, rather than a Captain's Log by Kirk, to provide context. In the voice-over, Spock surveys the conditions of Stratos, providing us an opportunity to understand the historical oppression on Ardana. Using Galtung's triangle, we can better appreciate the narrative about violence that this episode proposes. On Ardana, the main form of oppression seems to be exploitation. Spock observes: "This troubled planet is a place of the most violent contrasts. Those who receive the rewards are totally separated from those who shoulder the burdens. It is not a wise leadership." Spock also notes that it is this structural violence that is driving the anger of the Disrupters: "The young girl who led the attack against us when we beamed down was filled with the violence of desperation."

Moreover, as the episode progresses, we witness the powerful way in which cultural violence has shaped the minds of the Stratosians to the point that they do not even recognize the injuries they inflict. Droxine, Plasus's daughter, tells Kirk and Spock that Troglytes must live on the surface because they cannot physically bear the sunlight in the clouds and their minds are not evolved enough to engage in artistic and intellectual pursuits. Obviously, the young Stratosian elite have grown up with accounts that justify the relative social positions of Ardanians as grounded in natural evolutionary processes—something that Dr. McCoy reveals is entirely false. So completely is the hold of cultural violence on Droxine that she experiences no cognitive dissonance as she explains to Kirk and Spock how Stratos has completely eliminated violence, and in the next moment she assists her father in torturing Vanna. When Kirk and Spock protest and intervene on Vanna's behalf, Droxine scoffs and suggests that physical coercion is the only way to make Troglytes understand urgent matters. Spock replies that they can understand and are due what all other humanoid species require: to live with equality, kindness, and justice. Plasus assures them such concepts don't apply to the Troglytes, not only because they could not understand what they mean but because the Troglytes are simply not worthy of protection from violation: "Troglytes are not like Stratos dwellers, Mr. Spock. They're a conglomerate of inferior species. The abstract concepts of an intellectual society are beyond their comprehension."

Ira Steven Behr—who took over from Michael Piller as executive producer and writer when Piller left to work on *ST: VOY*—admitted that when he was developing the story for "Past Tense," he was thinking precisely about the effects of structural and cultural violence on US American society. Behr states he had in the back of his mind the Kent State University shootings in 1970 and the Attica Prison uprising in 1971. In the first incident, US National Guard soldiers were ordered to open fire on university students who were peacefully protesting the Vietnam War. Four students were killed and nine wounded. In the second case, some two thousand prisoners at the Attica State Prison in New York state rioted to protest their living conditions. State officials negotiated with the prisoners for several days before finally ordering police to storm the prison. Dozens of prisoners, guards, and civilians were killed. So for *ST: DS9*, Behr wanted to imagine the conditions that would prompt the US government to put homeless people into concentration camps and justify violence against them. As they began filming the episode, the mayor of Los Angeles at that time, Richard Riordan, floated the proposal of sectioning off part of the city for homeless encampments. Behr remarked: "That proposal, or remark, was on the front page of the

Los Angeles Times, and everyone on the show went insane when they saw that. Here we are shooting this thing, and it could have actually happened. I don't think we showed anything in that episode that wasn't a very possible future for this country."[27]

"Past Tense" premiered on television in 1995, just three years after the LA Riots. Ira Steven Behr expressed hope that there would be positive media attention on the episode because of its themes, but there was very little. Perhaps this was because the message of the episode—that positive political change and greater social justice can develop out of destructive riots—was something that was no longer welcome since the efforts for restoring the damaged city had already stalled out by that time.[28] Yet, "Past Tense" remains important because, like "The Cloud Minders," it tell us that when there are urban uprisings, it is crucial not to lose moral perspective by focusing entirely on restoring law and order and prosecuting criminal behavior. Indeed, both episodes suggest that official state responses to riots and uprisings—Plasus's interrogation of Vanna or the police attack on the San Francisco Sanctuary District— often exacerbate tensions and increase harm rather than implement justice. What matters more than condemning or punishing wrongdoers, both episodes say, is figuring out how to reveal the circumstances that generate the intolerable pressure that constrains people's understandings of their choices and making violent action seem like the best or only option. In the case of "The Cloud Minders," that means spending time in the mines to see how the zenite gas damages the cognitive and emotional capacities of the Troglytes thereby completely undermining the cultural violence the Stratosians have created over generations to validate their exploitation. In "Past Tense," it means that the district dwellers have their chance to explain their life stories to the general public through the Net, demonstrating that they are being marginalized and rendered powerless not because they are lazy or have made bad choices but because the economic system doesn't need them anymore in order to support the lavish lifestyles of the global elite. The STU seems to tell us that there is a morally appropriate response to violence and that is to step back and investigate the deeper wells from which it draws its generative and sustaining power.

This lesson from the STU aligns with the message from at least two significant theorists and practitioners of nonviolence: Cesar Chavez and Martin Luther King, Jr. In 1971, Chavez, the leader of the farmworker movement in California, spoke out for the first time against the US involvement in the Vietnam War. He was particularly concerned with the high levels of fatalities among Latinx and Black soldiers. It perplexed him, he admitted, that so many poor farmworkers were ready to go to war to kill other poor people on the other side of the world. Yet, then he realized how suffused our world is with cultural violence. Concentrating on those forces might help to understand the fascination with war. For instance, poor young men grow up in our society with extensive stories that masculinity is tied up with physical strength and the ability to dominate others: "Why does it happen? Perhaps they are afraid or perhaps they have come to believe in that in order to be fully men, to gain respect from other men and to have their way in the world, they must take up the gun and use brute force against other men."[29] There are numerous examples of authority figures wielding power with weapons: "in Delano and Salinas and Coachella all the growers carry gun racks in their trucks. The police all carry guns and use them to get their way. The security guards (rent-a-cops) carry guns and nightsticks."[30] But Chavez was clear that it is not just our leaders who are fascinated with violence—in our society we are all influenced by traditions and norms that make violence the default tool for the solution of conflict: "Some husbands prove to their children that might makes right by the way they beat on their own wives. Most of us honor violence in one way or another, in sports if not at home. We insist on our own way, grab for security, and trample on other people in the process."[31] The task of people committed to peace and justice, Chavez maintained, is to create movements that envision different values for a flourishing human life and different ways of dealing with disagreement: "If we provide alternatives for our young out of the way we use the energies and resources of our own lives, perhaps fewer and fewer of them will seek their manhood in affluence and war."[32]

Similarly, Martin Luther King, Jr., thought that attending to the structural and cultural foundations of spectacular violence in the United States not only makes sense sociologically, but we are morally obligated to do so. In a speech delivered just a few weeks before his murder in 1968, King was asked to comment on the urban riots that had rocked the United States since the previous year. He responded:

> But it is not enough for me to stand before you tonight and condemn riots. It would be morally irresponsible for me to do that without, at

the same time, condemning the contingent, intolerable conditions that exist in our society. These conditions are the things that cause individuals to feel that they have no other alternative than to engage in violent rebellions to get attention. And I must say tonight that a riot is the language of the unheard. And what is it America has failed to hear? It has failed to hear that the plight of the negro poor has worsened over the last twelve or fifteen years. It has failed to hear that the promises of freedom and justice have not been met. And it has failed to hear that large segments of white society are more concerned about tranquility and the status quo than about justice and humanity.[33]

Thinking of riots with a triangle of violence framework suggested to King that there were at least three ways to proceed morally. First, King criticized the tendency, particularly like that of President Bush in the aftermath of the LA Riots, to accentuate individual criminal liability during spectacular eruptions of violence, particularly those of people involved in the destruction of property. He argued that such a tendency by the state relies on a mistaken equivalence between violence toward people and property destruction: "A life is sacred. Property is intended to serve life, and no matter how much we surround it with rights and respect, it has no personal being. It is part of the earth man walks on; it is not man."[34] Second, acts of looting or vandalism, he cautioned, should more often be read not as proof of people being out of control, brutes, or "thuggish" but as signs that people are sending a message about the systems of violence they experience around them. In the case of the Detroit riot of 1967 in which looting occurred, Kind pointed out that police were inundated with calls afterward of people wanting to return items they had taken: "Why were people so violent with property then? Because property represents the white power structure, which they were attacking and trying to destroy. . . . Those people wanted the experience of taking, of redressing the power imbalance that property represents. Possession, afterward, was secondary."[35] Vicky Osterweil confirms that this kind of appropriation of property during protests is quite common in US history.[36] Third, he warned that official responses by the state to spectacular violence often make the situation worse. Referring again to the case of the Detroit, King declared: "It is clear that the riots were exacerbated by police action that was designed to injure or even kill people."[37] Researchers today attest to the fact that when police respond to protests with force or intimidation of crowds, the violence tends to escalate rather than diminish.[38]

Conclusion

If the Situational Ideal from Chapter 1 suggests to us that human beings often channel aggressive tendencies into violent actions depending on the way in which conditions around them circumscribe their choices, then it seems we should try to get a better sense of the relationship between external environmental conditions and violent behavior. In this chapter, I have examined two episodes, *ST: TOS* "The Cloud Minders" and *ST: DS9* "Past Tense," that maintain that the proper manner to understand violent actions is as spectacular events conditioned by underlying social and economic tensions that are often—like the zenite gas in the mines of Ardana—invisible but highly toxic to the well-being of human life. This lesson from the STU is supported by the theoretical work of peace and justice studies founder Johan Galtung, who argues that direct violence needs to be understood as a result of structural and cultural violence forces. It is a lesson that also aligns with the practical examples of nonviolence developed by social movement leaders Cesar Chavez and Martin Luther King, Jr. Indeed, Chavez and King add an important dimension to this investigation of violence: they point out that the building of a socially just and anti-racist society requires that we think of spectacles of violence as the result of deep structures constraining the life opportunities of individuals. Unless we focus our scholarly and activist work within peace studies on reforming those structures, then violence and war will always be thought of as natural, inevitable, or most effective for dealing with conflict.

Chapter 3

The Nature of Peace and Human Flourishing

Star Trek Episodes

ST: TOS: "The Apple"; "The Return of the Archons"; "Who Mourns for Adonais?"; "This Side of Paradise"; "Private Little War"; "Piece of the Action"; "Patterns of Force

ST: TNG: "Symbiosis"

ST: DS9: "The Maquis I"; "The Maquis II"

ST: ENT: "Dear Doctor"; "Cogenitor"

ST: DISC: "There Is a Tide . . . "

During the preproduction of the second season *ST: TOS* episode "The Apple," writer Dorothy (D.C.) Fontana expressed her concerns about it in a memo to producer Gene L. Coon. She felt the story line basically recycled the first season episode "The Return of the Archons," as well as the episode "Who Mourns for Adonais," which had already aired earlier in the second season.[1] In all three of the stories, Captain James T. Kirk thwarts some powerful being/artificial intelligence that he believes threaten the well-being of a group of humanoids by stunting their social or cultural growth. Kirk's willingness to destroy seemingly utopian and peaceful societies is almost a trademark of his character.[2] Indeed, the ease with which Kirk interferes with the development of alien societies is one of the things that separates him from other captains in the STU. In the *ST: TNG* episode "Symbiosis," for instance, Jean-Luc Picard expounds on the Prime Directive—the Starfleet rule that prohibits the kind of thing Kirk does again and again—this way: "The Prime Directive is not just a set of rules; it is a philosophy . . . and a very correct one. History has proven again and again that whenever mankind interferes with a less developed civilization, no matter how well intentioned that interference may be the results are invariably disastrous." Even Captain Jonathan Archer, who commands the *Enterprise* almost a hundred years before Kirk in the STU time line, reflects on the need for a noninterference principle in the *ST: ENT* episode "Dear Doctor": "Someday my people are going to come up with some sort of doctrine: something that tells us what we can and can't do out here—should and shouldn't do. But until somebody tells me that they've drafted that directive, I'm going to have to remind myself every day that we didn't come out here to play God."

So why is Kirk so willing to play God and overthrow what appear to be harmonious societies? Theorists approach this trope with a variety of explanations. Lincoln Geraughty argues that Kirk is enacting a long-standing story line within science fiction, going back to US American Westerns, of the lone cowboy hero who rides into a new scenario and saves the day.[3] Robert Chaires and Bradley Chilton maintain this story line is more a reflection of US political culture, namely the imperial project of the nineteenth-century Monroe Doctrine, which held that the United States would protect the right of nations to develop so long as they did so in very specific ways.[4] Mark Langon and Eric Green each hold that Kirk's actions are more clearly expressions of the mood within US foreign policy in the 1960s, which wanted to justify interference in developing societies as part of the Cold War against the Soviet Union.[5]

In this chapter, I examine several *ST: TOS* episodes including "The Return of the Archons," "The Apple," and "This Side of Paradise" to begin to make sense of Kirk's actions. I argue that the way to understand these stories is with a distinction that comes from Nobel Peace Prize winner and US American philosopher Jane Addams (1860–1935). Her philosophy of peace and justice recognizes a difference between negative and positive peace. The reduction, or elimination, of violence and war is important, but this condition—called "negative peace" by Addams—can be accomplished without also establishing a firm foundation for human rights, political participation, meaningful work, and a relationship to natural world. It is possible to imagine, for instance, a totalitarian regime accomplishing negative peace but not affording its inhabitants any say in their society or providing for the protection of rights or meaningful participation in society. To help us understand the content of positive peace, I turn to philosopher Martha Nussbaum's theory of human capabilities. Her work helps us to understand the requirements for a fully flourishing life for human beings. These capabilities match with the conditions laid out by the idea of positive peace in Addams's work. Negative peace might, then, be thought of as a necessary condition for a flourishing life, but it is not sufficient. When Kirk is destroying utopias, we ought to understand him laying the groundwork for a more comprehensive peace involving both negative and positive aspects. I then consider the question of whether Kirk is, in fact, justified to use force in the way he does to create peace. It is important to note that Kirk hardly ever intervenes to protect a society without first defending the *Enterprise* from attack—the flourishing of others comes after the protection of his crew. In this way, his decisions, and those of other captains in the STU, reflect contemporary debates about the controversial use of military force for humanitarian intervention and the protection of human rights in doctrines, such as the United Nations' Responsibility to Protect. I conclude by suggesting that more recent *Star Trek* stories are taking seriously the importance of standing up for aspects of positive peace as part of building a more just future.

Star Trek Episodes: "The Return of the Archons," "The Apple," and "This Side of Paradise"

In "The Return of the Archons," the *Enterprise* finds itself investigating Beta III, a planet where the starship *Archon* mysteriously crashed about one hundred years before. The initial landing party is attacked by hooded figures with wand-like weapons who reduce Lieutenant Sulu to a permanent state of drug-like euphoria. Later, Kirk and his team beam down to the planet surface and find a society populated by obedient, but eerily contented, individuals. The crew's unwillingness to participate in a bizarre and violent ritual called Festival—in which all social rules are put aside and violence and mayhem litter the streets—draws attention of the hooded lawgivers. These authorities arrest the crew and prepare them to "be absorbed" into "the body," that is, turned into mindless residents of the city. During their captivity, Kirk and Spock learn that the *Archon* crew arrived on the planet and was either killed or absorbed into the society by an absolute leader named Landru. Spock and Kirk manage to find their way to what they think is Landru's command center only to discover that no such person exists. Landru was leader over six thousand years ago. He programmed a computer to oversee the care of the Body—the people of Beta III—and now only exists as a holographic projection of the machine.

The artificial intelligence has shaped a community of complete peace and harmony; when Landru appears to the landing party he tells them: "Landru seeks tranquility. Peace for all. The universal good." When he threatens the *Enterprise* crew with brainwashing, he intones : "You will be absorbed. Your individuality will merge into the unity of good, and in your submergence, into the common being of the body, you will find contentment, fulfillment. You will experience the absolute good." Spock, however, comes to a different conclusion about the character of Beta III under Landru's control: "This is a soulless society, Captain. It has no spirit, no spark. All is indeed peace and tranquility—the peace of the factory; the tranquility of the machine; all parts working in unison." Kirk then embarks on a strategy he will employ regularly in dealing with other AI: he decides to snare Landru in logical contradictions. Realizing that Landru's primary orders are to maintain the health of the people of Beta III, Kirk asks it: "What have you done to do justice to the full potential of every individual of the body?" Landru admits that it has constructed a society in which creativity is reserved only for itself. Kirk and Spock posit that without the ability to express creative thought, humanoid creatures will wither and die. Thus, Landru realizes it has failed to fulfill its basic programming by stunting the full potential of the people of Beta III, so it must now shut itself down to protect the Body. With Landru destroyed, the *Enterprise* departs, leaving a landing party headed by Lieutenant Lindstrom, a sociologist, who is charged to bring the culture of Beta III back to a more "human form."

In "The Apple," the *Enterprise* begins to explore a new planet, Gamma Trianguli VI, which starts off looking like an ideal paradise. The soil is rich and fertile with a great variety of plant life and the temperature is even all across the planet. However, soon several members of the security team are killed by native plants and exploding rocks. Energy beams from the surface begin to drain the *Enterprise*'s engines high up in orbit. Not all is as peaceful as it first appears to be.

Soon the landing party encounters a humanoid individual by the name of Akuta. He informs them that he and his people exist to serve an all-powerful being named Vaal. It is Vaal who controls the planet and makes the conditions so perfect for humanoid life. Akuta takes the Starfleet officers to his village and introduces them to his people, the Feeders of Vaal. Dr. McCoy's scans reveal that everyone in the village is perfectly healthy and possibly tens of thousands of years old. Yet, the Feeders of Vaal are oddly different than human beings—they live in a simple community, without industrial technology, but they know nothing about the emotion of love, or about children, or of sexuality. Akuta says these things are forbidden by Vaal. The crew soon realizes that Vaal is not a living being but a machine located far below the surface, with a huge serpent's head as a cavernous entry point.

As they secretly observe the Feeders servicing Vaal by throwing fruit into the mouth of the serpent, Kirk, Spock, and Dr. McCoy debate about the conditions on Gamma Trianguli VI. Spock claims that the relationship of the Feeders to Vaal is one of perfect "reciprocity"— they service Vaal and it controls the environment to permit them to live in perfect health and harmony. McCoy objects: "There are certain absolutes, Mr. Spock, and one of them is the right of humanoids to a free and unchained environment; the right to have conditions that permit growth." Spock retorts that the right to self-determination is also an absolute and the Feeders seem to have a system that works for them very well. McCoy turns to Kirk then and argues: "Jim . . . these are humanoids, intelligent. They need to advance and grow. . . . There's been no change or progress here in at least 10,000 years. This isn't life, its stagnation."

As in "The Return of the Archons," Kirk is preoccupied both with the inhabitants of the planet and with the way in which his ship is being threatened by the machine. In the end, Kirk devises a plan to weaken Vaal's energy reserves by preventing the Feeders from doing their job. He then orders the *Enterprise* to blast Vaal's shields with phasers until it exhausts its batteries and dies. The Feeders rush to the husk of Vaal's serpent head and express their worries about living without Vaal's protection. Kirk promises that they will come to appreciate the experience of creating and working for themselves: "You'll learn to build for yourselves, think for yourselves, work for yourselves, and what you create is yours. That's what we call freedom. You'll like it a lot." He also assures them they will also learn to care intimately for one another and expand their emotional and sexual horizons through love with each other. The episode concludes back aboard the *Enterprise* with Spock noting that in destroying Vaal, and leaving the Feeders to their own efforts at survival, the *Enterprise* has essentially reenacted the biblical story of Genesis by introducing knowledge and driving them out of their tranquil paradise.

In yet another episode, "This Side of Paradise," Kirk must destroy what looks like a perfectly peaceful and serene society. The *Enterprise* sets course Omicron Ceti III to document the destruction of an Earth colony there by deadly Berthold rays—a kind of radiation only detected after the colony had been established and which is extremely dangerous to living tissue. However, when the ship gets there, it finds that the colony is still intact and the inhabitants very much alive. Again, Dr. McCoy is able to confirm that the colonists are completely healthy—almost too healthy. Several of them have, in fact, healed scar tissue from old wounds as if their bodies are transforming into picture-perfect versions of human well-being. Kirk soon realizes that the calmness of Omicron Ceti III is due to the fact that everyone is infected with alien spores that thrive on Berthold rays. The spores soak up the rays in the host body and, in turn, provide the host with happiness, comfort, and long life.

The spores eventually manage to infect Kirk and the entire crew of the *Enterprise*, but before Kirk beams down to join them in paradise he experiences a rush of emotions that destroys the spores in his body. With that knowledge, he tricks Spock (who had previously been infected) into a rage, freeing him as well. The two of them then devise a way to flood the planet with subsonic waves that provoke violent emotions in all the humans there. Upon being liberated from the spores' influence, the colony leader, Elias Sandoval, looks over the landscape and remarks: "We've done nothing here. No accomplishment, no progress. Three years wasted." As the *Enterprise* leaves the planet, McCoy again refers to the Garden of Eden: "Well, that's the second time man's been thrown out of Paradise." Kirk responds wistfully but ominously: "No, no Bones, this time we walked out on our own. Maybe we weren't made for paradise. Maybe we were meant to fight our way through, struggle, claw our way up, scratch for every inch of the way. Maybe we can't stroll to the music of the lute. We must march to the sound of drums."

Peace Studies Concepts: Negative and Positive Peace

In examining the history of peace studies since its inception in the mid-twentieth century, Robin J. Crews observes that, for the most part, the field has focused more on studying violence than actually explaining the nature of peace. More attention ought to be given, Crews maintains, toward filling out a conception of what a peaceful world would look like rather than simply defining it against what we wish to avoid: "The future of peace studies depends in large part on whether, in the coming years, those who teach about peace can succeed in publicly reclaiming the word 'peace' . . . to primarily mean something other than the absence of war and other manifestations of overt violence."[6] Johan Galtung's work is often taken as the pioneer in this kind of effort by offering a distinction between "negative" and "positive" peace. For Galtung, negative peace refers to conditions in which there is an absence of direct violence; positive peace refers to conditions in which there is an absence of structural/cultural violence.[7] Yet, Galtung is doing precisely what Crews warns against: defining peace in relationship to violence rather than delineating it robustly on its own terms. For a more complete conception of peace, I hold it would be better to turn to philosopher and social activist Jane Addams, the first US American woman to win a Nobel Peace Prize, in 1931, for her antiwar activism.

Addams, in fact, spoke about different versions of peace in terms of negative and positive elements decades before Galtung did in 1969. In her 1906 book *Newer Ideals of Peace*, Addams wants to separate older, more "dovelike" ideals of peace from what she considers to be newer, more "dynamic" ideals arising in the modern age. The older ideals seek to eliminate war, she argues, usually by envisioning elaborate systems of international law or commerce that constrain the actions of nations.[8] In that sense, they are attempting to create negative peace—a world without war. Yet, Addams feels these theories failed to think holistically about violence and oppression internally within states.

It would be possible to develop a world free from war between national governments, Addams maintains, but this does little to nothing to change the way political power is arranged within a society. Most modern democratic governments, Addams argues, draw their inspiration from the liberal philosophies of John Locke, Thomas Hobbes, and others. These thinkers conceive of the idea of government as the institution to establish law and order and protect the natural rights of individual human beings by monopolizing the legitimate exercise of force within a given jurisdiction. It is the government's job to create laws and punish those who violate those edicts, depending upon "penalties, coercion, compulsion, remnants of military codes, to hold the community together."[9] For Addams, this limited view of government's purpose may have been appropriate in the seventeenth century for fragile new societies coming out from under the yoke of absolute monarchy, but it seems inappropriate to say, some three hundred years later, that the main job of the state today is merely to keep people in line: "Having looked to the sword for independence from oppressive governmental control they came to regard the sword as an essential part of the government they had succeeded in establishing."[10] The older ideals of peace did not notice all the remnants of militarism and state coercion within society, concentrating mostly instead on how to prevent war between states. This way of thinking of peace would still permit national governments to be highly restrictive of liberty, and even internally violent toward its own people, just as long as they had not declared war on another national government. Failing to address these layers of internal violence and oppression could quickly undermine the longevity of any peace between states. As Oliver Richmond puts it, "A peace agreement based on narrow understanding of peace would probably not be satisfactory in anything other than the short term. Military force or an authoritarian government may maintain a basic security order—as in East Germany during the Cold War—but many deficits relating to human rights, democratic representation, and prosperity remain," and these ultimately create unstable societies that are more likely to go to war.[11]

Because of these limitations, Addams proposes conceptualizing peace in a more "dynamic" way that resembles what many peace scholars think of today as positive peace. Trying to move away from the old liberal models of societies from Locke, Hobbes, and the American founders, she looked for inspiration to the ways in which new urban municipal governments were dealing with questions of housing, public health, food safety, immigration, and fair labor laws and attempting "to make life possible and human in large cities" at the beginning of the twentieth century.[12] Rather than merely focusing on restricting unlawful behavior, new governments were experimenting with projects, such as public parks, libraries, baths, and gymnasiums, to address ever-changing social needs and to offer services that would nourish people's physical and mental well-being. Much of her own activist work in Chicago was in building community organizations that could secure the proper "outlet for the active faculties" of individuals living in major urban areas of the United States.[13] Out of these experiences, she believes, is developing an ideal of democratic community which sees each person as a "creative agent" with "dynamic power" and the responsibility of the society being "to free the powers of each man and connect him with the rest of life."[14] For Addams, "dynamic peace" refers to those conditions that allow a society to pursue this kind of community ideal. Dynamic peace, then, would refer to a society that had negative peace, but also established social and state institutions that prioritize the self-governance of the community, economic fairness and a nonexploitative economy, public education, and flourishing multicultural communities. She ended her book *Newer Ideals of Peace* by recalling the enthusiasm pervading the International Peace Conference in 1904, in which participants "foresaw that under an enlightened industrialism peace would no longer be an absence of war, but the unfolding of worldwide processes making for the nurture of human life."[15]

Philosopher Carol Hay notices a similarity between Addams's emphasis on flourishing and the "nurture of human life" with Martha Nussbaum's theory of human capabilities.[16] I believe this connection may help us to understand more specifically what Addams has in mind with nurturance in her notion of dynamic peace. Nussbaum's work attempts to define human well-being as the opportunity and ability to achieve a combination of various beneficial experiences in one's life. A good human life, for instance, is one in which the individual has the opportunity and ability to live in such a way that they undergo or come into contact with a variety of what Nussbaum calls "core capabilities." Conversely, an unhealthy or damaged life would be one in which the individual is unable to experience a threshold of core capabilities. We might say that a person unable to experience this threshold is living in "inhumane" conditions, a life not worthy of a human being. Nussbaum lists these core capabilities as follows:

1. **Life**. Being able to live to the end of a human life of normal length.

2. **Bodily Health**. Being able to have good health, nutrition, shelter, opportunities for choice in reproduction.

3. **Bodily Integrity**. Being able to move freely and avoid unnecessary violation of one's own body; experience pleasure, including sexual satisfaction.

4. **Senses, Imagination, and Thought**. Being able to use senses, imagine, think, and use reason; have the educational opportunities to nurture those faculties.

5. **Emotions**. Being able to have attachments to things and people outside ourselves; to express love, grief, gratitude, and anger.

6. **Practical Reason**. Being able to form a conception of the good for one's own life and engage in the critical thinking needed to plan it.

7. **Affiliation**. Being able to live with and for others, to recognize and show concerns for other human beings through interaction.

8. **Other Species**. Being able to live with and show concern for animals and the natural world.

9. **Play**. Being able to laugh, to play, to enjoy recreational activities.

10. **Control over One's Environment**. Being able to participate
     effectively in political choices that affect one's own life;
     being able to own and use one's own property and to seek
     employment.[17]

Amartya Sen, the Nobel Prize–winning economist with whom Nussbaum
began developing the theory of human capabilities, argues that we can
connect capabilities with specific human rights.[18] That is, human rights
are legal devices in which states commit to guaranteeing people's
access to certain capabilities within their societies. Governments which
enact policies that contravene human rights treaties or conventions
can be understood as prohibiting or damaging people's capacity to
experience core capabilities. This approach allows us to view the core
human capabilities as a kind of normative measurement tool by which
we can evaluate a state's responsibility toward providing a dignified
life for individuals. Protecting human rights means maintaining the
conditions for human beings to live good lives. Human rights violations
dehumanize people by forcing them to live in such a way that they merely
survive and cannot flourish in the ways human beings are capable.

Using this capabilities framework allows us to fill in more the kind
of world Addams envisions with her notion of dynamic peace. For
Addams, peace studies ought to seek a world with dynamic peace,
that is, with both negative and positive peace. Negative peace here
means a world with not just the absence of war but also the dedication
of society toward providing conditions that generate positive peace.
Positive peace means here a world in which state, social, and economic
institutions are arranged to guarantee opportunity and access to the
core capabilities of human life for individuals residing within society in a
way that allows them to flourish as dignified human beings.

But having this robust normative framework for human rights raises
an important question: Is there a moral obligation to intervene when a
nation engages in actions that violate negative and positive peace? Do
other nations have a responsibility to act if a country undermines the
core human capabilities of its own residents?

Some philosophers, such as Immanuel Kant (1724–1804), have
argued that global peace requires a strong adherence to noninterference
with the sovereign affairs of nations. Kant writes: "No nation shall forcibly
interfere with the constitution and government of another . . . a foreign

power's interference would violate the rights of an independent people struggling with its internal ills."[19] Yet, more recently, political theorist Michael Walzer has argued that the rights to autonomy and self-determination by a people, which are the rights Kant references in his work, can be violated by one's own government. In such cases, outside forces can legitimately intervene if a government threatens the human rights of its own citizens because that government has, in essence, declared war on its own people. The question becomes, then, what kinds of abuses justify foreign action. Walzer responds: "Humanitarian intervention is justified when it is a response (with reasonable expectations of success) to acts 'that shock the moral conscience of mankind.'"[20] The problem with this standard, however, is its vagueness. How do we define the parameters of the moral conscience of humanity?

After the Rwandan genocide of 1994, which led to the murder of almost a million Tutsis in the time frame of about four months, United Nations' Secretary General Kofi Annan called for the development of a new normative framework for preventing such atrocities in the future.[21] This has become what is now referred to, since 2005, as the Responsibility to Protect doctrine, or R2P. The main idea of R2P is that all member states of the United Nations have a duty to protect civilians, by force if necessary, if their own sovereign government fails to do so. It is believed that a state willing to abuse its own citizens has essentially abdicated its responsibilities and is no longer due respect as a sovereign entity. R2P is not necessarily international law now, but it is a growing outlook that has found its way into some charters.

As David Barash and Charles Webel explain, however:

R2P is especially concerned with preventing . . . four crimes: ethnic cleansing, crimes against humanity, war crimes, and genocide. It is thus rather conservative and limited, in that it does not include a governmental responsibility to protect people from disease, illiteracy, social injustice, or to protect the environment. Instead, it focuses on the four most egregious insults to a populace, which are identified as mass atrocity crimes.[22]

Thus, our most current attempt to articulate a global policy of protecting human rights holds that forceful intervention is usually only justified in cases where states are violating the bodily health or integrity of human beings and not so much the other of Nussbaum's core capabilities. Some recent interventions, such as the 2001 invasion of Afghanistan by the United States or the invasion of Iraq by the United States and the United Kingdom, have purportedly occurred for violations that do not obviously meet the threshold of "mass atrocity crimes," such as repression of political prisoners or the abusive treatment of women, but these are fairly controversial interventions.[23] Addams believes that for too long we have ignored the importance of positive peace, but no international agreements today justify intervention for violations of economic, social, or cultural rights associated with the flourishing of human beings.

Star Trek Lessons: Is Kirk Justified in Intervening in Peaceful Societies?

With this robust notion of peace furnished by Addams, and clarified by Nussbaum, we can begin to evaluate Kirk's actions in destroying what appear to be idyllic societies on three different planets. All three seem to be peaceful societies in that negative peace prevails over them. There is no war in the sense of organized group-on-group violence and very little, or no, direct violence among inhabitants of these worlds, except in the bizarre case of Beta III with its tradition of Festival. Yet, what the crew of the *Enterprise* quickly learn is that there is very little positive peace on any of them. All three planets contain various limitations of core capabilities, meaning that the inhabitants are not allowed to lead fully flourishing lives.

On Beta III, Landru admits to Kirk and Spock that it denies creativity, imagination, and free thought to the people. It also might be said that by allowing Festival, Landru compromises the bodily health and integrity of many individuals since assault, rape, and murder appear to be allowed once the Red Hour chimes. The Feeders of Vaal on Gamma Trianguli VI do indeed have their life, bodily health, and bodily integrity protected by Vaal, as Spock notes. However, Vaal denies the Feeders some very key components of a fully human life according to Nussbaum's framework. They are not allowed to experience sexual intimacy and pleasure, they are prohibited from experiencing love and other emotions related to a rich sense of affiliation with one another, and it is not clear they are free to engage in practical reason to envision any other life than that of servicing Vaal. Finally, the spores that affect Sandoval's colony on Omicron Ceti III do provide for perfect life and bodily health and integrity by protecting them from the effects of Berthold rays. Most of the time, the colonists are playing and enjoying recreational time with one another. But the mental high of the spores seems to affect the emotional range of the colonists; they are not able to access strong feelings of anger without killing the spores and dying from radiation. When Sandovel is finally released from the spores, he tells McCoy that they were living without any practical reason—they had given no thought for years about planning for the future. Finally, the colonists had very little interest in controlling their environment, in the sense of the opportunity to engage in meaningful work since they were content simply to survive and experience the spore elation. Thus, it is not obviously the case that Kirk was destroying societies that, in Spock's words, "were working for" their inhabitants. The framework of Addams, clarified by Nussbaum, allows us to see that each of them had serious deficiencies in providing for the conditions that allow for a dignified and flourishing human life.

Yet, even if these three planets failed to maintain positive peace, did that justify Kirk's use of force to destroy Landru, Vaal, or the spores? It's important to recognize that the limitations on positive peace were not sufficient reasons for Kirk to intervene in these three cases. In all of them, there was also a serious threat of destruction to the *Enterprise* by the controlling force on the planet. Kirk, in a sense, primarily acted out of duty as captain to defend his ship rather than out of a responsibility to protect the planet inhabitants. At least in one other case, Kirk does not directly intervene despite a lack of positive peace. In the episode "Bread and Circuses," Kirk refuses to use the *Enterprise* to rescue Spock and McCoy from deadly gladiatorial games because doing so would violate the Prime Directive. The planet in this case, 892-IV, existed in a state of global negative peace because of a dominating world empire but was rife with slavery, religious persecution, and torture. The outcome of this episode resembles several other examples, such as "Private Little War," "Piece of the Action," and "Patterns of Force," in which Kirk intervenes not so much to provide peace for the inhabitants, or even to protect the

Enterprise, but to reestablish a status quo after a previous intervention by Federation personnel ruptured a balance.

Kirk's unwillingness to intervene simply to assist people to lead flourishing lives is not unique in the STU. Captain Jean-Luc Picard in the *ST: TNG* episode "Symbiosis" refuses to intervene in a situation in which a planet of people, the Ornarans, have become addicted to a drug. His decision leaves them suffering, in despair, and in submission to the people of a neighboring planet, the Brekkians, who harvest the drug and had been taking advantage of the addiction. In the *ST: DS9* episodes "The Maquis" (Parts I and II), we learn that the Federation is willing to allow the positive peace of its former citizens in a demilitarized zone to be limited, as long as such toleration maintains the negative peace between the Federation and the Cardassian Empire. Finally, in *ST: ENT* "Cogenitor," we have perhaps the most shocking example of the Federations' unwillingness to help in cases of violation of positive peace. Commander Trip Tucker befriends a being that is essentially held captive by other members of their society because of their unique reproductive capacities. An advanced civilization, the Vissians reproduce in a manner that requires a male, female, and third gender individual, a cogenitor. However, the cogenitors are not considered people by the Vissians; they are not educated, spoken to except when given orders, and forced to participate in procreation by male and female couples. Tucker secretly tries to educate one cogenitor by providing them with books and helps them to imagine a life exercising Nussbaum's core capabilities of bodily health and integrity, practical reason, and sense and imagination. The cogenitor flees to the *Enterprise NX01* and asks Captain Archer for political asylum. He refuses, citing a moral duty not to interfere in the affairs of other civilizations (in the STU time line, this episode takes place before the formation of the United Federation of Planets and the establishment of the Prime Directive). The cogenitor is returned to the Vissians and the *Enterprise NX01* crew learn shortly afterwards that they committed suicide rather than continue living without being able to experience the elements of positive peace they had glimpsed briefly.

The decision by most Starfleet captains not to intervene in an alien society to protect positive peace is more than just a convenient trope from the STU. It is very much a reflection of today's international consensus on norms about intervention and human rights. Clearly, most Starfleet captains would feel very comfortable inhabiting the halls of our international human rights bodies, where there is much talk about protecting the well-being of human beings but as much skepticism and hesitancy about how to properly enforce any such agreements. Yet, I agree with philosopher David Boersma that there is a critical tension in STU that compels us to move beyond the contemporary hesitancy in being committed to the protection of positive peace. Even though *Star Trek* often contains depictions of violence and conflict, Boersma argues, it also consistently presents visions of a world grappling with the problems of peace-building that compel us to find alternatives to our dilemmas: "Valuing peace—believing in it and working for it—doesn't mean that we have to be unrealistic about conflict or violence. Rather, it means that we can see a better alternative and are committed to striving for a reality that reduces, if not eliminates, violence."[24] Indeed, more recent *Star Trek* warns us not to settle for easy solutions that compromise positive peace.

In season three of *ST: Discovery*, the crew of the *Discovery* find themselves permanently thrust into the 32nd century, some nine hundred years in their future. The Federation that they find there is very different from what it once was. Because of a mysterious effect that has come to be known as the Burn, faster-than-light warp travel is rare and costly. The Federation that once stood as an association of planets in the hundreds collapsed into a collection of a few dozen. Most of the galaxy retreated into lawlessness and isolation. In the power vacuum, another organization, the Emerald Chain, arose. The Chain is a syndicate of trading partners devoted to predatory capitalism. It is well known for running debt slave markets and violently extracting resources from vulnerable planets. These tendencies put it at odds with the Federation, but the latter is unable to do much because of its lack of resources.

In the episode "There Is a Tide . . . ," the minister for the Chain Osyraa secures a meeting with Starfleet Fleet Admiral Charles Vance to negotiate a peace treaty. The agreement would put an end to hostilities and allow the Federation to have access to the best scientific and research facilities in the galaxy that are owned and operated by the Chain. The Chain, in turn, would finally gain legitimacy by association with the Federation. Admiral Vance is sorely tempted by the treaty but insists that slavery would have to be abolished and the Prime Directive respected throughout the combined territories. In addition, he wants Osyraa to be tried for numerous atrocities across the galaxy. She refuses and a final battle ensues between the two powers.

What is striking about this interaction is the way in which Vance is willing to sacrifice negative peace to ensure that past abuses are not forgotten and that societies be released from myriad forms of oppression. He tells the Chain's leader:

> Osyraa, I want peace. I want the Federation to join the Chain and I want to learn from your great society. The Burn has left us with a legacy of fear, of isolation, or scarcity that still clouds our moral clarity, a clarity that I fight for on a daily basis and I ask my people to die for. So if that's the reason that we can't reach an accord today, well, . . . I can live with that.

Osyraa snarls that Vance is spouting abstractions that will cost the Federation material benefits. Vance responds by saying he can offer her peace but not at the expense of justice.

It's not clear other Starfleet officers would have insisted on Admiral Vance's conditions on eliminating exploitation and holding leaders accountable for atrocities. After all, Archer left in place the sexual exploitation of the cogenitor, Kirk allowed slavery to remain intact in "Bread and Circuses," and the Federation was willing to sign a peace treaty with the Cardassians even though they knew it would leave open some of its former citizens to abuses. Perhaps the STU, with Admiral Vance's 32nd-century brand of diplomacy, is now finally catching up with the insights of Addams from 1906: a stable society is one that centers justice and human flourishing as the basis for the absence of violence and war.

Conclusion

Among *Star Trek* fans, Captain Kirk often has the reputation of having the worst record of violating the Federation's directive of noninterference with developing societies.[25] Kirk does seem very much like a jerk, as David Kyle Johnson puts it, when it comes to demolishing utopian worlds. In this chapter, I've tried to explain this tendency by pointing out that the societies Kirk takes down in the *ST: TOS* episodes "The Return of the Archons," "The Apple," and "This Side of Paradise" are not as serene and tranquil as they first seem to be. Using the framework of negative and positive peace developed by Jane Addams, and supplemented by the notion of core human capabilities from Martha Nussbaum, we can see that these worlds may have had no war and very little violence, but they were not the kinds of places in which people would be allowed to flourish to their fullest potentials. At the same time, this distinction between negative and positive peace allows us to see that the Federation has always had a halfhearted devotion to the support of the conditions for human flourishing. In this way, the STU does mirror our contemporary world in which realpolitik considerations often compromise the protection of human rights. However, I believe that some of the newer stories in *Star Trek* demonstrate a renewed awareness that a more humane future can only really be built if the eradication of war is grounded in societies arranged to provide opportunities for humans to thrive intellectually, emotionally, economically, politically, and with strong imaginations to conceive of even better worlds. As we will see in Chapter 4, it will be a dedication to this ideal of dynamic peace that is required to confront head-on the trauma and legacy of white supremacy in the world today.

Chapter 4

Towards an Anti-Racist Future

Star Trek Episodes

ST: TOS: "Balance of Terror"; "Let That Be Your Last Battlefield"; "The Savage Curtain"; "Charlie X"; "By Any Other Name"; "Is There in Truth No Beauty"

ST: TNG: "Encounter at Farpoint"; "Cause and Effect"; "The Neutral Zone"

ST: DS9: "The Search I"; "Image in the Sand"; "Badda Bing, Badda Bang"; "Far Beyond the Stars"

ST: VOY: "Faces"; "Barge of the Dead"; Lineage"; "Scorpion II"; "Tattoo"; "The Cloud"; "Initiations"; "Mortal Coil"

ST: ENT: "Broken Bow"; "Fortunate Son"

ST: DISC: "That Hope Is You II"

ST: PIC: "The End Is the Beginning"

When *ST: TOS* premiered on television in September 1966, the United States was in a period of enormous social turmoil. Involvement of US forces in Vietnam was increasing; by the end of the year almost 400,000 troops were deployed there and American casualties topped off at more than six thousand with 30,000 wounded. Domestically, the Civil Rights Movement had accomplished two major legislative victories in the 1964 Civil Rights Act and the 1965 Voting Rights Act. But different communities continued to press for justice and social transformation. In California, Cesar Chavez mobilized thousands of Mexican American and Filipino supporters to march for an end to exploitative labor practices in agriculture. Major urban areas were experiencing urban riots, such as the Watts uprising of 1965, in which thirty-four people died. A major voice of the Black community, Malcolm X had been killed two years before, and many young African Americans were voicing displeasure with the slow pace of social change. They called for "Black Power" and their voices were heard when the Black Panther Party for Self-Defense would form in October 1966 in Oakland, California.

Gene Roddenberry originally pitched an idea for a groundbreaking science fiction series in which a woman would serve as second in command of a starship. When this pilot episode, "The Cage," was rejected by network executives, Roddenberry came back with a concept that responded to the tumultuous mood of US American society. The *USS Enterprise* would be the setting for a multiracial and multiethnic crew, with a Black woman communications officer, an Asian male helmsman, a Scottish engineer, and later, a Russian navigator. It pushed against dominant racist media stereotypes and rejected the tendency toward all-white casting that was common in science fiction television shows of the time.[1] Over its three-year run, *ST: TOS* continued to push the boundaries, including the infamous interracial kiss between Captain Kirk and Uhura, that got the show banned from affiliates in the South. Rod Roddenberry, Gene's son, remembers that his father adamantly rejected those sorts of complaints about his vision of the future: "Apparently, he would get letters from the TV stations in the South saying they won't show Star Trek because there is a black officer and he'd say 'Fuck off, then.'"[2]

How exactly radical were *ST: TOS*'s portrayals of race and an anti-racist future?[3] Several episodes, particularly in the third season, depict an almost colorblind emphasis in which racial identity and racism itself are ideas to be downplayed and forgotten in favor of more progressive ideals of belonging. This view seemed in line with the calls made by Dr. Martin Luther King, Jr., in his "I Have a Dream" speech at the Washington Monument in 1963. Many US Americans can today recite

King's famous line from this speech that articulates this ideal: "I have a dream that my four little children will one day live in a nation where they will not be judged by the color of their skin but by the content of their character."[4]

However, King himself soon started to change his focus about what racial justice would require in the United States and that meant toning down the talk of colorblindness. Like Jane Addams before him with her idea of "dynamic peace," he began to understand that dealing with violence in US society required stronger a focus on economic and social issues. In his "Letter from a Birmingham Jail," King criticized his white allies for not understanding that negative peace was not enough. True justice involved expanding social movements to include positive peace: "I had hoped that the white moderate would understand that the present tension in the South is a necessary phase of the transition from an obnoxious negative peace, in which the Negro passively accepted his unjust plight, to a substantive and positive peace in which all men will respect the dignity and worth of human personality."[5] By 1968, King was no longer talking about colorblindness as an ideal but instead, emphasized the need for Black people to become color conscious and to recognize the moral authority they possessed as a result of their common history and cultural perspective. Such a unique outlook, he believed, would be required to save the soul of the United States: "After all, no other minority has been so constantly, brutally, and deliberately exploited. But because of this very exploitation, Negroes bring a special spiritual and moral contribution to American life—a contribution without which America could not survive."[6]

In this chapter, I examine how these different ideals of racial justice are presented in the STU. I begin by analyzing how the ideal of colorblindness is depicted in the STU by focusing on the *ST: TOS* episodes: "Balance of Terror," "Let That Be Your Last Battlefield," and "The Savage Curtain." I argue that even though the Colorblind Ideal has been understood as the way to move society forward toward a more racially just future, recent research suggests that it might actually exacerbate, rather than alleviate, social conflict and oppression. I, then, indicate that King's other ideal, the multicultural perspective—which encourages individuals to take pride in, rather than ignore or erase, one's own racial or ethnic identity—is also represented in *ST: TOS*. This ideal is more fully articulated in later parts of the STU, particularly through the characters of *ST: PIC*'s Cristobal Rios, *ST: VOY*'s Commander Chakotay, and *ST: DS9*'s Captain Benjamin Sisko. Yet, while the Multicultural Ideal is favorably endorsed by the STU, recent research also suggests that it has serious limitations, namely, that it elicits violent reaction from many white US Americans in a way that threatens social stability and trust. I maintain that if we want to achieve a future in which we can imagine fully realized characters such as Rios, Chakotay, and Sisko we need to consider the third ideal—a critical anti-racist one—that is suggested by the STU. This ideal envisions a major transformation of our social, political, and economic institutions that undercuts support for white supremacy and makes a diverse and multiracial democratic society a real possibility.

Star Trek Episodes and the Colorblind Ideal: "Balance of Terror," "Let That Be Your Last Battlefield," and "The Savage Curtain"

The Colorblind Ideal of the Federation is hinted at in at least three episodes of *ST: TOS*. Colorblindness is the belief that "racial group membership and race-based differences should not be taken into account when decisions are made, impressions are formed and behaviors are enacted."[7] The justification for this ideal is that if racial group membership or differences are not noticed or made relevant in organizational or institutional decision making, then people will be unable to act in a racially biased way. The Colorblind Ideal has become an ideal for many different domains including legal, political, educational, and organizational contexts, as well as interpersonal relationships. Leonard Nimoy, who portrayed Spock for many years, believed that this approach is what makes the STU so attractive to viewers:

> I think one of the major reasons is that the whole structure of *Trek* is a moral one—it's a moral society that people are attracted to. It really is a meritocracy. If you do well, you advance. If you are good at what you do, you can have the job. It doesn't matter who you are or

what you are, what your origins are, your color or race. None of that matters. We need to get jobs done here, and if we have someone who can do the job, they have the job.[8]

In the first season episode "Balance of Terror," the *USS Enterprise* is sent on an emergency mission to investigate attacks on Federation outposts along the Romulan Neutral Zone. Sometime in the 22nd century, Earth and the Romulan Empire had engaged in a vicious and destructive war that ended with a treaty establishing a demilitarized zone between the two powers. Now, the *Enterprise* has evidence of a secret Romulan ship systematically destroying bases on the Federation side in an effort to spark another war. On the bridge of the *Enterprise* is Lt. Stiles, a navigator who had family members die in the war long ago. He still bears a grudge against the Romulans. It turns out the Romulans bear a striking resemblance to the Vulcans, and Stiles immediately raises suspicions that Mr. Spock may be a Romulan spy. During one tense moment, Stiles mutters a remark about Spock's loyalty and Kirk quickly reprimands him: "Leave any bigotry in your quarters. There's no room for it on the bridge."

In the third season episode "The Savage Curtain," the *USS Enterprise* encounters an unlikely alien presence as it is investigating an alien world. The figure of US president Abraham Lincoln appears outside the ship's hull, suspended in space, asking to be beamed into the ship. When he is brought aboard, the alien being acts and thinks of himself as President Lincoln, and so Captain Kirk decides to treat him as such until it can be determined who, or what, he actually is. During a tour of the bridge, Kirk and Lincoln are briefly interrupted by Lt. Uhura. Lincoln is momentarily taken aback at the sight of Uhura and blurts out: "What a charming Negress!" When he realizes from the faces of everyone around him that he has said something offensive, he apologizes: "Oh, forgive me, my dear. I know that in my time some used that term as a description of property." Unperturbed, Uhura responds: "But why should I object to that term, sir? You see, in our century, we've learned not to fear words."

It is not until the third season episode "Let That Be Your Last Battlefield" that we get our clearest expression of the colorblind ethos of the Federation. This episode aired in December 1968, at the end of year that saw the assassinations of Martin Luther King, Jr., eight months before, and Robert F. Kennedy just six months before. Race riots had torn through over 125 cities, including Baltimore, Washington, DC, and Chicago. *Star Trek's* response to this wave of political violence was the story of the *Enterprise* caught in the middle of race war, tens of thousands of years old. Two humanoid aliens, Lokai and Bele, both of which have skin that is black on one side and white on the other, appeal to the Kirk to intervene in their struggle. Bele claims that Lokai is a political extremist from the planet Cheron, where is he charged with treason and terrorism against the government. Lokai pleads for political asylum from the Federation—his people had once been enslaved by Bele's people. After their legal emancipation, they continued to be oppressed and marginalized. He says he is fighting for the complete liberation of his people and that his cause is just. While Kirk awaits a decision from Starfleet on Lokai's petition, he invites Bele and Spock for a drink to discuss the matter. When Bele finds out that Starfleet requires a due process hearing before it can hand over custody of Lokai, he retorts that Lokai is swaying the Federation to his campaign of violence. Kirk assures him that they will not be so obviously manipulated, and there is a crucial exchange among the three characters:

> **Bele:** It is obvious to the most simpleminded that Lokai is of an inferior breed.
> **Spock:** The obvious vision evidence, Commissioner, is that he is of the same breed as yourself.
> **Bele:** Are you blind, Commander Spock? Well? Look at me. Look at me.
> **Kirk:** You're black on one side and white on the other.
> **Bele:** I am black on the right side.
> **Kirk:** I fail to see the significant difference.
> **Bele:** Lokai is white on the right side. All of his people are white on the right side.

Kirk stops, shakes his head in disbelief at what he heard, and glances over at Spock to express his incredulity and frustration with Bele's racism. The episode ends with the *Enterprise* arriving at Cheron to find the entire planet in flames, and Bele and Lokai's people all dead from mutual annihilation.

When Kirk gets after Stiles for his xenophobia toward Spock in "Balance of Terror," he is clearly demonstrating the Colorblind Ideal as a standard for the organizational operation of a starship. Kirk recognizes that Stiles is a bigot and that he, as Captain, has no control over what goes on in his officer's heart and mind. But he can make it clear that those beliefs, and any actions that might result from those beliefs, are subject to official sanction if they are found to affect the cooperative efforts of the institution. Kirk is sending the message to his bridge officers that when they are on duty what matters is not their racial or humanoid differences but their "unifying organization identity" as Starfleet personnel and their ability to conduct their work with one another.[9]

In "The Savage Curtain," when Uhura reassures Lincoln that he has not offended her by using a 19th-century term associated with racial subjugation, she demonstrates colorblindness as a societal ideal prevalent among 23rd-century humans. That is, she seems to be saying that the Federation is truly a "post-racial" society in which racial-based differences are not particularly salient or noticed as a defining part of one's identity. As Lincoln explains, in his time, that term was used to mark a person as essentially property because of their racial identity. Uhura is not offended because she knows her own worth and self-esteem and does not experience her racial identity as completely and utterly defining who she is. She understands, as Nimoy suggests, that her world is structured to value people like her for the skills and aptitudes she brings to her work and not for immutable characteristics, such as her skin color.

The conversation between Bele, Kirk, and Spock in "Let That Be Your Last Battlefield" exhibits colorblindness as an interpersonal ideal. Here the goal is to arrive at a world in which racial differences are literally not perceived or at least recognized immediately in interpersonal interactions. Race becomes something like eye color—a trait that many people simply do not notice about other people or pay much attention to when looking at others. Kirk and Spock simply do not notice that Bele and Lokai are mirror images of one another—they merely see two dual-colored beings. But the seemingly minor difference makes all the difference to Bele; they represent alternative conceptions of culture, social status, intelligence, and moral worth. The reactions by Kirk and Spock to Bele's shock are meant to signal the irrelevance of such distinctions in skin color and of impatience with the narrow-mindedness that insists on making them important. The ending announces that holding on to the idea that race is important leads only to animosity, violence, and war.

Star Trek and the Multicultural Ideal: The Cases of Chakotay, Sisko, and Rios

Toward the end of this life, Martin Luther King, Jr., began to articulate his vision of a racially just society more clearly than he had done in his 1963 "I Have a Dream Speech." While many read that speech calling strictly for a Colorblind Ideal as the goal of racial justice, King clarifies that he expects much more: "When I speak of integration, I don't mean a romantic mixing of colors, I mean a real sharing of power and responsibility."[10] This sharing, for King, begins with the African American community learning their own history and gaining an appreciation of their contribution to US history. Through this reflection, King says African Americans will "stand up and say 'I'm black and I'm beautiful,' and this self-affirmation is the black man's need, made compelling by the white man's crimes against him."[11] Then, with this new self-esteem and knowledge, the Black community can engage in a social and political project to transform institutions and cultural ideas toward a racially just society: "The black man in America can provide a new soul force for all Americans, a new expression of the American dream that need not be realized at the expense of other men around the world, but a dream of opportunity and life that can be shared with the rest of the world."[12]

Many contemporary political theorists today refer to this kind of idea for a democracy as "multiculturalism."[13] It is a vision of multiple communities living within a democratic society and minority racial, cultural, or religious groups making moral claims on the government for the official recognition and support of their cultures, languages, and traditions "in the name of equal freedom, opportunity, and civic equality."[14] Instead of thinking about race or ethnicity as something to ignore or work to make irrelevant in social interaction or organizational operations, multiculturalism encourages us to think that race or ethnicity is one form of identity that is important for some people to embrace and express. In the past forty years, this idea has grown in popularity outside of North America and Europe, to involve theorists and political movements in Latin America, Asia, and the Middle East envisioning ways to build culturally pluralistic societies.[15]

While colorblindness is sometimes represented in *ST: TOS* as we have seen earlier, it seems clear that Starfleet is depicted as also embracing the Multicultural Ideal. In *ST: TOS*, not only are human crew members racially and ethnically diverse but they are also depicted as expressing or celebrating these differences. Lt. Uhura is not offended by 19th-century US American slurs, but she also feels free to express herself in Swahili in the episode "Charlie X." Ensign Pavel Chekov famously speaks with a Russian accent and frequently shares humorous tidbits of Russian history and culture that are clearly not true or are exaggerations. Lt. Commander Montgomery Scott also speaks with a Scottish accent and is allowed to wear a kilt as part of his dress uniform in the episodes "By Any Other Name," "Is There in Truth No Beauty," and "The Savage Curtain."

"Is There in Truth No Beauty" is perhaps the most important *ST: TOS* episode for the Multicultural Ideal, not necessarily for the narrative it tells but because of its production details. In this episode, Spock attends a dinner celebration for a visiting Federation psychologist, Miranda Jones. During the event, Dr. Jones notices that Spock is wearing a pin on his uniform that she calls his "IDIC." The meaning of the pendant is not explained in the episode other than Kirk saying it is the "most revered of all Vulcan symbols." The pendant was something designed by Gene Roddenberry to represent the ideal of "Infinite Diversity in Infinite Combinations." He introduced the pin in this episode apparently with hopes of marketing it as *Star Trek* merchandise. The catalog description for the pin from Roddenberry's company later explained that IDIC "represents a Vulcan belief that beauty, growth [and] progress all result from the union of the unlike. . . . The brotherhood of Man is an ideal based on learning to delight in our essential differences as well as learning to recognize our similarities."[16] Roddenberry himself explained how IDIC was an important element in his own philosophical perspective: "Until humans learn to tolerate—no, that's not enough; to positively value each other—until we can value the diversity on Earth, then we don't deserve to go into outer space and encounter infinite diversity out there."[17]

The Multicultural Ideal appears in later series within the STU. However, many of these later examinations of race and ethnicity, more often than not, rely on the traditional science fiction's tendency to explore identity issues through the stories of encounters with non-human aliens or with cyborgs.[18] *ST: TNG* has numerous episodes with Lt. Worf, a Klingon raised by humans, who struggles to define his identity as a warrior within the peaceful world of the Federation. Like Scotty, he is allowed to wear a Klingon baldric, or sash, with his uniform as a reminder of his heritage. *ST: TNG* also explores identity through the character of Lt. Commander Data, an android, who from the very beginning of the series in the episode "Encounter at Farpoint" announces that it is his eternal quest to understand and embody humanity, despite the limitation of not experiencing emotion.

Likewise, in *ST: VOY*, there are two characters whose development involves questions of identity conflict and eventual self-acceptance using this traditional science fiction trope. The first is B'Elanna Torres, who is half-Klingon and half-human. In the episode "Faces," she experiences an extreme identity crisis in which she is turned into two different people, one wholly Klingon and one wholly human, by having her DNA separated out by an alien doctor. Torres's experience is reminiscent of Kirk's in the episode "The Enemy Within"—her human version is weak and fearful and cannot survive without the aggressive and impulsive tendencies of her Klingon blood. At the end of "Faces," she realizes she must be reunited and come to psychological terms with mixed heritage, rather than try to ignore it. Over the course of the series, Torres learns to embrace and celebrate her complicated heritage in episodes such as "Barge of the Dead" and "Lineage." The second character is Seven of Nine, a human being who was kidnapped as a child by the Borg and turned into a cybernetic drone for most of her life. Captain Janeway separates Seven from the Borg Collective in the episode "Scorpion, Part II," and her character arc for the rest of the series is much like Data's—learning how to care for and adopt her humanity again.

By contrast, there are at least three human characters whose stories do exhibit the multicultural idea much more fully than has been done before in the STU. All individuals are conscious of their racial and cultural heritage and often demonstrate it in multiple story lines. The most recent character from the STU is Cristobal Rios, a former Starfleet commander from *ST: PIC*. His personality is the least developed since *ST: PIC* has had only one season, but we know that Rios is Latin American and depicted as a fluent Spanish speaker. He often uses colloquial phrases and has programmed his ship, named *La Sirena*, to recognize Latin American lullabies in Spanish as override codes. *La Sirena* contains a variety of emergency hologram crew members that are all programmed to be versions of Rios. One of them, the Emergency Tactical Hologram, nicknamed "Emmet," primarily speaks Spanish while conducting his duties. Rios displays various other cues to suggest that he is immersed in his Latin American heritage: he drinks pisco, a brandy popular in Chile and other Andean nations; he loves soccer; and, as we see in "The End Is the Beginning," he has a penchant for reading Spanish existentialist philosopher Miguel de Unamuno as a way of dealing with the trauma he suffered while serving in Starfleet.

Next is Commander Chakotay, the Native American second in command of the *USS Voyager*, who bears a prominent facial tattoo as a way to honor his indigenous ancestry. In the episode "Tattoo," we learn that Chakotay is a descendant of a fictional group of indigenous people from Central America called the Rubber Tree People. His internal struggle is with what it means to honor traditional spiritual beliefs in the technologically advanced civilization of the Federation. Yet, we see Chakotay blend these aspects of himself in "The Cloud," in which he reveals that he has a "medicine bundle" of objects that he uses to conduct spiritual ceremonies. This includes a device called an "akoonah" that allows him to enter into altered states of consciousness and to commune with an animal spirit guide. Following the Multicultural Ideal of allowing minority cultures to express their beliefs in the context of larger society, Captain Janeway, in the episode "Initiations," permits Chakotay to use a shuttlecraft to conduct a ritual honoring his father. While it has been noted that Chakotay's portrayal of indigeneity is sometimes stereotypical and problematic, it seems clear that the STU wanted to have a Native American character whose indigenous traditions and ceremonies are treated not merely as personal idiosyncrasies but as valuable assets that improve the mission of *Voyager* in at least two episodes: "The Cloud" and "Mortal Coil."[19]

Perhaps the most fully developed multicultural character is that of Captain Benjamin Sisko of *ST: DS9*. Sisko is important because he is Black, but more poignantly, because he is one of the few Black main characters rooted in African American culture and the history of the United States. Many of the Black characters in the STU are portrayed as part of the broad African diaspora, either African or raised away from Earth and its culture but not as African American per se. For instance, according to the *Star Trek* writer's guide from 1967, Uhura, for instance, is of African descent, having been born in the "United States of Africa." Similarly, the *ST: TNG* episode "Cause and Effect" establishes Geordi La Forge as being born in Mogadishu, Somalia. Travis Mayweather, the helmsman for the *Enterprise NX-01*, in *ST: ENT*, is Black but born in space. As we see in "Broken Bow" and "Fortunate Sone," Mayweather understands his cultural background more in terms of being a "boomer"—that is, someone who spends most of their life in space—than through the lens of his racial identity. Michael Burnham from *ST: DISC* is Black, but her identity story focuses more on her being raised by a Vulcan family. When we do see her childhood around her human parents, such as in the animated *Short Treks* film "The Girl Who Made the Stars," it is clear they were sharing African stories with her. Finally, Joann Owosekun, the navigator for *Discovery*, recounts stories of growing up near southeastern Nigeria in the *ST: DISC* episode "That Hope Is You, Part II."

Sisko, too, is rooted in African history and culture; in "The Search, Part I," we learn that he has a prized collection of Yoruban art. But, in several episodes, we see that Sisko's identity is deeply infused by the African American experience from the United States, including its history of racist oppression under white supremacy. He was born in the South—New Orleans—and his family has deep roots in Creole culture and cuisine. His father owns a well-known Creole restaurant in New Orleans and in "Image in the Sand," Sisko finds solace over the death of his colleague and friend Jadzia Dax by working there for a time. Most importantly, Sisko knows his history and has pride in his racial identity. In "Badda Bing, Badda Bang," Sisko demonstrates that he is familiar with the history of discrimination of African American people in the United States during the twentieth century. He tells his partner, Kasidy Yates, that he is reluctant to participate in a holosuite program set in a Las Vegas casino in the 1960s because he knows that Black people were not allowed to be guests in such spaces at that time, and it seems wrong to him to pretend otherwise. Finally, in "Far Beyond the Stars," Sisko is transfixed by a complex vision sent to him by the Prophets of Bajor in which he inhabits the life of an African American science fiction writer, Benny Russell, in the United States in the 1950s. The vision, which draws from Sisko's own ideas, memories, and beliefs, shows Russell as very familiar with Black authors and scholars, such as Ralph Ellison, Richard Wright, Langston Hughes, W. E. B Du Bois, and Zora Neal Hurston.

While both the colorblind and multicultural or color-conscious ideals appear in the STU, it is arguably the latter that gains more endorsement. IDIC obviously became more than a marketing ploy for Roddenberry, forming an integral part of how he viewed his creation. More recent characters of the STU, such as Rios, Chakotay, and Sisko, are positively portrayed as being deeply immersed in their racial and ethical heritage and use elements of their cultural background to enliven their missions as Starfleet officers. And, indeed, there are several good reasons to recommend the Multicultural Ideal over the colorblind because of the latter's serious limitations and undesirable social consequences.

First, the Multicultural Ideal is more sociologically accurate in terms of how many people of color in the United States understand their own identities. At least for Black, Latinx, and Asian US Americans, race and ethnicity are extremely important to how they think about themselves and as members of a larger cultural community.[20] Second, colorblindness, at least at an interpersonal ideal, is largely a fiction; research demonstrates that people do perceive racial differences almost immediately, and they begin to do so as early as six months of age.[21] Third, there is some evidence that exposure to colorblind messaging actually restricts people's abilities to identify acts of overt racial bias or to consider them very serious.[22] On the other hand, exposure to a multicultural messaging can heighten people's abilities to imagine other people's point of view.[23] Next, Eduardo Bonilla Silva and Ian Haney Lopez each argue that the Colorblind Ideal has become a kind of ideology used to undermine anti-racist efforts; if race is something that we ought to ignore or downplay in a democratic society, then it is impermissible to use racial categories in any laws and policies, even if they are designed to increase equal opportunity or social services for historically marginalized communities.[24] Most worrisome, however, is evidence that suggests that individuals who espouse higher levels of color blindness actually demonstrate greater racial prejudice and more easily accept incorrect views about racial and ethnic groups and race relations in society.[25]

Even though the Multicultural Ideal is preferable to colorblindness, it is not without its own drawbacks. In the past forty years, the Multicultural Ideal has come into disfavor in Europe. By 2010, major political leaders in the UK, France, and Germany had disavowed the idea of allowing immigrants to maintain their own cultural differences within a democratic society in favor of policies of forcing assimilation into a mainstream culture.[26] Research of anti-multicultural discourse in Europe reveals a sense of threat by some Europeans who feel that immigrants bring with them cultural and religious values that are incommensurable with European ideals or are inherently dangerous to the well-being of communities or the economic stability of society.[27]

In the United States, a focus on multiculturalism tends to make white US Americans feel alienated and threatened in society to such an extent that they are willing to abandon their commitment to a democratic society in order to preserve their group status. Political scientist Ashley Jardina argues that there is a growing sense of anxiety among many white people in the United States having to do with their loss of a demographic majority status.[28] The increasing economic, political, and social power of people of color means to them not an opportunity for living a rich and diverse community but a loss of dominance and control over the direction of their society. White Americans appear to feel more distrust than cooperation and altruism when faced with the idea of living among ethnic or racial minorities.[29] Indeed, when white Americans are reminded of the loss of demographic majority status, they tend to express more negative racial attitudes toward Blacks, Latinxs, and Asians and adopt more pro-white views.[30] White Americans who tend to express these negative racial views as a result of their perception of group status tend to be drawn more toward the Republican Party and more conservative views.[31] What is most troubling is that more and more white Republicans are increasingly drawn to the ideas that US political institutions do not serve their interests, but rather those of immigrants, African Americans, and Latinxs; and they are willing to entertain notions of violence, lawbreaking, and authoritarianism in order to reclaim a "traditional American way of life."[32] The events that occurred on January 6, 2021—when thousands of angry supporters of President Donald J. Trump stormed the US Capitol building in Washington, DC, to interrupt the certification of the Presidential Election—seem to bear these findings out.

Star Trek and Critical Antiracism

The challenge appears to be this: How do we design a multicultural democratic society that does not trigger a threat response in the dominant society? How can we imagine the empowerment of people of color in the United States that is not perceived as a zero-sum game? Historian Ibram X. Kendi points out that this kind of theorizing is difficult because it runs contrary to the flow of this nation's efforts. Quoting poet Audre Lorde, he writes:

> "We have all been programmed to respond to the human differences between us with fear and loathing and to handle that difference in one of three ways: ignore it, and if that is not possible, copy it if we think it is dominant, or destroy it if we think it is subordinate. But we have no patterns for relating across our human differences as equals." To be antiracist is a radical choice in the face of this history, requiring a radical reorientation of our consciousness.[33]

Martin Luther King, Jr., agreed, arguing in an essay that was published after his murder in 1968, that his vision of the integrated society was not simply colorblind but necessarily involved a radical alteration of national life, a "real sharing of power and responsibility."[34]

The STU may again be a way to help conceive what this kind of anti-racist integrated society might be like. As we have seen, the Federation is devoted to multiculturalism; it is a world that allows characters from Uhura to Rios, Chakotay, and Sisko to embody their racial and ethnic heritage and to share those aspects of themselves with others across their differences. But it is also a society with a very different economic system. In *ST: TNG* episode "The Neutral Zone," Captain Picard explains that in the Federation: "People are no longer obsessed with the accumulation of things. We've eliminated hunger, want, the need for possessions. We've grown out of our infancy."

Later, in the film *Star Trek: First Contact* (1996), Picard points out: "The economics of the future are somewhat different. You see, money doesn't exist in the 24th century. . . . The acquisition of wealth is no longer the driving force of our lives. We work to better ourselves and the rest of humanity." Rick Webb calls this a "proto post scarcity society" which has essentially decoupled labor from wages for a vast majority of society:

> Citizens have no financial need to work as their benefits are more than enough to provide for a comfortable life, and there is, clearly universal health care and education. The Federation has taken the plunge to the other side of people's fears about European socialist capitalism: yes, some people might not work. So what? Good for them. We think most still will.[35]

This kind of lifestyle is possible because of two technological advances, as Peter Frase points out: "One is the technology of the 'replicator' which is capable of materializing any object out of thin air, with only the press of a button. The other is a fuzzily described source of apparently free (or nearly free) energy, which runs the replicators as well as everything else on the show."[36]

Rios, Chakotay, and Sisko are possible because they live in post-"racial capitalist" society that has not only decoupled labor from wages but also eliminated white supremacy and the subjugation of racial groups for economic exploitation under capitalism. This kind of transformation is theorized by Martin Luther King, Jr., as he sketched out his idea of the integrated society. He warned that the United States would have to learn to see how *capitalism* is deeply intertwined with *racist subjugation* and *military imperialism* abroad in what he called "the triple evils."[37] Historian Ibram X. Kendi adds that capitalism is a form of market economics that arose in the modern era alongside racism to form a complex system called "racial capitalism." To build an anti-racist society now, Kendi argues, requires that activists must understand the history of the way that capitalist wealth first accumulated through the free labor of subjugated slaves, continues through the unfair exploitation of large numbers of working-class people of color, and relies on the extraction of resources from foreign countries with legacies of racist European colonization:

Markets and market rules and competition and benefits from winning existed long before the rise of capitalism in the modern world. What capitalism introduced into this mix was global theft, racially uneven playing fields, unidirectional wealth that rushes upward in unprecedented amounts. . . . Capitalism is essentially racist and racism is essentially capitalist. They were birthed together from the same unnatural causes and they shall one day die together from unnatural causes. Or racial capitalism will live into another epoch of theft and rapacious inequity, especially if activists naively fight the conjoined twins independently, as if they are not the same.[38]

The Federation's technological advances, thus, have essentially eliminated the need to continue racist subjugation for the maintenance of a cheap labor force needed for energy extraction and resource distribution.

More importantly, undercutting racial capitalism means eliminating what US American philosopher and sociologist W. E. B. Du Bois (1868–1963) called the "wages of whiteness." In his study of the success and limitations of the Reconstruction period in US American history (1860–80), W. E. B. Du Bois explains that solidarity between poor white workers and Black workers for better working conditions was not possible because the former was offered white social status by wealthy elites as compensation for low pay:

It must be remembered that the white group of laborers, while they received a low wage, were compensated in part by a sort of public and psychological wage. They were given public deference and tides of courtesy because they were white. They were admitted freely with all classes of white people to public functions, public parks, and the best schools. The police were drawn from their ranks, and the courts dependent on their votes, treated them with such leniency as to encourage lawlessness. Their vote selected public officials, and while this had small effect upon the economic situation, it had great effect upon their personal treatment and the deference shown them.[39]

This tactic of dividing poor whites from Blacks with the wages of whiteness continued after Reconstruction into the twentieth century, according to Du Bois, as industrialists "spend large sums of money to make laborers think that the most worthless white man is better than any colored man."[40] This ideology of whiteness also spread among the millions of immigrants who journeyed to the United States during the 1920s and 1930s, so that acceptance of anti-Black racism became like entry pass into elevated social status:

> Thus, in America we have seen a wild and ruthless scramble of labor groups over each other in order to climb to wealth on the backs of black labor and foreign immigrants. The Irish climbed on the Negroes. The Germans scrambled over the Negroes and emulated the Irish. The Scandinavians fought forward next to the Germans and Italians and "Bohunks" are crowding up, leaving Negroes still at the bottom chained to helplessness, first by slavery, then by disenfranchisement and always by the Color Bar.[41]

Historian David Roediger confirms this account and adds that it was not until the middle of the twentieth century, with the New Deal program and the beginning of the Second World War, that most European immigrants could ease scrambling for the wages of whiteness; but by that point, a majority of African Americans were firmly segregated from the US American mainstream socially, politically, and economically.[42] The legacy of struggles for white social status, according to critical race legal scholar Derrick Bell, has now sedimented itself in US American institutions, particularly the legal system, and affects policy decisions dealing with housing, schooling, employment, and higher education admissions:

> Whites have come to expect and rely on these benefits and over time these expectations have been affirmed, legitimated, and protected by the law. Even though the law is neither uniform nor explicit in all instances, in protecting settled expectations based on white privileges, American law has recognized a property interest in whiteness that, although unacknowledged, now forms the background against which legal disputes are framed, argued, and adjudicated.[43]

Thus, the STU presents the Federation as an anti-racist multicultural society in which human beings are able to embody, explore, and share their racial and cultural differences with one another because these differences are no longer aspects of identity used to create castes of oppression. The scientific and technological advances of the Federation, such as the replicator, allow individuals to exercise their basic human capabilities and flourish, as Nussbaum would put it, because they no longer have to worry about access to basic survival needs. The Federation's economic structure has eliminated wage labor as a means of sustenance for workers and as a source of profit making for elites. Work is done, or not done, for personal fulfillment. In decoupling labor from wages, the Federation has thereby undone the basis for the wages of whiteness. As historian Keenga Yamatta-Taylor explains:

> It is widely accepted that the racial oppression of slaves was rooted in the exploitation of the slave economy, but fewer recognize that under capitalism, wage slavery is the pivot around which all other inequalities and oppressions turn. Capitalism used racism to justify plunder, conquest, and slavery, but as Karl Marx pointed out, it would also come to racism to divide and rule—to put one section of the working class against another and in doing so, blunt the class consciousness of all.[44]

By eliminating this pivot point, the Federation has unraveled the racial caste system in the United States that puts a social premium on white identity, which has historically been used to compensate certain individuals for their economic exploitation and political disempowerment. And it is this fixation on whiteness as property that must be defended which is at the heart of so much white resistance to the multicultural idea in our era.

The Advantage of an Anti-Racist Future

Star Trek's vision of a different racial future is not something that only works to empower individuals who are marginalized in our current reality. It does indeed allow us imagine what it might be like to be a person of color who does not have to fear, on an everyday basis, the dangers of white supremacy. But it also allows us to imagine what it might be like to a person who does not have to suffer what philosopher Terrence MacMullan calls the "habits of whiteness"—the historical patterns of thinking and reacting to the presence of nonwhite people as personal and social threats to well-being that often result in direct personal violence or the creation of social policy, like segregation or housing redlining, which constitutes structural violence.[45] Philosopher George Yancy asks us to think of how George Zimmerman, the vigilante who shot and killed Treyvon Martin, or the officers who killed Eric Garner and Sandra Bland might have acted differently if they had not been programmed for years with a centuries-old cultural violence that taught them to react viscerally with fear to the presence of a Black human being. Thus, *Star Trek* asks us to imagine individuals who are freed from historical frameworks of perception and meaning—"white modes of being-in-the world, white bodily forms of comportment, white ways of occupying space, and white gazes"—that narrow their own self-understandings and potentials as people.[46] That, after all, seems to be Captain Kirk's message to Stiles in "Balance of Terror" when he tells him that the war between Earth and Romulus that killed his ancestors need not be his war too, and that his bigotry against Vulcans is a frame of reference that will ultimately inhibit his capacity as a Starfleet officer and as a human being.

Perhaps most importantly, this anti-racist ideal of the Federation can also offer more than just a vision of how individuals might possibly relate to one another's racial and ethnic differences without the social pressure of economic competition and survival looming over their heads. It can help to illuminate what forms of collective action and policy we can pursue now to bring that vision to bear. Keeanga Yamatta Taylor notes that as movements such as Black Lives Matter grow and mature, they start to make connections between social issues like police violence with racism, poverty, hunger, and economic inequality. Part of the work becomes how we weave these realizations into some "much larger vision of what a different world could look like."[47] Science fiction writer and scholar Walidah Imarisha tells us this can be the job of good science fiction in social justice work, to supply these visions and be an "exploring ground, a laboratory to try new tactics, strategies, and visions without real world costs."[48] I believe that the STU's rich depiction of an anti-racist future can assist anti-racist activist work by shedding light on the essential need to create robust social and economic safety nets. Widely available education, universal health care, and well-compensated and meaningful work are all policy goals that can help to reduce inequality and the violence that often accompany social despair and frustration. It is perhaps no coincidence, then, that Black Lives Matters protests have erupted across the United States at roughly the same era as widespread strikes by public school teachers, home health care providers, and minimum-wage service workers for better working conditions. There is a growing concern about economic precarity and the erosion of social networks that support a dignified life for individuals. *Star Trek* shows that even if we do not have replicator technology or unlimited energy from dilithium crystals, we can still struggle in our schools, workplaces, and communities to support individuals to experiment with, and maintain, vibrant identities and new forms of being with each other that we see represented in the lives of people like Uhura, Rios, Chakotay, and Benjamin Sisko.

Conclusion

Star Trek has always had a reputation among major science fiction franchises of being particularly progressive in terms of its representation of racial diversity and its portrayal of a future free from racial strife. In this chapter, I have tried to examine the STU for its lessons about how to imagine a future of racial justice. I maintain that there are three main ideals in *Star Trek* about the role that race should take in a democratic society that are presented over the course of fifty years: the Colorblind Ideal, the Multicultural Ideal, and the Critical Anti-Racist Ideal. The first ideal, colorblindness, seems straightforward to many people, but researchers point out that attempting to pretend that you don't notice race is psychologically dishonest, and there are adverse effects when society does not take racial identity into account in order to remedy past racial injustices. Multiculturalism, on the other hand, attempts to imagine a role for racial identity within a democratic society; it imagines a world in which individuals have the freedom to embody and express their racial and ethnic heritage and to feel those identities affirmed and welcomed by others. While this ideal is celebrated in the STU, researchers point that multiculturalism faces stiff opposition in the United States and Europe, particularly by white, European citizens in the majority, who feel that multiculturalism somehow diminishes the value of a white identity in their cultures. I argue that by taking a critical anti-racist perspective from within some of the stories of *Star Trek*, we learn that the core of this resistance has to do with the way that capitalist economic systems pit different racial and ethnic groups into competition over resources and status. If we can transform our societies to remove the foundation of these conflicts, then we can better imagine what it might be like to live in a society in which racial difference is valued and affirmed as a social good for the well-being of all members of society.

Chapter 5

Mercy, Forgiveness, and Justice

The *Star Trek* story that treats the destructiveness surrounding the emotion of vengeance best is undoubtedly that of the arch-villain Khan Noonian Singh in the film *Star Trek II: The Wrath of Khan* (1982). Khan made his appearance in the *ST: TOS* episode "Space Seed" as a genetically enhanced superhuman from the 20th century, exiled from the Earth for tyrannizing humanity during a period that came to be known in the STU as the Eugenics Wars. He wreaks havoc aboard the *Enterprise* in a quest to reassert his brutal authority until he is once again exiled by Kirk on a deserted planet. *Star Trek II* finds Khan again kidnapping a Federation starship several years later in order to hunt down and kill Kirk who he feels is the source of all his life's agony. Khan's followers do not completely understand his obsession with revenge once they have obtained a ship to take them away from their dying planet, but they display unblinking loyalty to his violent urges. Khan is not able to kill Kirk, but he sets in motion a series of events that leads to his own bitter end, along with all his crew. Tragically, his wrath releases ripples of destruction that spread out across the galaxy, causing the death of Captain Spock and, arguably, Kirk's son David in *Star Trek III: The Search for Spock* (1984).

For author Milovan Djilas, the story of Khan's vengeance would probably sound like a realistic description of the dangers he experienced in his world. Growing up in the Balkan nation of Montenegro in the early twentieth century meant, for Djilas, living in society suffused with the violence of vengeance. His great-grandfather and grandfather had been murdered as a result of blood feuds going back for generations. Djilas was born in 1911, and as he grew up, he soon came to realize that the snares of these vendettas endangered him and limited the possibilities his own life could take. He would eventually go on to become a top politician in the former Yugoslavia. But in his autobiography, *Land without Justice*, Djilas writes how the lives of his ancestors cast a shadow over his existence and created expectations about what duties his future self would have to fulfill in order to maintain family honor:

> I had a close friend in the seventh grade, the kin of those who had killed my grandfather, though I knew nothing of this kinship. I brought him home one night around Christmas time, so that he would not have to go home on a lonely road in the dark. When my father learned who he was, he forbade me to sleep with him because, has he said later, he did not want anyone with our blood on his hands to breathe into the soul of his son. . . . The next day I escorted my friend home, and only then did my father tell us that a male child of an enemy clan had spent the night in our house. After the recess I met my friend again, and he, too, had obviously learned the awful secret from his people. We avoided one another and our friendship was smothered, without either of us admitting the real reason, for our childish breasts were straining for revenge.

Djilas's experience demonstrates that living in a society without strong traditions of reconciliation leads to perpetual cycles of violence that can end only in humiliating subordination or, as in *The Wrath of Khan*, widespread destruction. The STU contains many such complex narratives about retaliation and vengeance. It also contains many stories about how we can work toward reconciling with one another and, more importantly, the values we need in order to heal from the harm we inflict upon one another.

In this chapter, I begin by examining two episodes that give us insight into the problem of vengeance: *ST: TOS* "The Conscience of the King" and *ST: VOY* "Nemesis." Both episodes assert that some kind of intervention is needed to prevent cycles of harm and retaliation from spiraling out of control. But what kind of intervention will be effective? Historically, the answer has been that justice needs to be done and people who harm others need to be punished. Yet, I think both these episodes end by suggesting that punishment of wrongdoers is not a perfect solution and often leaves traumatic aftereffects that are not solved by a system of retributive justice. This is the assessment offered by peace philosophers, such as Gandhi and Martin Luther King, Jr.: punishing people for causing harm to others is not lasting solution for a stable and just society. We need some other kinds of values to intervene and stop cycles of violence and revenge.

I then consider *Star Trek* story lines that offer three different possibilities for the responses to address the problem of harm and revenge. The *ST: TOS* episode "Arena" offers that of mercy; the *ST: DS9* episodes "Return to Grace" and "Waltz" introduce the notion of grace; and finally *ST: VOY* "Jetrel" suggests forgiveness. I contend that mercy and grace are indeed values that intervene to halt cycles of retaliation, but they are not particularly transformative of conditions in society that would lead to lasting peace and justice. Instead, I suggest that the work of Desmond Tutu and the Truth and Reconciliation Commission (TRC) of South Africa indicates that forgiveness is more effective for helping societies ravaged by collective violence to give survivors and perpetrators a way to change the dynamics of their interactions and create a basis for a more just future with one another.

Star Trek Episodes: "The Conscience of the King" and "Nemesis"

In his story outline for "The Conscience of the King," writer Barry Trivers broadcast the theme he wanted to achieve this way: "Our story deals with the question: When does the search for Justice become a drive for Vengeance?"[1] As the episode opens, the *Enterprise* is diverted from its normal mission to Planet Q by Captain Kirk's childhood friend, Dr. Thomas Leighton, who has promised Kirk a scientific breakthrough to assist a famine on another planet. However, when Kirk arrives he finds that Leighton has lured him there under false pretenses. Leighton tells Kirk that he is convinced that there is a person on Planet Q who is actually a long missing fugitive named Kodos. Twenty years before, Kodos was governor of the Earth colony on the planet Tarsus IV. During an emergency food shortage, Kodos systematically murdered over four thousand inhabitants, in hopes of saving enough supplies to keep the rest of the colony alive. Relief from the Federation arrived soon after the killings and Kodos fled Tarsus IV rather than face the consequences of his commands. Leighton and Kirk were both on the planet during the massacre and are among the last handful of people in the galaxy who were eye witnesses to Kodos's reign of terror. Now, Leighton has called Kirk because he believes that Kodos is disguising himself as an acclaimed actor who is performing on Planet Q: Anton Karidian. He wants Kirk to help him apprehend this disguised tyrant. When Leighton is later found murdered, Kirk feels the urgency to determine Karidian's true identity and trap the killer.

Much of the dramatic tension in this episode arises because of Spock and Dr. McCoy's concern with Kirk's single-minded preoccupation to solve the mystery. In one scene, they both confront Kirk because of his erratic behavior. Spock worries that it might interfere with Kirk's ability to carry out his duties and informs him that he has also done some background research on the matter. Spock is convinced that Karidian is Kodos. He advises Kirk to act decisively. The captain admits his hesitation:

Kirk: I'm interested in justice.
McCoy: Are you? Are you sure it's not vengeance?

Kirk: No, I'm not sure. I wish I was. I've done things I've never done before. I've placed my command in jeopardy. From here on, I've got to determine whether or not Karidian is Kodos.

Spock: He is.

Kirk: You sound certain. I wish I could be. Before I accuse a man of that, I've got to be. I saw him once, twenty years ago. Men change. Memory changes . . .

McCoy: What if you decide he is Kodos? What then? Do you play God, carry his head through the corridors in triumph? That won't bring back the dead, Jim.

Kirk: No. But they may rest easier.

Karidian is, in fact, Kodos. He hid his past expertly from everyone except, it turns out, his daughter, Leonore. In order to protect her father, she has been systematically murdering all of the remaining eye witnesses to the massacre on Tarsus IV. When she admits this to her father, he is horrified and exclaims: "You've left me nothing. You were the one thing in my life untouched by what I'd done." Kodos realizes that his one hope for doing good in the world is ruined. Leonore's compulsion to shield her father from punishment for his past crimes has driven her insane. Kirk overhears Leonore's confession and orders them apprehended. But before they can be arrested by security, Leonore steals a phaser and threatens Kirk. As she fires the weapon, Kodos leaps in front of the captain and takes the blast. At the end of the episode, Kirk sits somberly on the bridge, reading a medical report about Leonore. She apparently remembers nothing about killing her own father. In fact, she believes he is still alive, giving performances to adoring fans. Kodos died in a moment of poetic justice, but Kirk appears more weary than triumphant. We are left to ponder whether the dead rest easier now that Kodos is dead or whether we should continue to be unsettled by the way his legacy continued to ruin lives until his very last moments.

In *ST: VOY* "Nemesis," Commander Chakotay's shuttle is shot down over a planet while on a survey mission. He is captured by a group of soldiers from a species named the Vori. Chakotay learns that the Vori are in a vicious war with another species called the Kradin, a brutal enemy that relishes killing the Vori and desecrating their war dead. Over the next few days, Chakotay experiences Kradin attacks on the Vori that result in the death of all the soldiers. Chakotay manages to find safety in a Vori village which welcomes him as one of their own defenders. However, the next day the Kradin attack the village and march all the civilians to extermination camps. As he witnesses the ruthlessness of the Kradin, Chakotay increasingly comes to identify with the Vori cause. His hatred of the Kradin is so complete that he refuses to return to search for his shuttle and his life aboard *Voyager*.

Eventually, Chakotay is rescued by the *Voyager* crew. In a surprising twist, we learn that Captain Janeway had been working with the Kradin government to locate Chakotay. She finds out that Chakotay's experiences were really part of an elaborate holographic simulation conducted by the Vori to train kidnapped victims to fight for them. The Doctor informs Chakotay that he has undergone massive brainwashing. A confused Chakotay asks if anything he underwent was true and Janeway admits she does not know whether the Kradin are as brutal as the Vori claim. The Kradin ambassador who assisted the *Voyager* rescue mission enters the sickbay at that moment and apologizes to Chakotay for not being able to extricate him sooner. Chakotay, obviously uncomfortable, excuses himself and bursts out of the room. Janeway runs after him in the hallway. He turns to her to explain: "I wish it were as easy to stop hating as it was to start." Despite knowing the truth about the war and being able to understand rationally what happened to him, Chakotay cannot shake the emotional trauma the war simulation inflicted upon him. Without a way to process his feelings, his hatred smolders under the surface, leaving him vulnerable and angry.

Peace Studies Concepts: Revenge and Retribution

For Martin Luther King, Jr., the autobiography of Djilas, the story of Karidian/Kodos, and Chakotay's lingering unease all illustrate his view that there is a kind of metaphysical law about the use of violence. When violence is inflicted upon someone, we should expect a reaction from them. Violence begets retaliation, which then sets the condition for another round of retaliation. This cycle will continue even if one of the parties is either incapacitated or killed. As we see in the case of Djilas's family in Montenegro, or with Leonore Karidian, the cycle of violence can be taken up by descendants and perpetuated with increasing devastation generation after generation. King maintains that the cycle of violence is something that can only be ended by changing the dynamic of harm/retaliation and introducing a new force into the mix:

> In struggling for human dignity the oppressed people of the world must not allow themselves to become bitter or indulge in hate campaigns. To retaliate with hate and bitterness would do nothing but intensify the hate in the world. Along the way of life, someone must have sense enough and morality enough to cut off the chain of hate.[2]

King claims he learned this lesson from Mohandas Gandhi (1869–1948), one of the leaders of the Indian independence movement. Gandhi calls what King referred to as the "chain of hate" as "the law of the jungle," and he similarly describes it in cyclical and generational terms: "Hatred increases. The defeated party vows vengeance and simply bides its time. The spirit of revenge thus descends from father to son."[3]

Martha Nussbaum reminds us that the ancient Greeks were also particularly fascinated with how to end repeating chains of violence. One of the most classic stories of ancient Greek culture focuses precisely on the question of transforming revenge into a legal system involving just punishment or retribution against wrongdoers. The playwright Aeschylus' fifth-century BCE trilogy *Oresteia* explores the destructive potential of unchecked feelings of vengeance and the need of society to create a stable way to channel anger for harm done.[4] Many other societies, including the medieval Vikings and Japan of the samurai, for instance, also built norms of community deliberation or complex honor codes to contain the violence of blood feuds.[5] Indeed, this urgency to regulate retaliatory violence is perhaps one of the oldest concerns of the earliest city-states in human history. The Babylonian Code of Hammurabi from ancient Mesopotamia in 1700 BCE, for instance, detailed a precise formula of punishment for crimes that have come to be known as *lex talionis,* or the principle of "eye for an eye."[6]

For some, the Code of Hammurabi, or the Laws of Moses which borrow from the Babylonian ideals, appears to be merely vengeance codified into law. Retribution for crime does resemble vengeance, in that it answers harm with harm. But despite this similarity, the point of *lex talionis* is actually to put an end to the cycle of harm and retaliation.[7] When the legal system of the state punishes someone for a crime, the matter is supposed to be over. Further retaliation by the victim on the perpetrator is not allowed—when you take out my eye, you deserve to have your eye taken—by the state. I am not justified, after you are punished, in also taking your tooth and breaking your bone. Retributive punishment, then, is a kind of harm—but it is not the same thing as vengeance or retaliation.

While the creation of a system of retributive punishment might have been one tool that human beings developed to break the cycle of vengeance, King and Gandhi both maintain that more progress is needed for truly peaceful societies. King believes that the problem of social conflict requires going to the root causes of violence in society. Instead of merely trying to regulate cycles of violence, we should instead try to find ways to transform the social conditions that lead individuals to feel that violence is something they need to exercise in order to satisfy their desires and interests or to calm their fears and insecurities.[8] Gandhi provides two reasons for thinking we need to move beyond retribution.

On the one hand, he thinks the story of human civilization is that of the increasing rejection of violence and coercion as a way to coordinate human action and the adoption of principles of nonviolence in more of our social relationships and institutions:

> If we turn our eyes to the time of which history has any record down to our own time, we shall find that man has been steadily progressing towards ahimsa [principle of no-harm]. Our remote ancestors were cannibals. Then came a time when they were fed up with cannibalism and they began to live on chase. Next came a stage when man was ashamed of leading the life of a wandering hunter. He therefore took to agriculture and depended principally on mother earth for his food. Thus from being a nomad he settled down to civilized stable life, founded villages and towns, and from member of a family he became member of a community and a nation. All these are signs of progressing ahimsa and diminishing himsa [commitment to force and violence]. Had it been otherwise, the human species should

have been extinct by now, even as many of the lower species have disappeared.[9]

Retribution might then be seen as one step in this evolution, but there is no reason to believe we cannot continue to work to remove violence from our society, even if violence justified as punishment for wrongdoing. The other reason Gandhi feels we need to imagine beyond retributive justice is his view that most of the world's religions call on human beings to draw deep on their spiritual and moral abilities to find new values that eschew the urge for retaliation, even in the case of wrongful harms. He writes:

> In our present state, we are partly men and partly beasts and, in our ignorance and even arrogance, say that we truly fulfill the purpose of our species when we deliver blow for blow and develop the measure of anger required for the purpose. We pretend to believe that retaliation is the law of our being, whereas in every scripture we find that retaliation is the law of our being, whereas in ever scripture we find that retaliation is nowhere obligatory but only permissible. It is restraint that is obligatory. Retaliation is indulgence requiring elaborate regulating. Restraint is the law of our being. For, highest perfection is unattainable without highest restraint. Suffering is the badge of the human tribe.[10]

In what follows, then, I want to explore several story lines from the STU that present three different alternatives to retribution, namely mercy, grace, and forgiveness. While they all try to break the chain of hate, I argue they are not equally effective in transforming the underlying social conditions that lead to violence and, thus, for laying the foundations for a more peaceful and just future.

"Arena": The Value of Mercy

In the *ST: TOS* episode "Arena," Captain Kirk, Spock, and Dr. McCoy are invited to beam down to the planet Cestus III, where there is a Federation outpost, for a relaxing dinner with the outpost's leaders. However, when they arrive they realize that the invitation is a trap to get them on the planet; the outpost had been destroyed days earlier by an unknown foe. As they search the ruins, they are once again attacked by an unseen enemy, who kills a member of the security detail on the landing party. The *Enterprise* is attacked in orbit at the same time by an unidentified craft.

Kirk and his team are able to bring an outpost survivor on board as the ship gives pursuit to the enemy vessel. The survivor tells them they were attacked unprovoked and the enemy then sent a fake message to lure to *Enterprise* into an ambush. Kirk surmises that such actions are a prelude to an invasion of the Federation. Spock points out there could be other explanations for the attack, but Kirk shuts him down and orders a high warp speed pursuit. Spock asks Kirk if he means to destroy the enemy ship and Kirk answers affirmatively. Yet, Spock again wants his captain to consider other alternatives:

> **Spock:** The destruction of the alien vessel will not help that colony, Jim.
>
> **Kirk:** If the aliens go unpunished, they'll be back, attacking other Federation installations.
>
> **Spock:** I merely suggest that a regard for sentient life—
>
> **Kirk:** There's no time for that! It's a matter of policy. Out here, we're the only policemen around. And a crime has been committed. Do I make myself clear?

However, before Kirk can become a policeman, judge, and executioner, both the *Enterprise* and the alien ship are stopped in space and scanned. Another alien presence, calling themselves the Metrons, appears to both ships and announces that they are the ones responsible for subduing them. Kirk and the alien captain are then whisked away by the Metrons and placed on a faraway arid planet. The Metrons tell their abductees that they will settle their dispute by engaging in a battle to the death. Kirk finally learns the identity of the alien that destroyed the outpost on Cestus III—it is a sentient reptilian species called the Gorn. Kirk quickly realizes that the Gorn captain is stronger and more vicious than he is. He begins to doubt whether he will survive the trial by combat.

Very quickly, however, Kirk notices that the planet surface is rich with a variety of minerals. It dawns on him that these deposits can be combined to form a powerful gunpowder weapon. At the last crucial moment, Kirk ignites his crude cannon and blasts the Gorn with diamond projectiles. The attack leaves the Gorn helpless and supine, so Kirk approaches to finish him off. But at the last minute, Kirk throws away his stone knife, refusing to execute his enemy. The wounded Gorn immediately disappears and a shining, almost angelic, being materializes. This Metron declares: "You surprise me, Captain. . . . By sparing your helpless enemy, who surely would have destroyed you, you demonstrated the advanced trait of mercy, something we hardly expected. We feel that there may be hope for your kind. Therefore, you will not be destroyed. It would not be civilized." The Metron tells Kirk that his species still considers human beings to be "half-savage," but believe that their two peoples may be able to find agreement in a few thousand years.

The Metrons should not have been so surprised to find Kirk displaying mercy to the Gorn. As Martha Nussbaum points out, mercy—"an inclination of the mind toward leniency in exacting punishment"—is a very old idea that goes back at least to Greek and Roman societies.[11] Usually, mercy was a trait associated with state officials, such as monarchs and judges, who were in a position to mete out retribution. However, moral reformers, such as Christ and the Prophet Muhammad, speak of mercy as a component of a spiritually righteous and ethical life for ordinary people. In the *Sermon on the Mount* from the Gospel of Matthew, Christ tells his followers: "You have learned that they were told, 'Eye for eye, tooth for tooth.'[12] But what I tell you is this: Do not set yourself against the man who wrongs you. If someone slaps you on the right cheek, turn and offer him your left." In Surah 12 of the Koran, it is stated:

> O ye who believe! The law of equality is prescribed to you in cases of murder; The free for free, the slave for slave, the woman for woman. But if any remission is made by the brother of the slain, then grant any reasonable demand and compensate him with handsome gratitude. This is a concession and a Mercy from your Lord.[13]

Clearly, in these cases Christ and the Prophet Muhammad recognize the long-standing authority of the *lex talionis*. Yet, they, like King and Gandhi much later, suggest that there might be a better way to end the chain of hate than through retribution. Instead, it might be preferable not to allow oneself to be engulfed by a punitive spirit and the urge to make those who harm you suffer, even if the perpetrators deserve it for inflicting unjustified harm.

Yet, Kirk is merciful not because he wishes to exercise spiritual fortitude but because he realizes that he might be wrong about whether the Gorn deserves punishment. During the combat, he begins to wonder whether his initial theories about an unprovoked attack on Cestus III, and the possibility of a Gorn invasion, are warranted. Perhaps the Gorn were acting in self-defense? While the Metron was pleased with Kirk's show of mercy, Gandhi and King might not see this decision as one that really works to undermine the chain of hatred or the system of retributive justice in general. In exercising mercy, Kirk is not questioning the use of retribution at all; he is just not sure if the Gorn entirely deserves punishment in this particular case. If there were clearer proof that the Gorn had attacked for no good reason, then Kirk might not have hesitated to execute the enemy captain.

Kirk's merciful display is an exception to the rule of retribution and, thus, keeps in place the status quo which Gandhi and King implore us to transcend. They seek an alternative that can transform social conditions and relationships in a way that prevents violent eruptions and the need for punishment in the first place. Mercy, as a way to react to violence that has already taken place, is not quite the catalyst for the ethical revolution toward a more peaceful society.

"Return to Grace" and "Waltz": The Value of Grace

These two *ST: DS9* episodes deal with Dukat, the Cardassian military commander who is the former governor of the planet Bajor during the last years of the Cardassian occupation. Under his rule, several million Bajorans died in concentration camps or were executed as prisoners of war. Dukat never faced any consequences for these deaths when the Cardassians withdrew from Bajor and left the planet in the care of the Federation. His reputation for brutality nonetheless follows him throughout the *ST: DS9* series.

In the fourth season episode "Return to Grace," Dukat has been demoted to a freighter captain because it is revealed that he fathered a half-Bajoran-half-Cardassian daughter, Tora Ziyal, with one of his Bajoran sex slaves. He finds himself in common cause with Major Kira, the Bajoran commander serving on *Deep Space Nine*, as they work together to hunt down a Klingon ship that killed Cardassian and Bajoran politicians. Throughout the episode, Dukat attempts to either seduce Kira or convince her to join him in his military expeditions against the Klingons (we learn in a later season six episode, "Wrongs Darker Than Death or Night," that Kira's mother had been Dukat's sex slave during the Occupation, making the interactions in "Return to Grace" particularly unsettling). Kira continually rejects all his overtures. She recalls the long trail of murders for which he is responsible, but she grudgingly admires his leadership ability and the affection he has for his daughter. For her part, Ziyal deeply loves her father and tells Kira that Dukat seeks Kira's respect because he sees her as a kind of kindred soul. Both of them killed people during the Occupation. Kira replies: "Ziyal, what your father wants from me is forgiveness. That's one thing I can never give him." Kira is clearly shaken by Ziyal's reminder of her actions during the Occupation and at the end of the episode she asks Dukat permission to take Ziyal back to *Deep Space Nine*. She tells him that she wants to protect Ziyal from becoming a killer like she and her father are.

A similar personal dynamic plays out in the sixth season episode "Waltz." By this point in the series, Dukat had redeemed himself in Cardassian society and become a leader once again. But he has led Cardassia into alliance with the Dominion empire against the Federation. Ziyal is killed in a skirmish as she helps some of her Federation friends escape the Dominion. Dukat has a mental breakdown as a result of her death. He is captured by Federation forces and taken to face war crime charges, with Captain Benjamin Sisko as his escort. However, on the way to the tribunal, their ship is attacked by Dominion ships. Dukat and Sisko are marooned on a planet together. Sisko is seriously injured, but Dukat tends to his wounds and tells him he will find a way to get them both off the planet. This promise, however, is a carefully crafted lie. Dukat is still crazed. He has sabotaged the emergency beacon and is simply seeking to manipulate a situation in which Sisko can announce his approval for Dukat's deeds during the Occupation. After being severely beaten by Dukat, Sisko goads him on to hear what amounts to Dukat's confession about his crimes on Bajor. Dukat admits that he does not feel responsible for what he did because he believes that the Bajorans brought the repression upon themselves:

> **Dukat:** Oh because they were blind ignorant fools. If only they had cooperated with us, we could have turned their world into a paradise. From the moment we arrived on Bajor, it was clear we were the superior race, but they couldn't accept that. They wanted to be treated as equals when they most certainly were not. . . . We did not choose to be the superior race. Fate handed us that role. And it would have been so much easier for everyone if the Bajorans had simply accepted their role . . .
> **Sisko:** And you hated them for it?
> **Dukat:** Of course I hated them! I hated everything about them! . . .
> **Sisko:** You should have killed them all, hmm?
> **Dukat:** Yes! Yes! That's it, isn't it?! I should have killed every last one of them. I should have turned their planet into a graveyard the likes of which the galaxy had never seen! I should have killed them all!

Hans Beimler, who wrote the episode "Return to Grace," observes: "There are so many facets to Dukat. He's a very complicated character. But he's always a Nazi, *always*. In this episode you're aware of different shades to his personality. But, if you think about it, they're all very self-serving. This is not a pleasant man. He's done a lot of terrible things."[14] With these two episodes together, we understand that Dukat does not think of himself as a villain or believe that what he did on Bajor is "terrible." He does not believe he must atone for his crimes. Rather, he wants gratitude from Kira, and respect from Sisko, for the acts of grace he believes he committed while prefect of Bajor.

Grace is usually thought of as a Christian theological concept, but Peter King reminds us that there are more ordinary and secular versions. Acts of grace involve bestowing benefits on a recipient who is not entitled to, or has done nothing particular to deserve, good rewards: "Everyday examples include leaving a 'tip' or gratuity (etymologically linked to 'grace'); giving money to charity; helping an infirm person to cross the street; volunteer work. The conferred benefit is a gift freely given with no strings attached; grace is thus often called a gift."[15] Dukat's declarations in "Waltz" reveal that he sometimes gave the Bajorans extra food rations or reduced work hours. Yet, he also considered the violence he inflicted on the Bajoran people as a kind of gracious discipline they needed for their own good, a sort of punishment a parent might inflict on a misbehaving child. The Bajorans, in his mind, certainly did not deserve these acts of kindness since they were an inferior race in his estimation. His indignation arose when he couldn't get them to realize that they were not entitled to respond to his oppression with rebellious violence. It would eventually lead to his frustration and bitterness, with people such as Kira and Sisko failing to appreciate the grace he supposedly showed during the Occupation.

Dukat's moral failure is clearly highlighted in "Return to Grace" by contrasting him with Kira's decision to rescue Ziyal. Dukat believes that he will regain his leadership in Cardassian society if he hunts down and kills the Klingon enemies his government refuses to pursue. He is willing to embroil Ziyal in his crusades. Kira however thinks that there is still time to extricate Ziyal from the cycle of violence her father is about to inaugurate. She displays true grace by gifting Ziyal an opportunity to find a path other than becoming a Cardassian terrorist in her father's war. Kira tries to build a future with a little less violence. In that way, Kira is doing penance for the deaths she caused while she was in the Resistance in a way that Dukat is not willing to do for his crimes. Sadly, Ziyal is later murdered because she is caught in the wake of the violence unleashed by her father's actions, and her death leads to Dukat's mental breakdown witnessed in "Waltz."

Yet, it is not clear from these episodes that grace is any better than mercy at being the kind of disposition that can successfully cut off the cycles of violence that concern Gandhi and King. Kira exercises true grace and, for a time, changes the life of an innocent woman who would have gone down a morally treacherous road otherwise. But it is not quite enough to transform conditions around Ziyal that lead to her death. Like mercy, grace works by being an exception to the system of retribution. But the idea of grace does not entail we ought to do away with retribution altogether.

Moreover, Dukat illustrates another particular failure of grace. He considered the oppression he unleashed as a favor to the Bajoran people, a kind of charity of which they were not worthy. His inclination to "gift" the Bajorans with discipline was not meant in any way to transform relationships of power or unequal social standing between Cardassians and Bajorans. Indeed, it was meant to reinforce the lesson that the Bajorans ought simply to accept the power and social hierarchy imposed by the Cardassians. Dukat's actions suggest that acts of grace are compatible with feelings of pity, condescension, or even contempt for the people receiving grace. In short, grace does not necessarily work to radically transform unjust power relationships that might be the cause of the violence calling for grace in the first place.

Theologian Reinhold Niebuhr seemed to notice this problematic feature of grace when he wrote: "We have previously suggested that philanthropy combines genuine pity with the display of power and that the later element explains why the powerful are more inclined to be generous than to grant social justice."[16] One particular example Niebuhr offered was the charitable assistance that privileged white people provided for Black schools during Jim Crow segregation in the United States: "The Negro schools, conducted under the auspices of white philanthropy, encourage individual Negroes to higher forms of self-realization; but they do not make a frontal attack upon the social injustices from which the Negro suffers."[17] The segregated schools, in other words, helped to uplift a few individuals, but they did not do much to undermine the systems of racist discrimination that created them in the first place. More recent data on charitable giving suggests that the problem is even more pronounced today; a significant amount of charity given by the wealthy is not for the alleviation of the poor but for causes that directly benefit the rich such as elite universities, schools, and museums: "The common assumption that philanthropy automatically results in a redistribution of money is wrong. A lot of elite philanthropy is about elite causes. Rather than making the world a better place, it largely reinforces the world as it is."[18] Such examples do not entail that all charity is demeaning or done out of motives of contempt. It does suggest that grace is best thought of as a kind of intervention into a system of inequalities that is meant to ameliorate, rather than transform, conditions. Again, Gandhi and King implore us to imagine a better, less punitive, alternative.

"Jetrel": The Value of Forgiveness

"Jetrel" begins with the USS Voyager being intercepted by a Haakon Ian shuttle bearing a single passenger named Dr. Ma'Bor Jetrel. The Haakonian urgently asks to speak to Neelix. When Neelix learns that this person wishes to talk with him he becomes visibly disturbed, revealing that he knows who this stranger really is. Some fifteen years before, the Haakonians were at war with the Talaxian people. Jetrel was a scientist working for the Haakonian military, and he invented a weapon of mass destruction called the Metreon Cascade. The weapon was deployed against the Talaxian moon of Rinax. It immediately disintegrated over 300, 000 people, including members of Neelix's family. More died as a result of the poisoning from the weapon. Neelix was not with his family on the moon at the time because he claimed he was on his home world with the defense forces. However, Neelix did go to Rinax to help in relief efforts. Jetrel tells the Voyager crew that he has been studying the long-term effects of the Metreon Cascade and has identified a fatal blood disease among survivors, including Neelix.

Jetrel's presence on the ship deeply upsets Neelix, not only because he holds Jetrel responsible for the death of his family but because of the shame he feels about the war. It turns out that on the day of the Metreon Cascade, Neelix was not preparing with the defense forces after all. Instead, he was hiding from them because he did not want to serve in a war he considered unjust. He long felt he was a coward since he did not help to defend his people against the atrocity. He feels ashamed to have lied for so many years about his own lack of military service. Kes tries to soothe him by sorting out his emotions:

Kes: What an awful burden you've carried all these years. No wonder you're so angry with Jetrel.

Neelix: Of course I am! He killed them all, my mother, my father, my little brothers.

Kes: Is that really why?. . . . Ever since Jetrel came on board, you've despised him. The hurt and anger you've held in all these years was vented right at him, but was it really Jetrel you were angry with? Is he the one you blame for what happened?

Neelix: I . . . I don't know.

It turns out that Jetrel's mission to *Voyager* is a lie. Neelix does not have the disease, but Jetrel does. He made up the story to lure *Voyager* so that he could use their transporter technology to test a hypothesis. He believes that he can use *Voyager's* systems to reconstitute the victims of Rinax. Captain Janeway agrees to assist Jetrel, but their attempts to materialize biomatter from the Cascade cloud that surrounds Rinax do not succeed. Jetrel collapses from the advanced poisoning and the episode winds down with him and Neelix talking in sickbay.

> **Jetrel:** Neelix, I suppose you think this is a fitting punishment for me.
>
> **Neelix:** Maybe the Cascade was a punishment for all of us, for our hatred, our brutality. There's something I need to tell you. I tried to tell you before, but . . .
>
> **Jetrel:** What . . . What is it?
>
> **Neelix:** I want to tell you that I forgive you.

Forgiveness and the Truth and Reconciliation Commission of South Africa

"Jetrel" was first aired in May 1995, almost a year before the TRC of South Africa first began its hearings, but just about a year after South Africa ended its decades-long system of racial segregation known as apartheid. In 1994, the white dominant government dissolved and the Black and Asian South African majority elected Nelson Mandela as its president. The white South African minority had held onto power for years through brutal repression which, in turn, had spawned vicious retaliation against government forces. With the end of apartheid, the question was how to deal with the hatred and possibility of unlimited cycles of vengeance that had built up. Two options immediately appeared: (1) a Nuremburg Trials retributive justice approach, similar to what the Allies imposed on the Nazis after the Second World War, that would punish society's worst human rights offenders; or (2) issue a blanket amnesty law, as had been passed in Chile in 1978, to shield all state officials from criminal prosecution.

South Africa found both of these options unappealing and chose to pursue a third path, guided by the moral foundation of Archbishop Desmond Tutu's notion of forgiveness.[19] The belief was that pursuing a retributive path would only lead to more resentment and retaliation and not end the extensive chains of violence that wove through so much of society. The amnesty route, on the other hand, seemed like an attempt to simply forget the violence. As Tutu notes, the TRC goal instead was to expose "the awfulness, the abuse, the pain, the degradation," in hopes that new relationships could be established based on a mutual understanding of the truth of what had occurred.[20] The work of the TRC involved hearing and recording human rights abuses by state officials and antigovernment forces that occurred during the apartheid era. It had the authority to grant amnesty to some witnesses in exchange for full testimony of the crimes committed, and it could also order certain kinds of restitution for victims. Guiding Tutu's vision in this process is the South African concept of ubuntu, which philosopher Mogobe Ramose interprets as maintaining that "to be human is to affirm one's humanity by recognizing the humanity of others, and on that basis, establish human relations with them."[21] Thus, by revealing the truth of what had happened, and how people had participated in violence, victims and perpetrators could work together in a process that would allow them to see each other with new identities. That transformative process was forgiveness.

For Tutu, it is important to think about forgiveness first in terms of what it is not. First, forgiveness is not purely an emotional or sentimental process but an interactive process involving action and behavior. Second, forgiveness is not something that is, or should be, automatically given when someone harms another—a perpetrator cannot take for granted that they will be absolved. Moreover, forgiveness does not mean that a survivor of violence must somehow forget what happened and put things behind them in order to move on: "On the contrary, it is important that we should not let such atrocities happen again."[22] In addition, forgiveness does not mean condoning the violence that occurred, or minimizing the harm that the survivor suffered, but about delving deeper into the violent act in order "to understand the perpetrator and so have empathy, to try to stand in their shoes and appreciate the sort of pressures and influences that might have conditioned them."[23] Forgiveness, then, "means abandoning your right to pay back the perpetrator in his own coin," forgoing the right to engage in retaliation or retribution for harm suffered.[24]

Not only is forgiveness about rejecting both the practice of retaliation and *lex talionis* as ways to respond to violence, but it is different than mercy and grace as well. As I have argued, mercy does not necessarily reject a system of retribution altogether; instead, it suggests that circumstances might mitigate punishment in particular cases. Kirk doesn't kill the Gorn because he's not completely sure the Gorn acted out of malice or out of a need to protect itself. Grace is an unmerited gift, a benefit given to someone who does not deserve it. Yet, relations between a gracious benefactor and beneficiary are not necessarily changed by the act of grace; grace is compatible with a benefactor's pity, contempt, or feeling of superiority over the beneficiary, and the act of grace can be used to reinforce the inequality between them. Dukat graciously provided the Bajoran prisoners in his labor camps with more food rations and less working hours, but he did so in order for them to better understand that he ultimately controlled their lives and they needed to learn their place.

Forgiveness, on the other hand, works to transform relationships between people related by violence. When a person forgives, they send a message to the perpetrator that they will not seek retaliation or retribution. For Tutu, this communication does not first require an apology from the perpetrator. The forgiveness can be gifted. But in order for gift to be effective, the perpetrator has to be able to take the gift, which means acknowledging that they have violated someone. They cannot accept it as forgiveness if they avoid responsibility or deny that the harm took place. In the case of genuine forgiveness, both survivor and perpetrator are transforming who they think they are and how they can relate to one another. For the survivor, the hope is that forgiving the perpetrator can release themselves from feelings of anger, resentment, or from the need to build a life around the moment that they can exact the right vengeance. For the perpetrator, the hope is that once forgiven, they can understand themselves as being given an opportunity to come back into the moral community and form new connections with people: "In the act of forgiveness we are declaring our faith in the future of a relationship and in the capacity of the wrongdoer to make a new beginning on a course that will be different from the one that caused us the wrong. We are saying here is a chance to make a new beginning."[25] One survivor of the apartheid era violence—a woman whose son was killed by police—explained her hope for this kind of reconciliation:

> What we are hoping for when we embrace the notion of reconciliation is that we restore the humanity to those who were perpetrators. We do not want to return evil by another evil. . . . I think that all South Africans should be committed to the idea of reaccepting these people back into the community. . . . We want to demonstrate humaneness towards them, so that they in turn may restore their own humanity.[26]

We can see these dynamics portrayed in "Jetrel." Both Neelix and Jetrel find themselves in different relationships to their own pasts and to one another by the end of the episode. In forgiving Jetrel, Neelix is able to find a way to release himself from the anger and pain of losing his family to Cascade. More importantly, however, he can process his own shame and self-hatred brought about by years of lying about his actions the day Rinax was destroyed. Jetrel, for a few moments before he dies, is able to experience the sense of being accepted once again. After living for years as a pariah among the Haakonian people, and having his family leave him for his responsibility in the weapons program, Jetrel can finally feel that he is not a "monster" but a part of a community of moral beings.

Tutu is clear that cases of great social conflict often require more than public professions of guilt and forgiveness. Material reparation, redistribution of wealth, and institutional reform are often also needed to transform relationships wherein there are great inequalities of power and money. Forgiveness then is a long and complicated process, and the work of the TRC has taken on a special place of study in the growing field called "transitional justice." This area of study is concerned with charting the ethical and political considerations involved in transitioning societies from widespread violence and injustice to situations of more negative and positive peace.[27] Research within transitional justice studies does indicate that there were limits to what the TRC was able to accomplish. For instance, one early study indicated that few people who participated in the TRC felt satisfied with their cases and those who did feel the most satisfaction were the ones granted amnesty from criminal prosecution.[28] Another study pointed out that very few survivors, around 2 percent of cases, actually offered forgiveness to those who harmed them.[29] And while the exposure of hideous abuses was the goal of the TRC, some high-profile cases were not brought forward because of the political costs. Terry Bell points out that Frederick de Klerk, the last white president of South Africa, ordered a strike on anti-apartheid militants in 1993 as he was on route to receive the Nobel Peace Prize. State forces killed several youths in their sleep. This case, for example, was never brought forward to the TRC.[30]

Despite some of these practical limitations, the work of the TRC remains an important example for truth commissions in other nations, such as Rwanda and Colombia, and for more numerous attempts in the United States and Canada to deal with the legacy of slavery, lynching, and Native/indigenous/First Nation oppression.[31] Undoubtedly, its enduring power comes from its commitment to build a public forum for arriving at the truth of collective violence in society. Gandhi would have appreciated this dedication because he holds that pacifism and nonviolence have a special reverence for the value of the truth. His theory of nonviolence literally means "holding on to truth" not because he thinks that nonviolent activists can have a monopoly on the truth but because he believes that knowing what's true about the world is always a continual struggle for human beings to achieve.[32] Absolute truth is always just out of reach and that limitation should temper how we act toward one another, especially when it comes to retribution: "Satygraha then . . . means Truth force. Truth is soul or spirit. It is, therefore, known as soul force. It excludes the use of violence because man is not capable of knowing the absolute truth and, therefore, not competent to punish."[33] The TRC took as its charge, first and foremost, the hard work of preserving decades worth of stories of human rights abuses. This task was especially important considering that the apartheid government made it a point to destroy as many records of the intelligence services as it could before the transition of power in 1994 in order to erase any memory of the past.[34] Tutu realized that getting to the truth about collective violence in South Africa was a necessary, but not sufficient, condition for achieving a just future.[35]

Without having the truth of what happened, it would be impossible to acknowledge the seriousness of the wrongdoing inflicted on survivors. Such recognition is often the catalyst for both survivors and the perpetrators to reassess their self-understandings and develop the possibility for new relationships based on trust, dignity, and hope.[36] This is demonstrated at the end of "Nemesis." We are left there with the image of a haunted Chakotay—wandering the hallway after his ordeal with the Vori—not having a way to process his experiences of trauma and confused over not knowing what is real. His situation suggests that without a way to bring the truth forward emotions like hatred, anger, and vengeance will remain vivid and biting. And that kind of lingering effect makes the prospects of social stability unlikely. Neelix and Jetrel, on the other hand, through their bitter interactions with one another were able to share parts of their histories they had never been able to tell anyone. While their plan to repair the tragedy of Rinax never materialized, the point was made clear that it is a future free of revenge through forgiveness that matters for creating lasting peace.

Conclusion

One of the most enduring struggles in human history is the endeavor to find ways to end cycles of harm and retaliation. Some of the earliest written legal codes represent attempts to replace destructive vengeful vendettas and blood feuds with political institutional arrangements that dispense retributive justice. Yet, major ethical reformers such as the Prophet Muhammad and Jesus Christ, and significant nonviolent theorists in peace studies such as Gandhi and Martin Luther King, Jr., implore us to find means to respond to cycles of revenge that do not rely on injecting even more violence, in the form of punishment, into the world. In this chapter, I have shown how this enduring struggle has been a major source of reflection for tales within the STU. Episodes such as ST: TOS "The Conscience of the King" and ST: VOY "Nemesis" demonstrate the various destructive paths unresolved revenge and anger can take that make peaceful societies fragile. I have argued that the STU also presents several stories that operate like thought experiments on the effectiveness of different responses to the problem of retaliation, namely the values of mercy, grace, and, finally, forgiveness. However, only forgiveness, I argue, is a process that is transformative and future looking enough to bring about lasting peace.

The work of the TRC in South Africa and its ongoing legacy in numerous commissions in a variety of nations demonstrate the enduring need to develop institutional forums to process trauma, both individual and group, separate from systems of retributive punishment. It was Gandhi and Martin Luther King Jr.'s hope that doing so would reduce our reliance on punitive violence as a means for settling conflict. This hope seems especially appropriate in a world such as ours with millions of people languishing in systems of mass incarceration and social reality fragmented by political polarization and, increasingly, disagreements about what counts as objective fact.

Chapter 6

Imagining a Better World

Up to now, I have discussed violence mostly in terms of harm committed by human beings upon other human beings, usually in direct and spectacular ways, though acknowledging that such events most often have deeper structural and/or cultural causes. Literary theorist Rob Nixon cautions us against holding onto this understanding of violence too strongly, however, because he worries that it inhibits us from being able to conceive of a particularly dangerous and pervasive form of violence. Rather than the spectacular violence we witness in riots, terrorist attacks, or genocides and war crimes, Nixon advises us to be aware of a kind of "violence that is neither spectacular nor instantaneous but instead incremental and accretive, its calamitous repercussions playing out across a range of temporal scales."[1] He calls this "slow violence" and offers the following of what he has in mind: "Climate change, the thawing cryosphere, toxic drift, biomagnification, deforestation, the radioactive aftermaths of wars, acidifying oceans and a host of other slowly unfolding environmental crises [that] present formidable representational obstacles that can hinder our efforts to mobilize and act decisively."[2] Nixon calls on authors, particularly in the Global North, to consider how to dramatize the "long dyings" of people, animals, and ecosystems in ways that can capture people's imaginations and motivate intervention before human action generates unstoppable extinction level effects.

Since the publication of Nixon's work on slow violence there has been an eruption of works in a new literary field known as "climate fiction," or cli-fi, that attempts to meet his challenge.[3] One of the preeminent authors in this genre is Kim Stanley Robinson. In his novel *The Ministry of the Future* (2020), Robinson begins with a horrifying account of a heat wave in India that kills 20 million people in a two-week period. The devastation sparks global political and economic upheaval as humanity scrambles to avoid similar catastrophes. New international institutions are chartered, novel economic systems formed, and change is spurred, in part, by ecoterrorist cells that engage in sabotage and targeted assassinations. Robinson's work does not justify the use of political violence, but it demonstrates how messy and imprecise distinctions between spectacular and slow violence really are. Slow violence can be punctuated by spectacular tragedies, such as the heat wave, as well as explosions by human beings attempting to change the course of human civilization. Robinson makes clear that his novel puts forth the idea that trying to contain the spiral of all these intertwined forms of violence, and to avoid mass extinction events, will require significant political, economic, and cultural transformation, focused especially on altering some of our foundational attitudes about how we relate to the natural world: "I want to argue that humanity is now a major player in Earth's biosphere, and anything we can do to help Earth's biosphere at scale—in other words, the whole civilization doing it on purpose—could be defined as geoengineering. . . . What we're really talking about is civilization, as such, as a form of biosphere management."[4]

But it is not just novelists and literary theorists who are urging for more attention on the effects of slow violence and the need for major social transformation in the face of environmental deterioration. In 2017, the Alliance of World Scientists issued a "Warning to Humanity," endorsed by over 15,000 scientists, outlining the vast damage to the environment caused by human activity, including ozone depletion, marine life depletion, forest loss, destruction of freshwater sources, ocean acidification, and climate change. They called for fundamental changes "urgently needed to avoid the consequences our present course would bring."[5] Two years later, over 11,000 scientists from all across the planet signed onto similar warning of a "climate emergency" to come unless we commit to protect biodiversity, altering agricultural practices and radically transforming our global economic processes and institutions: "Excessive extraction of materials and overexploitation of ecosystems, driven by economic growth, must be quickly curtailed to maintain long-term sustainability of the biosphere. . . . Our goals need to shift from GDP growth and the pursuit of affluence toward sustaining ecosystems and improving human well being by prioritizing basic needs and reducing inequality."[6] More recently, however, a group of scientists have released a list of what they call "ghastly predictions," including massive species extinction and global warming, that will confront humanity if we do not struggle immediately to intervene with substantial modifications to our way of life on Earth: "The gravity of the situation requires fundamental changes to global capitalism, education, and equality, which include inter alia the abolition of perpetual economic growth, properly pricing externalities, a rapid exit from fossil fuel use, strict regulation of markets and property acquisition, reigning in corporate lobbying, and the empowerment of women."[7]

In this chapter, I examine how *Star Trek* might contribute to this intervention by presenting narratives that urge us to revise our understanding of the relationship of human beings to the natural world. We can identify at least three different environmentalist ideals in the STU. The first, which I term the "Ecosystems Services Ideal," is evident in the *ST: TOS* episodes "Man Trap" and "Devil in the Dark" and the 1986 film *Star Trek IV: The Voyage Home*. This ideal holds that we need to position ourselves as stewards of the natural world, understood primarily as resources for the well-being of human life. Under this view, we have a special obligation to preserve particular animal species. The second ideal, which I call the "Biotic Community

Ideal," stems from the *ST: TNG* episodes "Home Soil" and "Force of Nature." This ideal holds that we ought to position ourselves more as what nature writer and conservationist Aldo Leopold called "citizens of the biotic community." We ought to think of ourselves not necessarily as stewards apart from natural resources but as integral parts of the life cycles of biospheres, with special obligations to keep whole ecosystems in harmonious and regenerating balance. Finally, the third ideal, which I term the "Earth Democracy Ideal," is hinted at *ST: DISC* "Choose Your Pain" and in an episode of the animated series *Lower Decks*: "Second Contact." This ideal argues, along with ecofeminist philosopher Vandana Shiva, that animals and ecosystems possess their own agency that deserves ethical and political recognition by human beings. This acknowledgment entails radically altering our political and economic systems to encompass the interests of animals and the natural world as coequal rights bearers who deserve to have a say in decisions that would affect their well-being. My analysis of these ideals suggests that if we want to begin to engage in considerable institutional changes that scientists are calling for in order to avoid ghastly futures full of the long dyings, we need to adopt the Earth Democracy perspective.

The Ecosystems Services Ideal: "The Man Trap," "The Devil in the Dark," *Star Trek IV: The Voyage Home*

The very first *Star Trek* episode that US audiences would ever have seen in September 1966, "The Man Trap," grapples with the question about how to deal with an endangered alien life-form that is killing the crew of the *Enterprise*. "The Man Trap" begins with Captain Kirk and Dr. McCoy beaming down to planet M-113 to provide routine medical check-ups to Federation personnel doing archaeological research on the surface. The expedition is headed by Professor Robert Crater and his wife, Nancy. Many years before, Nancy and Dr. McCoy were romantically involved. When he is reunited with her, he is surprised to see that she has apparently not aged at all. When he comments on this to Kirk, the captain suggests that McCoy's perception is clouded by his memories. But crisis immediately ensues when one of the security team is found murdered out in the ruins. The dead man is covered in strange spots and an autopsy eventually reveals that all the salt has been removed from his body through some unknown process. Professor Crater and Nancy are brought on board the *Enterprise* for their own protection. More murders then begin to occur on the ship.

As the investigation proceeds, Crater admits that a shapeshifting alien being is responsible for the killings. The creature—which has come to be referred to officially in the STU as a "salt vampire" or a "salt succubus" (*ST: LD* "Cupid's Errant Arrow")—feeds on human beings by sucking the salt out of their bodies with its fingers. It once existed by the millions on M-113 before the salt reserves there disappeared, causing a mass extinction. By the time Crater and Nancy arrived, there was only one left on the planet. It eventually killed Nancy. Crater realized what had happened, but he also recognized that the creature was the last of its kind. He admits to Kirk and Spock that he took pity on the creature and lived with it for a long while, feeding it salt from his stores, while it took on the form of Nancy to keep him company. Crater defends his actions:

> **Crater:** She was the last of her kind.
> **Kirk:** The last of her kind?
> **Crater:** The last of its kind. Earth history, remember? Like the passenger pigeon or the buffalo.
> **Spock:** The Earth buffalo. What about it?
> **Crater:** Once there were millions of them; prairies black with them. One herd covered three whole states, and when they moved, they were like thunder.
> **Spock:** And now they're gone. Is that what you mean?
> **Crater:** Like the creatures here. Once there were millions of them. Now there's one left.

The salt vampire becomes desperately hungry aboard the *Enterprise* as it's being hunted. It kills Crater and seeks out Kirk. Spock and McCoy rush to Kirk's rescue as the vampire descends on him in Nancy's form. It displays enormous strength by beating Spock almost senseless and McCoy is left to shoot it with a phaser, killing it. The episode ends with

Spock and Kirk on the bridge after the incident. Spock enquires about his captain's somber mood and Kirk responds, "I was thinking about the buffalo, Mr. Spock."

Kirk is struck by the tragedy of having to put human welfare above the survival of the salt vampire species, but a similar conflict presents itself in "The Devil in the Dark." In this episode, the *Enterprise* responds to a distress call from a mining colony on the planet Janus Six. More than fifty people have been killed in the mines, and machinery crucial to the operation has been sabotaged. The miners report that some sort of creature is preying upon them, disintegrating them with a highly acidic substance. Kirk and Spock are eventually able to track the creature and Spock initiates a Vulcan mind meld with it. The creature calls itself a Horta. It informs them that it has killed the miners in self-defense. The mining operation has been destroying the Horta's eggs, which the miners thought were useless silicon spheres in the caverns. Kirk gets the miners to comprehend that the Horta is not a mindless monster but an intelligent being, acting in a justified manner to preserve its species against the human incursion into its habitat. Unlike "The Man Trap," "The Devil in the Dark" ends with the humans and the endangered alien coming to a mutually beneficial arrangement: the miners cease destroying the Horta eggs, and the newly hatched baby Hortas assist in the mineral extraction process by scoring new underground tunnels with their acid-infused bodies.

The theme about the importance of preserving endangered species arises again in the STU some twenty years after "The Man Trap" in the 1986 movie *Star Trek IV: The Voyage Home*. In this story, a mysterious alien probe invades the Sol System and overwhelms Earth with unknown energy transmissions that drain power systems and create cataclysmic weather forces. Kirk and his crew, aboard a stolen Klingon ship they commandeered in *Star Trek III: The Search for Spock* (1984), are able to decipher the probe's transmissions as humpback whale song. They surmise that the probe is searching for whales. The tragedy is that according to the STU, the humpback went extinct on Earth sometime in the 21st century.[8] Kirk and his crew must, therefore, travel back into the past to retrieve whales so that they can communicate with the probe. A bonded pair of humpback whales, named George and Gracie by their human caretakers, are brought back to the 23rd century, and they are able to avert the destruction of the Earth. Toward the end of the film,

Kirk reflects: "It's ironic. When man was killing these creatures, he was destroying his own future."

According to historian Dolly Jorgensen, these three stories display an anthropocentric view of what is worth saving in the natural world that is congruent with much mainstream environmentalist thinking since the 1970s: "Endangered and threatened species were not seen as valuable in and of themselves, but rather because of their 'educational, historical, recreational, and scientific' value to humans, a concept we now call 'ecosystem services.'"[9] Indeed, in 2001, United Nations Secretary Kofi Annan initiated a four-year project called the Millennium Ecosystem Assessment (MEA), which brought together almost two thousand scientists to "assess the consequences of ecosystem change for human well-being and to establish the scientific basis for actions needed to enhance the conservation and sustainable use of ecosystems and their contributions to human well-being."[10] The MEA specified that ecosystem services under review included: (1) *provisioning services* such as food, water, and timber; (2) *regulating services* that affect climate, floods, water quality, and so on; (3) *providing cultural services* that offer recreational, aesthetic, and spiritual benefits for humans; and (4) *lending supporting services* which include soil formation, photosynthesis, and nutrient cycling. While the final report of the MEA recognized that species and ecosystems may have intrinsic value apart of their utility, the thrust of the investigation was to provide insight for policy makers on how human beings can be better stewards of the natural world largely conceived in terms of resources for human life.[11]

All three *Star Trek* narratives reinforce the assumptions of ecosystem services in that they portray the balance between human and animal welfare always being struck in favor of human life. When the salt vampire attacks Kirk in "The Man Trap" there is no question that it needs to be put down by McCoy, even if that means eradicating the species. In "The Devil in the Dark," Spock and Kirk do have a brief exchange, before they realize the Horta is acting out of self-defense, about possibly saving the *it*:

> **Spock:** . . . If it is the only survivor of a dead race, to kill it would be a crime against science.

Kirk: Mr. Spock, our mission is to protect this colony, to get the pergium moving again. This is not a zoological expedition. . . . I'm sorry Mr. Spock, but I'm afraid the creature must die.
Spock: I see no alternative myself, Captain. It merely seems a pity.

The end solution, to have the miners coexist with the Horta, only works as long as the life processes of the Horta coincide with the production schedules and market needs of mineral extraction on Janus Six. Finally, the rescue of the whales George and Gracie only occurs because of the threat posed by the alien probe to human life in the 23rd century. Numerous other species have perished throughout history and none have received the kind of salvation that humpback whales do in the STU.

While the Ecosystems Services model has gained popularity among global political and economic leaders when dealing with environmental issues, researchers point to serious limitations. The model often relies on the capacity of scientists to explain the use value of the natural world in terms of some monetary measure. This allows states to be able to calculate trade-offs between the needs of human beings and the interests of species or ecosystems. Yet, researchers indicate that the economic and banking systems needed to commodify scientific data are imprecise and limited.[12] Moreover, some of the benefits of the natural world recognized by the Ecosystems Services model, such as aesthetic or spiritual well-being, are not commodifiable in the same way, or at all, as something like the provisioning benefits of food, water, or timber.[13] In the end, however, this way of thinking ultimately privileges human well-being above all else, even to the detriment of animals and the natural world. One of the most notable cases exemplifying the Ecosystems Services model came in the 1970s when US environmentalists took a legal battle all the way to the Supreme Court to protect the snail darter fish as an endangered species.[14] The snail darter habitat was threatened with destruction by the state of Tennessee, which wanted to build an important hydroelectric dam in key rivers supporting the fish. While the snail darter won the legal battle in Court, the US Congress passed laws specifically removing its designation as an endangered species. The dam project went ahead to provide electricity for human beings, but the case went on to stand as an example of the problems with trying to value the natural world through a cost-benefit analysis framework.[15]

The Biotic Community Ideal: "Home Soil" and "Force of Nature"

The *ST: TNG* episode "Home Soil" is remarkable because, at first, it simply looks like a retelling of the story on Janus Six. Captain Picard and the *Enterprise-D* are called to check on a terraforming expedition on the dead planet Velara III. While the away team is visiting the terraforming facility, they witness an attack by a laser drill on one of the expedition's technicians. He is brought back to the *Enterprise-D* and dies of his injuries. When Data and Geordi return to investigate the equipment on the planet, the laser drill attacks Data. They begin to suspect that the drill is being programmed to murder. Further investigation of the drill site locates a strange inorganic object that pulses with light. The object is brought back to the ship and is found to be silicon crystals that appear to be reproducing and growing. Dr. Crusher hypothesizes that the object is alive.

Her hunch is validated when the object causes power fluctuations and merges with the ship's computer system, including its universal translator. Soon the object broadcasts a message, calling the human beings "ugly bags of mostly water" and informing Picard that it kills them in order to protect itself. When Picard confronts the terraformers about the alien, they admit that they did not think the crystals were alive, but they begin to piece together that the attack happened as they started to siphon off a layer of saltwater under the planet's surface. Data suggests that the saline acted as a conduit for the crystals, linking them as a single consciousness through electrical charges. Picard determines that the best thing to do is to return the crystal object to the saline layer. However, unlike the result with the Horta, the alien life-form tells the humans that it does not want to have contact with them because it does not trust them completely: "You are still too arrogant, too primitive. Come back three centuries. Perhaps then we trust." Picard and crew signal their apologies, and respect, and beam the alien back to the planet, which is then put on indefinite quarantine to prevent any further Federation involvement.

Habitat destruction is also central to *ST: TNG* "Force of Nature." While on a mission to locate a missing ship near the Hakaran Corridor, the *Enterprise-D* is commandeered by two Hekarans, Rabal and Serova. They are scientists who believe they have evidence that warp field energy damages their area of space and threatens the extinction of their home world. Initially, Picard hears them out and informs them that the Federation Science Council has already reviewed the claims and found them to be insufficiently supported. Data reviews the theory and says that it could only be proven by exposing the area to high warp energy burst much greater than could be created by any one ship. Rabal and Serova imply that the effect is cumulative over time and Picard agrees to recommend more research. Serova, however, feels that more waiting means more damage and she decides on a dramatic course. She takes her ship and detonates a warp core explosion, killing herself and creating an enormous subspace rift. Once the *Enterprise-D* is able to get to safety and the rift investigated, Rabal reports that more instabilities will be created over the next few decades, eventually enveloping the entire sector and possibly destroying his planet. The Federation Council immediately imposes a speed limit of warp five on all Starfleet vessels traveling in areas of space found to be susceptible to damage. A solemn Picard confesses to Geordi at the end of the episode: "I've spent the better part of my life exploring space. I've charted new worlds, I've met dozens of new species and I believe that these were all valuable ends in themselves. And now it seems that . . . all this while I was helping to damage the thing that I hold most dear." Geordi reassures him: "It won't turn out that way, Captain. We still have time to make it better."

Both these episodes suggest a different environmental consciousness than the Ecosystems Services Ideal most evident in the episodes from *ST: TOS* some twenty years before. Such stories represent an environmental perspective that I call the Biotic Community Ideal. The notion of the biotic community is drawn from the work of the environmental philosopher Aldo Leopold (1887–1948). In the preface to his major work *A Sand County Almanac*, Leopold took direct aim at the central assumption underlying the Ecosystems Services Ideal, namely that the natural world should be conceived primarily as commodities for human survival:

Conservation is getting nowhere because it is incompatible with our Abrahamic concept of land. We abuse land because we regard it as a commodity belonging to us. . . . There is no other way for land to survive the impact of mechanized man, nor for us to reap from it the esthetic harvest it is capable, under science, of contributing to culture.[16]

In lecture notes he prepared in the 1940s, Leopold reflected on the kind of worldview that would be needed to make conservation efforts more effective:

> There must be some force behind conservation. . . . More universal than profit, less awkward than government, less ephemeral than sport something that reaches into all time and places. . . . I can see only one such force: a respect for land as an organism; a voluntary decency in land use exercised by every citizen and every land owner out of a sense of love for and obligation to the great biota we call America.[17]

He called this perspective the "land ethic."

The land ethic begins with some important ecological concepts as a base. First, "land" is defined not as inert ground or simple place but as an interconnected community of interconnected elements through which energy flows by means of food chains. Land is a complex organism or biosphere consisting of humans, plants, animals, soils, water, insects, and all the processes that relate them to one another. Second, land is a dynamic entity, involving energy traversing through the different elements at various speeds and directions. Thus, land can grow or shrink in its biodiversity; for instance, better climate supports abundant plant life which supports more insect and animal life and so on. Finally, it is possible to speak of the health of the land, which Leopold defines as the capacity of the land to generate energy and self-renew.[18] Unhealthy, or diseased, land, then, is that in which there are blockages or disconnections among the different components of this biotic community leading to a decrease in their well-being as a conduit of energy. Drought, for instance, affects the amount of plant and animal life the land can support. Yet, Leopold was most concerned with the way in which human intervention, such as deforestation, destabilizes the land and affects its overall ability to conduct life energy. A biotic community can be resilient, but it is not infinitely so.[19]

With these ecological ideas in place, Leopold proposes the principles behind the sense of "voluntary decency" he wanted to see take root in the world. First, we must expand our moral sense of concern beyond our individual selves, other human beings, and other human communities to include the biotic community of the land. As Leopold put it, we need to reorient the "role of Homo sapiens from conqueror of the land community to plain member and citizen of it."[20] This means altering long-held cultural and religious views that human beings are independent of the natural world and its systems. Instead, we must learn to see ourselves more humbly as one species among others and interrelated to them all. Second, we must learn how to extend ethical respect not just to other humans in the land but to all other components and species in the biotic community. We ought to judge whether our actions are harmful or beneficial to other human beings and communities, of course, but as well as to animals, birds, insects, watersheds, and forests. Third, we need to understand that commodification of the natural world is not always the appropriate way to measure the worth of, or to show respect for, elements within the biotic community. Leopold points out that some tree species, some animals, and some biospheres—particularly deserts or bogs—have little commercial value but are often nonetheless important components of a much larger ecosystem:

> A system of conservation based solely on economic self-interest is hopelessly lopsided. It tends to ignore, and thus eventually to eliminate, many elements in the land community that lack commercial value, but that are (as far as we know) essential to its healthy functioning. It assumes, falsely, I think, that the economic parts of the biotic clock will function without the uneconomic parts.[21]

While both "Home Soil" and "Force of Nature" involve stories of species threatened by human action, the focus is more on the damage being done to their wider biotic communities. The crystal alien of "Home Soil" is literally fighting to defend the land and water which permit it to flourish. Rabal and Serova are convinced that warp drive fields will eventually upset the delicate balance of the Hekaren Corridor, leading to gravity shifts and climate change on their planet. And unlike the solutions from the older episodes depicting the Ecosystems Services model, the *ST: TNG* episodes do not portray human needs as having primary importance over and above the well-being of the aliens and their ecosystems. Instead, the crew of the *Enterprise-D* craft resolutions that display the land ethic principles. The crystal entity, for instance, is not the Horta; it has no interest in cooperating with the terraformers to transform the planet for Federation colonization or economic exploitation. Indeed, Data's interest in having more scientific information about the salt crystal entity is not enough to convince Picard to stay on Velara III; he orders them to leave the planet as a form of respect to the creatures. Even Picard's curiosity for exploration—something that defined his life's worth for decades—must take a backseat to protect the fragile balance of subspace with a decision that is likely to have severe effects on the growth of the Federation and any possible future interactions with the Hekarans.

Despite its foundational status in the field of environmental ethics, Leopold's land ethic is not without criticism. Some philosophers feel that the ethical requirements of the Biotic Community Ideal are too vague or imprecise to be effective for moral action.[22] Others feel that Leopold's work is not attentive to social justice issues; indeed, some suggest that his exposition of the functioning of the biotic community relies on white supremacist assumptions and concepts.[23] However, the most bothersome question seems to be one that Leopold was aware of himself: Is the Biotic Community Ideal forceful enough to reorient our ways of life to prevent wide-scale damage to the health of global ecosystems? Leopold felt that, in the United States at least, there are examples of people subsidizing common goods that they individually do not use but recognize as valuable for society, such as public schools, libraries, roads. He hoped that the support for these kinds of goods could be extended to include the natural world as a kind of public good. But he understood that this educational effort takes time. This raises two crucial questions for the Biotic Community Ideal. First, do political and economic conditions in the world today—some seventy years after the first publication of *A Sand County Almanac*—facilitate or inhibit the spread of this ethical consciousness? Second, do we really have the time to wait for this cultural revolution in biotic awareness, given the increasing damage done to the Earth's climate?

The Earth Democracy Ideal: "Choose Your Pain," and "Second Contact"

During the first season of *ST: DISC*, a unique creature called a tardigrade is introduced into the STU. This alien being resembles microscopic Earth tardigrade, which are hearty creatures that can withstand extreme environments. The macroscopic tardigrade, however, is a huge and fearsome creature, twice the size of a bull, with claws that can shred metal. It is also a trans-dimensional being that can travel on the mycelial network—a vast subspace web made of fungus that extends throughout the galaxy. The crew of the *Discovery* realize that reliable and safe instantaneous travel is possible over vast distances by moving through the network, using the tardigrade as an organic navigator.

Yet, as becomes clear in "Choose Your Pain," doing so causes extreme discomfort to the animal. Commander Burnham, Lt. Stamets, and Cadet Tilly work, contrary to Captain Saru's orders, to find an alternative way to journey along the network. They have realized the tardigrade is sentient and believe that using it against its will is morally inappropriate. Saru is not pleased with this disobedience since *Discovery*'s wartime mission to rescue Captain Lorca is time-sensitive. He relieves Burnham of duty and confines her to quarters. He then orders the rest to use the tardigrade. The *Discovery* is able to rescue Lorca from Klingon forces, but only because Lt. Stamets injects himself with tardigrade DNA and substitutes himself for the creature in the spore drive mechanism. Once Lorca is safely aboard, Saru orders Burnham to free the tardigrade. Cadet Tilly and Burnham conduct a short ceremony before they sprinkle the tardigrade with fungal spores and jettison it into space:

> **Tilly:** May the sun and moon watch your comings and goings in the endless nights and days that are before you. [Turning to Burnham] Are you sure this will work?
>
> **Burnham:** No. . . . This creature has traveled to the far ends of the universe. My hope is that what makes it most happy is to be free.

ST: LD also contains a story that evokes the Earth Democracy Ideal. *ST: LD* is an animated series that premiered in 2020. *ST: LD* is different from all previous *Star Trek* series in that its focus is not so much on the heroics of the commanding officers but, instead, on the adventures of the most junior officers aboard a second-rate Starfleet vessel, the *USS Cerritos*. *ST: LD* is also different in tone; it is primarily a comedy, and its ironic, sarcastic storytelling allows it to playfully explore well-worn themes and ideas in the STU. It also can amplify and make fun of small details and throwaway lines from the previous series. One such example is the idea of Cetacean Operations.

In "Second Contact"—the first episode of the series—Ensigns Brad Boimler and Beckett Mariner introduce the newly arrived Ensign D'Vana Tendi to the *Cerritos*. While on the tour, Boimler lists all the areas of the ship he considers the best: the warp core, the bridge, the photon torpedo tubes, and then Cetacean Ops. In *ST: TNG* "Yesterday's Enterprise," Cetacean Ops is mentioned in a throwaway line as an area on the ship, but it is never shown. Rick Sternbach's 1996 book *Star Trek: The Next Generation USS Enterprise NCC-1701-D Blueprints* contains designs for a section on Deck 13 of the *Enterprise-D* to house dolphins and whales.[24] However, its purpose is not explained or mentioned ever again in the STU until "Second Contact." It seems significant, though, that Cetacean Ops is thought of as an important facility, even on a second-rate ship such as the *Cerritos*. For some reason, Starfleet ships of the 24th century have aquatic mammals as a standard complement of their crew.

These two episodes illustrate an environmental awareness that I term the "Earth Democracy Ideal." Earth Democracy is a concept drawn from the work of ecofeminist author Vandana Shiva. She explains that Earth Democracy is a social and political framework for a society that moves from anthropocentrism to eco-centrism and from human rights to the rights of species and nature:

> Earth Democracy enables us to envision and create living democracies. Living democracy enables democratic participation in all matters of life and death—the food we eat or do not have access to; the water we drink or are denied due to privatization or pollution; the air we breathe or are poisoned by. Living democracies are based on the intrinsic worth of all species, all peoples, all cultures; a just and equal sharing of this earth's vital resources; and sharing the decisions about the use of the earth's resources.[25]

According to Shiva, the Earth Democracy Ideal is grounded in a rejection of a European idea that was deployed as validation for the colonization of the planet beginning in the sixteenth century and that continues today in the form of corporate economic globalization. In order to justify the takeover of Asia, Africa, and the Americas, European societies replaced the view of indigenous societies of the Earth as *terra madre* (mother Earth) with the view of Earth as *terra nullius* (empty land): "The colonial construct of the passivity of the earth and the consequent creation of the colonial category of land as *terra nullius* (empty land) served two purposes: it denied the existence and prior rights of the original inhabitants and it obscured the regenerative capacity and processes of the earth."[26] After all, if the land is "empty," then it can be appropriated as property. If the land is not a being, an organism, but an inert thing, then it can be broken up and used as natural resources by those who own the property. With this mindset, Shiva argues that European societies began to enclose large swaths of areas, from England to India, that were traditionally considered commons and turned them into private holdings by wealthy elites.[27] Today's economic globalization, in which corporations increasingly control access to vital resources such as water, through privatization of public utilities, or access to food, through intellectual property rights over seeds, continues this process around the globe:

> Colonialism led to the violent separation of people from their land, resources and territories. It continues to this day, as greed for land and water, and for timber and minerals feeds an extractive economy, while globalisation's rules for deregulation and the "ease of doing business" make uprooting communities easy. Old colonialism violently appropriated the wealth of societies in Africa, Asia, and the Americas and transferred it to Europe. . . . If the British grabbed land and institutionalized lagaan (tax) in India, the contemporary 1% are using "intellectual property" to create monopolies over our seeds and food, our communications, our financial transactions, and our friendships.[28]

The Earth Democratic Ideal rejects the notion of the Earth as terra nullius and attempts to reimagine the world as a democratic community between human beings, animals, plants, and living soil and water. Shiva reveals that one of the inspirations for her vision was the Chipko movement in the Garhwal Himalayas. During the 1970s, peasant women in this region organized to defend the forests from large-scale logging efforts. The deforestation upset the ecology and social relationships in the area—hills without trees meant landslides, floods, scarcity of fuel, and heavier burdens on the women responsible for feeding families. So rather than allow companies to destroy more forests, groups of women began coordinated nonviolent direct-action campaigns to prevent logging from taking place. They would gather together and literally hug trees (Chipko means "to hug"), preventing loggers from being able to do their work. After many years of this kind of nonviolent intervention, the government prohibited logging in the high Himalayas. Shiva claims this example illuminated what Earth Democracy could mean: human beings cooperating and deliberating together to protect their environment against powerful corporate interests by treating the natural world as a being with which they have a deep and intimate relationship: "In the act of embracing trees as their kin, ordinary women mobilized an energy more powerful than the police and the brute strength of the logging interests."[29]

For Shiva, treating trees as kin is more than a metaphor for connection. Part of the Earth Democracy Ideal is about treating the natural world as a living and rights-bearing being. It is commonplace to think of human beings, and even some animals, as having moral and legal rights that others must respect. Usually this means that if a person or animal has rights, they are allowed to do certain actions or have access to certain goods without interference from others in society. Shiva maintains that if we are to think of animals and the natural world as an organism, then we ought to recognize their agency and rights. She points to examples in India, Bolivia, and Ecuador as a growing global movement in which courts and legislatures have established that mountain ranges, rivers, lakes, forests, and jungles are not only living beings but legal entities with rights that must be represented in any state proceedings having to deal with their future interests.[30] In the United States as well, such a strategy has gained a foothold. In 2019, residents of Toledo, Ohio, passed a ballot giving rights normally associated with a person to Lake Erie.[31] Researchers who have studied the national constitutions of Latin American nations that have enshrined Earth Democracy provisions suggest that the alterations to legal and economic processes have so far been modest but that "the legal protection of the rights of non-human entities provides an opportunity for society to redirect its behavior away from growth-without-limits paradigms toward an altogether more careful ecological approach."[32]

"Second Contact" does not contain a story line that explicitly illustrates the Earth Democracy Ideal, but it does insinuate that it is embodied in the workings of Starfleet in the 24th century. Much of the humor of *ST: LD* lies in its jokes, what it assumes the audience of Trekkies knows or take for granted from years of watching the different series or reading novelizations, comic books, or technical manuals. As I mentioned earlier, the existence of a facility for aquatic mammals was apocryphal for years until it was affirmed as STU canon in "Second Contact." Viewers of *ST: LD* who are not hard-core *Star Trek* nerds may wonder: Why is Cetacean Ops so important that Boimler—someone who is depicted as on the verge of obsessive compulsive about Starfleet operations—would list it as a crucial ship system on the *Cerritos*? It is obviously more than just entertainment for the crew, like an aquarium. The *Cerritos* is not like the *Enterprise-D*—it is a workhorse ship without much of the state-of-the-art technology that is found on other Starfleet vessels, as we find out in the *ST: LD* episode "Cupid's Errant Arrow." The answer is hidden in a detail in *The Star Trek: The Next Generation Technical Manual* from 1991: dolphins and whales are official crew members of Starfleet vessels who assist in the guidance and navigation of Starfleet ships in the 24th century.[33] The animals are more than just resources to the human crew member because they apparently have a rank structure. The *Technical Manual* discusses how some whales act as supervisors over a complement of other aquatic mammals. Thus, "Second Contact" alludes to the notion that each Starfleet vessel is a biotic community in which humans and aquatic animals live and cooperate together to explore the galaxy and to promote Federation values.

In "Choose Your Pain," we see the crew of the *Discovery* much more clearly enact the Earth Democracy Ideal of treating animals as kin and of speaking for the interests of the natural world when they decide to disobey Saru's orders. Instead of accepting the brutal reality of choices in wartime, they work on finding an alternative way to travel the mycelial network and to protect the tardigrade's life, even if it means they will be punished for it. Through their collective dedication to the tardigrade's well-being, the crew is finally able to convince Saru that the creature has a right to autonomy and deserves to be released. Saru realizes that the right thing to do is not simply to treat the tardigrade as a means to their ends and tells Burnham: "We have no claim on its soul. Go save its life Burnham." And when Tilly and Burnham do let the tardigrade loose, Tilly offers it a poetic farewell, an incantation that imparts kindness to a being she clearly respects and that she and Burnham hold in awe. Vandana Shiva remarks that folk songs sung for the trees were centerpieces of the Chipko movement in the 1970s.[34]

Glancing at the representations of the Earth Democracy Ideal in these episodes, it may not seem that it is significantly different from the Biotic Community Ideal. It is true that both reject the Ecosystems Services Ideal notion of considering animals and nature as resources for human use and well-being. Both Biotic Community and Earth Democracy urge a transformation of our conception of the human world to encompass animals and natures as part of our sphere of ethical concern. Yet, Earth Democracy surpasses the Biotic Community Ideal by not only maintaining that animals and the natural world deserve our moral attention but also insisting that we see them as legal persons that deserve their own autonomy and freedom. More importantly, they have rights that the rest of us need to respect and that may curb or limit how we can behave. In this sense, Earth Democracy extends the terms of the liberal social contact—with its vocabulary of rights, freedom, and citizenship—as well as our ethical awareness. This may mean that animals, water, soil, and forests require formal human legal representation of their interests before political and economic institutions for legal decisions and democratic deliberation. Leopold, perhaps idealistically, assumed that the conservation of the natural world could only happen if human beings evolved a larger moral conscience to spur their action. Earth Democracy, on the other hand, holds that we cannot wait for that project of moral education to take root. Patterns of European colonization, and now neoliberal economic globalization, threaten to decimate the natural world in ways that could possibly exterminate human life in a century or so. With this sense of urgency, Earth Democracy wants to transform our conceptions of democratic community to provide the political tools necessary for the material protection of nature against human economic interests for constant commodification and profit making. In other words, the Earth Democratic Ideal supplements the moral perspective of the Biotic Community Ideal with a framework that grasps the enormous political and economic global transformations that have happened in the last hundred years and outlines the legal apparatuses needed to make our ethical ideals effective. Thus, the STU calls on us to act by providing a vision of a possible future in which the fullest potential of humanity is realized by living in democratic solidarity with animals and the rest of the natural world.

Conclusion

Our global systems of resource extraction and distribution produce exceptional quality of life for a few human beings but result in enormous wealth inequality and depleted well-being for billions of other human beings, animals, and biospheres. Imaginative authors and literary theorists working in the field of climate fiction are skillfully revealing the different kinds of violence that are inflicted as a result of modern human intervention into the natural world. From the idea of "slow violence" which describes the long processes of decay and degradation of vital ecosystems to spectacular eruptions of direct violence that are likely under conditions of environmental and social collapse, cli-fi gives us glimpses of a dystopian future world that a field such as peace studies cannot avoid.

In this chapter, I have argued that the STU presents at least three different ideals for how to envision transformative relationships between humans and the natural world that might confront these myriad deteriorations. The Ecosystems Services Ideal calls for human beings to be more responsible stewards of the nature in order to create a more sustainable use of natural resources. This ideal is perhaps one of the most popular approach in international bodies concerned with issues such as climate change. The Biotic Community Ideal challenges this approach by arguing that conservation cannot proceed effectively unless we move away from an anthropocentric worldview that puts human needs at the forefront. It calls for a revolution in human ethical consciousness that envisions a wholistic community between humans, animals, plants, and soil in which human beings acknowledge the natural world and its processes as worthy of moral respect and consideration. I argue that the STU does contain stories that support the Biotic Community Ideal, but more recent narratives in the STU seem to suggest the need for a more complex perspective that preserves the insights of Leopold's land ethic and is also cognizant of imbalances in political and economic power in the world today. The Earth Democracy Ideal also calls for a moral transformation in human culture in regard to the conception of human beings in the natural world. But, in addition, it holds we need a change in our political conceptions of democratic community so that animals, plants, water, and soil can have access to legal tools to protect their integrity and regenerative processes much better than with mere economic trade-off calculations or moral suasion.

Conclusion

In March 2021, William Shatner was asked why he thought *Star Trek* remained such a popular science fiction franchise after almost sixty years since it first appeared on network television. He responded:

> We're on the verge of extinction. We are poisoning ourselves out of life and Mother Earth . . . and the fact that *Star Trek* exists 400 years from now is a promise that if you do those things, your children and your grandchildren will continue to live and live in fairly decent circumstances. . . . We exist 400 years from now . . . and there's hope. I think that's what the audience gets—is the hope. That's the message of *Star Trek* and that's why I think *Star Trek* is popular.[1]

In this book, I have argued that the STU does, indeed, stand out among popular science fiction universes in this dystopian era because it presents a vision of the future of humanity in which technology is not our enemy. Instead, it is harnessed for well-being. Values such as equality, curiosity, acceptance of difference, reason, freedom, peace, and justice inform institutions and our everyday lives. Shatner is correct: *Star Trek* stands out today, in other words, because it is utopian at a time that we are inundated with news about our dystopian reality.

Yet, Frederick Jameson maintains that we have reached a point in history in which utopian dreams are exhausted and most dystopian visions are just boring: "We have seen a marked diminution in the production of new utopias over the last decades (along with an overwhelming increase in all manner of conceivable dystopias most of which look monotonously alike)."[2] He thinks we find it almost impossible to imagine what a new perfect world might look like or the politics needed to get there. After all, for almost fifty or so years, neoliberal politicians, such as Margaret Thatcher, and political theorists like Francis Fukayama have told us there are no more alternatives and that history has come to an end. What other world is there but this one; what other political systems are there than the ones we already have?

Star Trek, I believe, warns us about thinking of utopia in this way, that is, as the ideal place to get to from where we are now. One of the most hated episodes of *ST: TOS* (hated almost universally even by its actors, writers, producers) is "The Way to Eden."[3] Many people dislike this episode because parts of it are corny and its attempt at making a comment about intergenerational conflict is clumsy. Yet, I think it presents a noteworthy approach to the issue of utopian politics. In this episode, the crew of the *Enterprise* must apprehend a group of people who have stolen a ship. The robbers turn out to be the young followers of a former professor, Dr. Sevrin, who rejects the technological utopia of the Federation. He has a bacterial infection caused by the antiseptic environments of the Federation. Sevrin seeks to find a new planet, Eden, away from its confines. His followers include former Starfleet cadets and the son of a prominent diplomat. They all consider the *Enterprise* crew to be rigid and uncreative bureaucrats of an authoritarian machine. Sevrin's followers want only to sing, dance, and enjoy sensuous pleasures. As Adam, one of the "space hippies," sings in front of a crowd of off-duty Starfleet personnel: "Stepping into Eden / Yea brother / No more trouble in my body or my mind / Gonna live like a king on whatever I find / Eat all the fruit and throw away the rind / Yea brother."

However, Sevrin's disciples are not as simple as they seem. They are, in fact, violent zealots who plot to take over the *Enterprise* and render the entire crew unconscious so that they can steal a shuttlecraft. Once the *Enterprise* crew is revived from the attack, they track Sevrin to the planet Eden, only to find it is no paradise. The surface is beautiful, but the plant life is toxic to humanoids. By the time Kirk and the landing party arrives, Adam is dead and Sevrin kills himself by eating an apple. The rest of the followers are brought back to the *Enterprise* for medical care and then are allowed to continue on their way to locate a new planet for themselves. Spock encourages them on their quest for utopia and says to a former Starfleet cadet scientist among them named Irina: "I have no doubt you will find it . . . or make it yourselves."

One way to read this episode is that it affirms the position of theorists, such as Karl Popper, who believe that utopian impulses are inherently dangerous.[4] In Popper's view, utopian thinking promotes a kind of instrumental rationality in which political ideas only make sense in terms of means to ends. If you seek a future utopian world, everything, even the use of violence and the sacrifice of innocent lives, can be justified as a way to realize it. All utopians, therefore, are really like Sevrin's admirers—willing to do all sorts of underhanded and ghastly things in order to get to Eden. Indeed, as sociologist Ruth Levitas points out, many respected political theorists, such as Hannah Arendt and Isaiah Berlin, have written about the connection of utopian thinking to totalitarian tendencies in the twentieth century.[5] The lesson appears to be this: a desire to seek a better world causes conflict with those who have other ideas about how the world should be and that, inevitably, leads to terror, violence, and war by utopians.

However, I think this is not the message of "The Way to Eden," given Spock's last reflection. He leaves Irina open to the possibility that Eden is not an already existing place but an ideal that she can attempt with her companions to define. In this way, *Star Trek's* warning here is not about utopianism in general but about a certain manner of engaging in utopian thinking. Borrowing a distinction from Russell Jacoby, I think that "The Way to Eden" asks us to avoid "blueprint" utopianism and to consider "iconoclastic" utopianism. The former variety is about detailing the contours of a perfect society, maybe even laying out the "blueprint" of the steps to achieve it. This is the kind of vision that drove Sevrin and his followers to their doom and disillusion: a drive to reach a specific place and a willingness to push anything aside that stood in the way. Iconoclastic utopianism, on the other hand, focuses on dreaming of a better society without always giving "its precise measurements."[6] This usually means conceiving of the values, sensations, and emotions afforded in a better world, but not specifying the exact structures necessary to embody them. Adam's song captures this iconoclasm by conjuring up a dream of a kind of existence with no hunger or thirst and full of autonomy, bodily health, and mental peace. The danger came when they were convinced by Sevrin that those values would definitely be found on the planet Eden and that they needed to get there as soon as they could.

Star Trek is utopian, but it is not a simple or naïve utopianism that is present in its stories. Rather, I think the STU corresponds to what Tom

Moylan calls the tradition of "critical utopia." For Moylan, a critical utopia rejects the emphasis of utopia-as-blueprint but nourishes the aspiration for a better society. He adds that novels in this genre

> dwell on the conflict between the ordinary world and the utopian society opposed to it so that the process of social change is more directly articulated. Finally, the novels focus on the continuing presence of difference and imperfection within utopian society itself and thus render more recognizable and dynamic alternatives.[7]

I believe this understanding of utopia is present in the story line laid out in season one of *ST: PIC*. This series is set some fourteen years after Jean-Luc Picard retired from Starfleet in protest. His last major mission was to save the planet Romulus from destruction by a nearby sun going supernova. When the fleet that was designated to evacuate the planet is destroyed in an attack by a malfunctioning robotic workforce, Starfleet decided not to continue its relief efforts. It let the Romulans to sort out the death of their solar system alone. In the episode "Remembrance," Picard admits he lost faith in Starfleet at that moment: "Because it was no longer Starfleet! We withdrew. The galaxy was in mourning, burying its dead, and Starfleet slunk from its duties. The decision to call off the rescue and to abandon those people we had sworn to save was not just dishonorable, it was downright criminal!" During the rest of the season, Picard continues to run into characters who, for one reason or another, have become disenchanted with Starfleet as an institution and the Federation as a repository of peace and justice. Yet, rather than give in to cynicism or nihilism, Picard attempts to remain true to the spirit of the Federation, even if the institution itself has diminished. For instance, in the episode "Broken Pieces," when Cristobal Rios admits his fear in the face of possible destruction by Romulan forces and hostile synthetic life-forms, Picard responds: "The past is written, but the future is left for us to write and we have powerful tools, Rios: openness, optimism, and the spirit of curiosity. All they have is secrecy, and fear, and fear is the great destroyer, Rios."

ST: PIC speaks, then, to our current dystopian moment that is characterized by political polarization and the widespread feeling that our political leaders are corrupt, out of touch, and unable to direct our societies to provide care and well-being for people. As a critical utopian work, this new series reminds us that utopia is not a static place or a description of an unchanging social system. It is not about honoring particular people or maintaining particular institutions. Utopia is more the name for an attitude, or a disposition of struggle, that strives for a better world, using the best capacities within us as resources. What made the United Federation of Planets and Starfleet noble throughout most of the STU timeline was not the magnificent technology, powerful ships, or great captains but the yearning to live flourishing lives in a galaxy devoted to peace and justice. As Michael Burnham says in *ST: DISC*, "That Hope is You I": "The Federation isn't just about ships and warp drive. It's about a vision and all those who believe in that vision." Holding onto those hopes can bring people together to define for themselves what a better world will look like, as when Picard is able to gather and unify a rag-tag crew about *La Sirena* to defend the universe from xenophobic life-forms; or in *ST: DISC*, when Admiral Vance is able to rally what is left of Starfleet in the 32nd century to hold on to ideals of justice rather than give in to the Emerald Chain's offer of material satisfaction after so much deprivation. What the better world is that might result from the resolution of these story lines is unclear. What matters more is that the characters have found it within themselves not to give in to hate, fear, and despair. Instead, they hold on to hope for a more decent way of life through solidarity with one another.

So I would agree with Shatner that *Star Trek* is popular because it is hopeful. Yet, to borrow a distinction from philosopher Cornel West, I think *Star Trek* is *hopeful* but not *optimistic*.[8] There is no guarantee that the future of *Star Trek* will happen or that technology will just simply evolve to the point at which we find the values of the STU realized around us. There is no promise that the world will get better and the future be more just than the past. But we can be *hopeful* that something like *Star Trek* will be ahead of us, meaning that if we think hard and imagine together, and engage with one another in serious social action, then we just might be able to transform institutions and entrenched ways of thinking toward a more just and humane society, whatever shape it may take for us. We might be able to form something like a world built around the values of the Federation and Starfleet, but it depends on our ethical perspectives and political action today.

The stories within the STU can be thought of as tools in that effort in two ways. First, as a form of science fiction, *Star Trek* can help to inform our imagination about what kind of futures are possible. I have argued that the STU contains numerous stories in which concepts such as peace, justice, and nonviolence are examined. Thus, they can help us to understand better what those concepts mean today. In that sense, *Star Trek* can be useful for instructors and practitioners within peace studies, helping students to comprehend material better with vivid narrative illustrations of the theories of this academic field.

But, more importantly, I think the vision of the STU, as a critical utopia, is also a diagnostic lens on the present. Obviously, *Star Trek* does not offer a complete social theory or an account of comprehensive justice. It can suggest to us some—not necessarily all—of the obstacles that stand in the way of a peaceful, just, and more humane future. If we want to aspire to a society that embodies the utopian values of the Federation, then we need to adopt today a politics of critical antiracism, egalitarianism, and anticolonialism—a politics that centers ecological renewability over market priorities and globalized capitalist development. We may not know what a completely peaceful and just world will look like exactly, but we can get a good sense of the systems, values, and ways of life that make peace and justice less likely. In that sense, then, *Star Trek* isn't boring, naïve, or corny, but perhaps one of the richest repositories in popular culture for revolutionary stories of social change. And as we have seen, the STU is still growing strong with new series in development. Hopefully, more stories can open new meanings and new vistas in our imagination about the possibilities for peace and justice. We can hope these narratives will provoke us to break with unjust traditions today and build the movements, and the strategies of action, to meet our newly emancipated needs and desires.

Notes

Introduction

1 I refer to each of the series with the following acronyms:

- *ST: TOS*: *Star Trek: The Original Series* (1966–9)
- *ST: TAS*: *Star Trek: The Animated Series* (1973–4)
- *ST: TNG*: *Star Trek: The Next Generation* (1987–94)
- *ST: DS9*: *Star Trek: Deep Space Nine* (1993–9)
- *ST: VOY*: *Star Trek: Voyager* (1995–2001)
- *ST: ENT*: *Star Trek: Enterprise* (2001–5)
- *ST: DISC*: *Star Trek: Discovery* (2017–Present)
- *ST: PIC*: *Star Trek: Picard* (2019–Present)
- *ST: LD*: *Star Trek: Lower Decks* (2020–Present)

2 In this book, I will use the term "Star Trek Universe" to refer to the collection of stories told in over fifty years of television series and feature films. I do not include here narratives that are based on novels, short fiction, or fan-based productions.

3 See Lawrence Krauss, *The Physics of Star Trek* (New York: Basic Books, 2007); Rick Hanley, *The Metaphysics of Star Trek* (New York: Basic Books, 1997); Mohammed A. F. Noor, *Live Long and Evolve: What Star Trek Can Teach Us about Evolution, Genetics, and Life on Other Worlds* (Princeton: Princeton University Press, 2018); George Gonzalez, *Star Trek and the Politics of Globalism* (New York: Palgrave Macmillan, 2018); Manu Saadia, *Trekonomics: The Economics of Star Trek* (San Francisco: Pipertexts, 2016); Jennifer Porter, *Star Trek and Sacred Ground: Explorations of Star Trek, Religion and American Culture* (Albany: State University of New York Press, 1999).

4 Robert H. Chaires and Bradley Chilton, *Star Trek Visions of Law and Justice* (Dallas: Adios Press, 2003), 9.

5 Judith Barad and Ed Robertson, *The Ethics of Star Trek* (New York: HarperCollins, 2000), xi.

6 Gregory Claeys and Lyman Tower Sargent, *The Utopia Reader*, 2nd edn (New York: New York University Press, 2017), 1.

7 Oliver P. Richmond, *Peace: A Very Short Introduction* (Oxford: Oxford University Press, 2014), 23–6.

8 Michael Allen Fox, "Nonviolence and Pacifism in the Long Nineteenth Century." In *The Routledge Handbook of Pacifism and Nonviolence*. Edited by Andrew Fiala (New York and London 2014), 23–4.

9 David P. Barash and Charles P. Webel, *Peace and Conflict Studies,* 3rd edn (Los Angeles: Sage, 2014), 20.

10 Houston Wood, *Current Debates in Peace and Conflict Studies* (New York: Oxford University Press, 2018), 1.

11 Elise Boulding, *Cultures of Peace: The Hidden Side of History* (Syracuse: Syracuse University Press, 2000), 25.

12 David Barash and Charles Webel, *Peace and Conflict Studies*, 3rd edn (Los Angeles: SAGE, 2014), 24.

13 Barash and Webel. *Peace and Conflict Studies*, 25.

14 See the *School Directory of Peace Studies and Conflict Resolutions Programs* for the Peace and Justice Studies Association at its website: https://www.peacejusticestudies.org/school-directory/.

15 Kent D. Shiffern, *From War to Peace: A Guide to the Next One Hundred Years* (Jefferson, NC: McFarland, 2011).

16 Richmond, *Peace: A Very Short Introduction*, 76–7.

17 Jacques Maritain, "The Grounds for an International Declaration of Human Rights (1947)." In *The Human Rights Reader*, 2nd edn. Edited by Micheline R. Ishay (New York: Routledge, 2007), 2–3.

18 Barash and Webel, *Peace and Conflict Studies*, 413.

19 Alex J. Bellamy, *World Peace: And How We Can Achieve It* (Oxford: Oxford University Press, 2019), 30–40.

20 Vaclav Havel, "The Politics of Responsibility." *World Policy Forum*. Vol. 12, No. 3 (1995), 81–7.

21 Richard Falk, *On Humane Governance: Toward a Global Politics* (Oxford: Polity Press, 1995), 241.

22 Boulding, *Cultures of Peace*, 257.

23 Nichelle Nichols, *Beyond Uhura: Star Trek and Other Memories* (London: Boxtree, 1994), 164–5.

24 Martin Luther King, Jr., *Letter to Coretta Scott* (July 18, 1952). https://ki nginstitute.stanford.edu/king-papers/documents/coretta-scott

25 James M. Lawson, Jr., "Nonviolence and the Non-Existent County." In *The Routledge Handbook of Pacifism and Nonviolence*. Edited by Andrew Fiala (New York and London: Routledge, 2018), 386.

26 Drew D. Hansen, *The Dream: Martin Luther King, Jr. and the Speech that Inspired a Nation* (New York: HarperCollins, 2003), 164–5.

27 Kimiko de Freytas-Tamura, "George Orwell's '1984' Is Suddenly a Best Seller," *The New York Times* (January 25, 2017) https://www.nytimes.com /2017/01/25/books/1984-george-orwell-donald-trump.html.

28 See Jeffrey C. Kinkley, *Visions of Dystopia in China's New Historical Novels* (New York: Columbia University Press, 2014); Ivan Fernando Rodrigo Mendizabal, "Andean Dystopias: When the Future Clashes with Desire." *Latin American Literature Today*, Vol. 1, No. 7 (August 2018), http://www.latinamericanliteraturetoday.org/en/2018/august/andean -dystopias-when-future-clashes-desire-iv%C3%A1n-rodrigo-mendiz %C3%A1bal; Moradewun Adejunmobi, "Introduction: African Science Fiction." *The Cambridge Journal of Postcolonial Literary Inquiry*, Vol. 3, No. 3 (2016), 265–72. doi:10.1017/pli.2016.28.

29 Jennifer Maas, "'Outbreak' Is Netflix's 9th Most Popular Overall Title in the US Right Now." The Wrap.com (March 14, 2020). https://www.thewrap. com/outbreak-movie-top-10-netflix-titles-movies-pandemic-tv-series-cor onavirus/

30 Blaka Basu, Katherine Broad, and Carrie Hintz, *Contemporary Dystopian Fiction for Young Adults: Brave New Teenagers* (New York: Routledge, 2013), 2.

31 See Gregory Claeys, *Dystopia: A Natural History* (Oxford: Oxford University Press, 2017), 501.

32 Amy L. Atchison and Shauna L. Shames, *Survive and Resist: The Definitive Guide to Dystopian Politics* (New York: Columbia University Press, 2019).

33 In this book, I will refer to residents living in the United States as "US Americans" rather than simply as "Americans" to recognize that residents of Latin American societies have also referred to themselves as "Americans" and a narrowing of this label to the United States erases this historical memory. See Elizabeth Martinez, "Don't Call This Country 'America.'" *Z Magazine* (August 1, 2003), https://zcomm.org/zmagazine /dont-call-this-country-and-quot-america-and-quot-by-elizabeth-marti nez/.

34 Rachel Janfranza, "'We're Tired of Waiting': Gen Z Is Ready for a Revolution." *CNN* (June 22, 2020). https://edition.cnn.com/2020/06 /16/politics/genz-voters-2020-election/index.html: "Absentee and Early

Voting by Youth in the 2020 Election. CIRCLE: The Center for Information Research on Civic Learning and Engagement" (October 30, 2020). https:/ /circle.tufts.edu/latest-research/absentee-and-early-voting-youth-2020-el ection.

35 Jeremy Bauer-Wolf, "Activists, but Not for Political Parties." *Inside Higher Education* (October 29, 2018). https://www.insidehighered.com/news /2018/10/29/report-students-prefer-issue-based-groups-rather-political -parties

36 James Sloam, "'Voice and Equality': Young People's Politics in the European Union," *West European Politics*, Vol. 36, No. 4 (March 2013), 836–58; Magdelina Kitanova, "Youth Political Participation in the EU: Evidence from a Cross-National Analysis." *Journal of Youth Studies*, Vol. 23, No. 7 (2020), 819–36; Cristian Leon, Antonella Perini, and Matthias Bianchi, "Transforming Political Participation in Latin America." *Open Democracy* (July 5, 2017), https://www.opendemocracy.net/en/de mocraciaabierta/transforming-political-participation/; Danielle Resnick and Daniela Casale, "Political Participation of Africa's Youth: Turnout, Partisanship and Protest." *Afrobarometer*, Afrobarometer Working Paper/136 (2011), https://afrobarometer.org/publications/political-partic ipation-africa%E2%80%99s-youth-turnout-partisanship-and-protest.

37 Steve LeVine, "The Coming Reckoning for Capitalism." *Axios.com* (December 20, 2018), https://www.axios.com/coming-reckoning-capita lism-2020-presidential-election-7f55e9f7-ab90-45a9-9cc1-47e1a102f 4bb.html.; Marie Solis, "Why Gen Z Is Turning to Socialism." Vice.com (May 4, 2020). https://www.vice.com/en/article/g5xz7j/gen-z-socialism-ydsa.

38 Cristian Leon, Antonella Perini, and Matthias Bianchi, "Transforming Political Participation in Latin America." *Open Democracy* (July 5, 2017), https://www.opendemocracy.net/en/democraciaabierta/transforming-p olitical-participation/; Tafadzwa Maganga, "Youth Demonstrations and Their Impact on Political Change and Development in Africa." *Accord.org* .za (2020), https://www.accord.org.za/conflict-trends/youth-demonstratio ns-and-their-impact-on-political-change-and-development-in-africa/.

39 Lauren Young, "Gen Z Is the Most Progressive—and Least Partisan— Generation." *Teen Vogue* (October 2, 2019), https://www.teenvogue.com /story/how-will-gen-z-vote

40 See "Youth Voting Rose in 2018 Despite Concerns about American Democracy." CIRCLE: Center for Information, Research on Civic Learning and Engagement (April 17, 2019). https://circle.tufts.edu/latest-research/ youth-voting-rose-2018-despite-concerns-about-american-democracy

41 Richard Wike and Shannon Schumacher, "Democratic Rights Popular Globally but Commitment to Them Not Always Strong." *Pew Research*

Center (February 27, 2020), https://www.pewresearch.org/global/2020/02/27/democratic-rights-popular-globally-but-commitment-to-them-not-always-strong/#many-are-frustrated-with-how-democracy-is-functioning.

42 Lauren Duca, *How to Start a Revolution: Young People and the Future of American Politics* (New York: Simon and Schuster, 2019), 127.

43 Duca, *How to Start a Revolution*, 134–5.

44 Darko Suvin, *Positions and Presuppositions in Science Fiction* (Kent, OH: Kent State University, 1988), 111.

45 Sherryl Vint, *Science Fiction* (Cambridge and London: MIT Press, 2021), 10–11.

46 Brookes Landon, *Science Fiction after 1900: From the Steam Man to the Stars* (New York; Twayne, 1997), 33.

47 Esther Jones, "Science Fiction Builds Mental Resiliency in Young Minds." The Conversation (May 11, 2020). https://theconversation.com/science-fiction-builds-mental-resiliency-in-young-readers-135513

48 Ericka Hoagland and Reema Sarwal. *Science Fiction, Imperialism, and the Third World: Essays on Postcolonial Literature and Film* (Jefferson, NC: McFarland and Co., 2010), 12.

49 Ursula K. Le Guin, "Science Fiction and the Future." In *Dancing at the Edge of the World: Thoughts on Words, Women, Places* (New York: Harper & Row, 1989), 143 (142–3).

50 David Kyle Johnson, "What Sci Phi Is All About: Treating Science Fiction as Philosophy," *Sci Phi Journal* (2019). https://www.sciphijournal.org/index.php/2019/02/14/sci-phi-journal-2019-1-for-printing/

51 See Mark Johnson, *Moral Imagination: Implications of Cognitive Science for Ethics* (Chicago: University of Chicago Press, 1993).

52 Mary Warnock, *Imagination* (Berkeley: University of California Press, 1978), 196.

53 See Helen De Cruz, Johan De Smedt, and Eric Schwitzgebel, *Philosophy through Science Fiction Stories: Exploring the Boundaries of the Possible* (London: Bloomsbury, 2021).

54 Elisabeth Anne Leonard, "Race and Ethnicity in Science Fiction." In *The Cambridge Companion to Science Fiction*. Edited by Edward James and Farah Mendelsohn (Cambridge: Cambridge University Press, 2003), 253–63.

55 Ursula K. Le Guin, "A War without End." In *Utopia by Thomas More*. Edited and Introduction by China Mieville (New York: Verso, 2016), 210 (199–210).

56 Shelley Streeby, *Imagining the Future of Climate Change: World Making through Science Fiction and Activism* (Berkeley and Los Angeles: University of California Press, 2018), 15–18.

57   Lauren Levitt, "The Hunger Games and the Dystopian Imagination." In
     Popular Culture and the Civic Imagination. Edited by Henry Jenkins,
     Gabriel Peters-Lazaro, and Sangita Shresthova (New York: New York
     University, 2020), 49–50.

58   Calvert Jones and Celia Paris, "It's the End of the World and They Know
     It: How Dystopian Fiction Shapes Political Attitudes." *Perspectives on
     Politics*, Vol. 16, No. 4 (December 2018), 969–89.

59   Calvery Jones and Celia Paris, "How Dystopian Narratives Can Incite Real
     World Radicalism." *Aeon* (April 15, 2020), https://aeon.co/ideas/how-dyst
     opian-narratives-can-incite-real-world-radicalism.

60   Brianna Rennix, "The Regrettable Decline of Space Utopias." *Current
     Affairs* (June 14, 2017). https://www.currentaffairs.org/2017/03/the-re
     grettable-decline-of-space-utopias

61   George Gonzalez, *Justice and Popular Culture: Star Trek as Philosophical
     Text* (Lanham: Rowman and Littlefield, 2019).

62   Peter Frase, *Four Futures: Life after Capitalism* (New York: Verso, 2016),
     48–9.

63   Yvonne Fern, *Gene Roddenberry: The Last Conversation* (New York:
     Pocket Books, 1996), 12–13.

64   George Gonzales, *Star Trek and the Politics of Globalism* (New York:
     Palgrave Macmillan 2018), 39.

65   Fern, *Gene Roddenberry: The Last Conversation*, 75.

66   Fern, *Gene Roddenberry: The Last Conversation*, 134–5.

67   David Gerrold, "Foreword: Still Trekkin' after All These Years." In *Boarding
     the Enterprise: Transporters, Tribbles, and the Vulcan Death Grip in Gene
     Roddenberry's Star Trek*. Edited by David Gerrold and Robert J. Sawyer
     (Dallas: Ben Bella Books, 2016), 8.

Chapter 1

1   Marc Cushman and Susan Osborn, *These Are the Voyages: TOS Season
    Three* (San Diego: Jacobs/Brown Press, 2014), 592–4.

2   Cushman and Osborn, *These Are the Voyages: TOS Season One*, 168.

3   Marc Cushman and Susan Osborn, *These Are the Voyages: TOS Season
    One* (San Diego: Jacobs/Brown Press, 2013), 168.

4   Thomas Hobbes, *Leviathan*. Edited by A.R. Waller. (Cambridge:
    Cambridge University Press, 1904), 84.

5 Albert Einstein, "Why War?" In *The Standard Edition of the Complete Psychological Works of Sigmund Freud*, Volume XXII. Edited by Sigmund Freud (1932–1936), 198–201.

6 Sigmund Freud, "Why War to 'Why War?,'" 208.

7 Sigmund Freud, "Why War to 'Why War?,'" 210–11.

8 Freud, "Why War to 'Why War?,'" 214.

9 William James, "The Moral Equivalent of War." In *The Works of William James: Essays in Religion and Morality* (Cambridge, MA: Harvard University Press, 1982), 170 (162–73).

10 James, "The Moral Equivalent of War," 171–2.

11 Majorie S. Campbell et al. "Postdeployment PTSD and Addictive Combat Attachment Behaviors in U.S. Military Service Members." *American Journal of Psychiatry*, Vol. 173, No. 12 (December 2016), 1171–6.

12 Chris Hedges, *War Is a Force That Gives Us Meaning* (New York: Anchor, 2003), 173.

13 Hedges, *War Is a Force That Gives Us Meaning*, 5.

14 E. O. Wilson, *The Meaning of Human Existence* (New York: W. W. Norton, 2015), 24–5.

15 Richard Dawkins, *The Selfish Gene* (Oxford: Oxford University Press, 1989), 3.

16 E. O. Wilson, *The Social Conquest of Earth* (New York: W. W. Norton, 2012).

17 John Horgan, *The End of War* (New York: McSweeneys, 2014).

18 David Adams, "The Seville Statement on Violence: A Progress Report." *Journal of Peace Research*, Vol. 26, No. 2 (1989), 113.

19 "The Seville Statement on Violence." *American Psychologist*, Vol. 45, No. 10 (1990), 1167–8.

20 David Barash and Charles Webel, *Peace and Conflict Studies,* 3rd edn (Thousand Oaks, CA: SAGE, 2014), 134.

21 Andrew Fitz-Gibbon, "Becoming Nonviolent: Sociobiological, Neurophysiological, and Spiritual Perspectives." In *The Routledge Handbook of Pacifism and Nonviolence*. Edited by Andrew Fiala (New York and London: Routledge, 2018), 311.

22 Brian Morris, *Kropotkin: The Politics of Community* (Oakland, CA: PM Press, 2018), 129–50.

23 Peter Kropotkin, *Mutual Aid: A Factor of Evolution* (London: Heinemann, 1902), 24.

24 Yuval Noah Harari, *Sapiens: A Brief History of Humankind* (New York: Harper Perennial, 2018), 23.

25 Philip Zimbardo, *The Lucifer Effect: Understanding How Good People Turn Evil* (New York: Random House, 2008), 5.

26 Alex J. Bellamy, *World Peace: And How We Can Achieve It* (Oxford: Oxford University Press, 2019), 89–90.

27 Douglas P. Fry, "Life without War?." *Science*, Vol. 336, No. 6083 (May 18, 2012), 879–84.

28 Raymond C. Kelly, "The Evolution of Lethal Intergroup Violence." *Proceedings of the National Academy of Sciences of the United States*, Vol. 102, No. 43 (October 25, 2005), 15294–8.

29 Jonathan Haas and Matthew Piscitelli, "The Prehistory of Warfare: Misled by Ethnography." In *War, Peace, and Human Nature: The Convergence of Evolutionary and Cultural Views*. Edited by Douglas P. Fry (Oxford: Oxford University Press, 2013), 181–2.

30 Raymond C. Kelly, "The Evolution of Lethal Intergroup Violence," 15298; see also, Lawrence Keely, *War before Civilization: The Myth of the Peaceful Savage* (New York: Oxford University Press, 1997), 38.

31 James C. Scott, *Against the Grain: A Deep History of the Earliest States* (New Haven and London: Yale University Press, 2017), 158–9.

32 Hannah Devlin, "Earliest Known Cave Art by Modern Humans Found in Indonesia." *The Guardian* (December 11, 2019), https://www.theguardian.com/science/2019/dec/11/earliest-known-cave-art-by-modern-humans-found-in-indonesia; Yuval Harrai, *Sapiens*, 23.

33 Ursula K. Le Guin, "The Carrier Bag Theory of Fiction." In *Dancing at the Edge of the World: Thoughts on Words, Woman, and Places* (New York: Grove Press, 1989), 165–70.

Chapter 2

1 Michael Piller in *The Fifty Year Mission: The Complete, Uncensored, Unauthorized Oral History of Star Trek; The Next 25 Years from The Next Generation to J.J. Abrams*. Edited by Mark A. Altman and Edward Gross (New York: St. Martin's Press, 2016), 414.

2 Rick Berman in *The Fifty Year Mission: The Complete, Uncensored, Unauthorized Oral History of Star Trek; The Next 25 Years from The Next Generation to J.J. Abrams*, 416.

3 Rick Berman in *The Fifty Year Mission: The Complete, Uncensored, Unauthorized Oral History of Star Trek; The Next 25 Years from The Next Generation to J.J. Abrams*, 424.

4 Michael Piller in *The Fifty Year Mission: The Complete, Uncensored, Unauthorized Oral History of Star Trek; The Next 25 Years from The Next Generation to J.J. Abrams, 425.*

5 Krishnadev Calamur, Ayesha Rascoe, Alana Wise, "Trump Says He Spoke with Floyd's Family, Understands Hurt and Pain of Community." *National Public Radio.* Npr.org (May 29, 2020). https://www.npr.org/2020/05/29 /864722348/twitter-hides-trumps-tweet-on-minneapolis-saying-it-glorifies -violence

6 Adrian Horton, "John Oliver: When Trump 'Uses the Word Thugs, You Know What It's Code For.'" *The Guardian.com* (June 1, 2020). https://www.theguardian.com/culture/2020/jun/01/john-oliver-when-trump-uses-thugs-code-racism-george-floyd-protests; See also, Melissa Block, "The Racially Charged Meaning behind the Word 'Thug.'" All Things Considered. Npr. Org (April 20, 2015) https://www.npr.org/2015/04/30/403362626/the-racially-charged-meaning-behind-the-word-thug

7 President George H. W. Bush, "Address to the Nation on the Civil Disturbances in Los Angeles, California." https://bush41library.tamu.edu/ archives/public-papers/4252

8 David Jackson, "Obama Stands by the Term 'Thugs,' White House Says." USA Today.com (April 29, 2015). https://www.usatoday.com/story/theo val/2015/04/29/obama-white-house-baltimore-stephanie-rawlings-blake /26585143/

9 Andrew Fiala, *Nonviolence: A Quick Immersion* (New York: Tibidabo, 2020) 59.

10 Danielle Kilgo, "Riot or Resistance? The Way the Media Frames the Unrest in Minneapolis Will Share the Public's View of Protest." Nieman Lab (May 30, 2020). https://www.niemanlab.org/2020/05/riot-or-resistan ce-the-way-the-media-frames-the-unrest-in-minneapolis-will-shape-the-p ublics-view-of-protest/

11 Aaron Morrison and Kat Stafford, "AP-NORC Poll: Support for Racial Injustice Protests Declines." *AP News* (September 24, 2020). https://ap news.com/article/breonna-taylor-race-and-ethnicity-shootings-police-new -york-24af876f135f529d95c9c857ad9aaa0e

12 Fiala, *Nonviolence: A Quick Immersion*, 60.

13 Johan Galtung, "Cultural Violence." *Journal of Peace Research*, Vol. 27, No. 3 (August 1990), 294

14 Galtung, "Cultural Violence," 292.

15 Fiala, *Nonviolence: A Quick Immersion*, 54.

16 Johan Galtung, "Violence, Peace, and Peace Research." *Journal of Peace Research*, Vol. 6, No. 3 (1969), 169.

17 Kit R. Christensen, *Nonviolence, Peace, and Justice: A Philosophical Introduction* (Ontario: Broadview Press, 2010), 35.

18 See Paul McGorrery and Marilyn McMahon, *Criminalising Coercive Control: Family Violence and Criminal Law* (Singapore: Springer, 2020).

19 Huston Wood, *Invitation to Peace Studies* (Oxford: Oxford University Press, 2016), 20.

20 Christensen, *Nonviolence, Peace, and Justice*, 35–6.

21 Galtung, "Cultural Violence," 293.

22 Iris Marion Young. *Justice and the Politics of Difference*. (Princeton: Princeton University Press, 2011) 39-65.

23 Galtung, "Cultural Violence," 292.

24 Wood, *Invitation to Peace Studies*, 19.

25 Christensen, *Nonviolence, Peace, and Justice*, 37.

26 Johan Galtung, "Twenty Five Years of Peace Research: Ten Challenges and Responses." *Journal of Peace Research*, Vol. 22, No. (1985).

27 Ira Steven Behr in *The Fifty Year Mission: The Complete, Uncensored, Unauthorized Oral History of Star Trek; The Next 25 Years from The Next Generation to J.J. Abrams, 479.*

28 Ina Jaffe, "After the L.A. Riots, A Failed Effort for a Broken City." National Public Radio. Com (April 29, 2012), https://www.npr.org/2012/04/29/151608071/after-l-a-riots-an-effort-to-rebuild-a-broken-city

29 Cesar Chavez, "At Exposition Park." In *Cesar Chavez: An Organizer's Tale*. Edited by Ilan Stavans (New York: Penguin, 2008), 120.

30 Chavez, "At Exposition Park," 120.

31 Chavez, "At Exposition Park," 120.

32 Chavez, "At Exposition Park," 121.

33 Martin Luther King, Jr. "The Other America." Speech Delivered at Gross Pointe High School, March 14, 1968. https://www.gphistorical.org/mlk/mlkspeech/mlk-gp-speech.pdf

34 Martin Luther King, Jr., "Nonviolence and Social Change." In *The Radical King*. Edited by Cornel West (Boston: Beacon Press, 2015), 149.

35 King, Jr. "Nonviolence and Social Change," 150.

36 Vickey Osterweil, *In Defense of Looting: A Riotous History of Uncivil Action* (New York: Bold Type Books, 2020).

37 King, Jr. "Nonviolence and Social Change," 149.

38 Edward Maguire, "New Directions in Protest Policing," Saint Louis University Public Law Review, Vol. 35, No. 1, Article 6. https://scholarship.law.slu.edu/plr/vol35/iss1/6

Chapter 3

1 Marc Cushman and Susan Osborn, *These Are the Voyages TOS: Season Two* (Los Angeles: Jacobs/Brown, 2014), 209.

2 David Kyle Johnson, "Destroying Utopias: Why Kirk Is a Jerk." In *The Ultimate Star Trek and Philosophy: The Search for Socrates*. Edited by Kevin S. Decker and Jason T. Eberl (Malden, MA: Wiley Blackwell 2016), 47–58.

3 Lincoln Geraughty, *Living with Star Trek: American Culture and the Star Trek Universe* (London: I. B. Tauris, 2007), 55–60.

4 Robert H. Chaires and Bradley Chilton, "Law, Justice, and Star Trek." In *Star Trek Visions of Law and Justice*. Edited by Robert Chaires and Bradley Chilton (Dallas: Adios Press, 2003), 22.

5 Mark P. Lagon, "'We Owe It to Them Not to Interfere': *Star Trek* and U.S. Statecraft in the 1960s and 1990s." *Extrapolation*, Vol. 34, No. 3 (1993), 262; Eric Greene, "The Prime Question." In *Boarding the Enterprise: Transporters, Tribbles, and the Vulcan Death Grip in Gene Roddenberry's Star Trek*. Edited by David Gerrold and Robert J. Sawyer (Dallas: Smart Pop, 2016), 55–80.

6 Robin J. Crews, "A Modest Proposal for Peace Studies." *Peace Review: A Journal of Social Justice*, Vol. 14, No. 1 (2002), 73.

7 Johan Galtung, "Violence, Peace, and Peace Research." *Journal of Peace Research*, Vol. 6, No. 3 (1969), 183.

8 Jane Addams, *Newer Ideals of Peace*. Introduction by Berenice A. Carroll and Clinton F. Fink (Urbana and Chicago: University of Illinois Press 2007), 15.

9 Addams, *Newer Ideals of Peace*, 21.

10 Addams, *Newer Ideals of Peace*, 22.

11 Oliver P. Richmond, *Peace: A Very Short Introduction* (Oxford: Oxford University Press, 2014), 7.

12 Addams, *Newer Ideals of Peace*, 11.

13 Jane Addams, *Twenty Years at Hull House* (New York: Macmillan, 1911), 120.

14 Jane Addams, *Democracy and Social Ethics* (New York: Macmillan, 1902) 178–9.

15 Addams, *Newer Ideals of Peace*, 131.

16 Carol Hay, "Justice and Objectivity for Pragmatists: Cosmopolitanism in the Work of Marth Nussbaum and Jane Addams." *The Pluralist*, Vol. 7, No. 3 (Fall 2012), 86–95.

17 Martha Nussbaum, *Creating Capabilities: The Human Development Approach* (Cambridge, MA: Harvard University Press, 2011), 33–4.

18 Amartya Sen, "Human Rights and Capabilities." *Journal of Human Development*, Vol. 6, No. 2 (July 2005), 151–66.

19 Immanuel Kant, *Perpetual Peace and Other Essays on Politics, History, and Morals*. Translated with Introduction by T. Humphrey (Indianapolis: Hackett Publishing, 1983), 109.

20 Michael Walzer, *Just and Unjust Wars*, 4th edn (New York: Basic Books, 1977), 107.

21 Kofi Annan, "Two Concepts of Sovereignty." *The Economist* (September 16, 1999). https://www.economist.com/international/1999/09/16/two-concepts-of-sovereignty

22 David Barash and Charles Webel, *Peace and Conflict Studies*, 3rd edn (Los Angeles: SAGE Publications, 2014), 421.

23 Alex J. Bellamy, *Just Wars* (Cambridge, UK: Polity Books 2006), 219–21.

24 David Boersma, "'We Are Not Going to Kill Today?': Star Trek and the Philosophy of Peace." In *The Ultimate Star Trek and Philosophy: The Search for Socrates*. Edited by Kevin S. Decker and Jason T. Eberl (Malden, MA: Wiley Blackwell, 2016), 67.

25 A poll of 27,000 fans done by the website startrek.com found that only 5 percent of them thought Kirk had any respect for the Prime Directive. Only Captain Jonathan Archer did worse, with 3 percent. But, of course, Archer served in Starfleet before there was a Prime Directive! See "Poll Says Captain with the Most Respect for the Prime Directive is . . . ," startrek.com (September 29, 2013). https://www.startrek.com/article/poll-says-captain-with-the-most-respect-for-the-prime-directive-is

Chapter 4

1 Margaret A. Weitekamp, "More than 'Just Uhura': Understanding *Star Trek*'s Lt. Uhura, Civil Rights, and Space History." In *Star Trek and History*. Edited by Nancy R. Reagin (Hoboken, NJ: Wiley, 2013), 24–5.

2 Quoted in *The Fifty Year Mission: The Complete, Uncensored, Unauthorized Oral History of Star Trek; The First 25 Years*. Edited by Edward Gross and Mark A. Altman (New York: St. Martin's Press, 2016), 36.

3 At least two studies argue that there are important tensions between the anti-racist message of *Star Trek* episodes and the manner in which they are dramatically portrayed which significantly dampen their anti-

racist potential. I think these critiques are important, but both were
written without incorporating *ST: DS9*. See Daniel L. Bernardi, *Star
Trek and History: Race-ing toward a White Future* (New Brunswick,
NJ: Rutgers University Press, 1998); Michael Pounds, *Race in Space:
The Representation of Ethnicity in Star Trek and Star Trek: The Next
Generation* (Lanham, MD: Scarecrow Press, 1999).

4 Martin Luther King, Jr., "I Have a Dream." In *A Testament of Hope: The
Essential Writing and Speeches of Martin Luther King, Jr.* Edited by
James W. Washington (San Francisco: Harper 1986), 219.

5 Martin Luther King, Jr., "Letter from a Birmingham City Jail." In *A
Testament of Hope: The Essential Writing and Speeches of Martin Luther
King, Jr.* Edited by James W. Washington (San Francisco: Harper 1986),
295.

6 Martin Luther King, Jr., "A Testament of Hope." In *A Testament of Hope:
The Essential Writing and Speeches of Martin Luther King, Jr.* Edited by
James W. Washington (San Francisco: Harper 1986), 317.

7 Evan P. Apfelbaum et al., "Racial Color Blindness: Emergence, Practice,
and Implications." *Current Directions in Psychological Science*, Vol. 21,
No. 3. (2012), 205 (205–9).

8 Quoted in *The Fifty Year Mission: The Complete, Uncensored,
Unauthorized Oral History of Star Trek; The First 25 Years*. Edited by
Edward Gross and Mark A. Altman (New York: St. Martin's Press, 2016),
39.

9 Apfelbaum et al., "Racial Color Blindness: Emergence, Practice, and
Implications," 206.

10 King, Jr., "A Testament of Hope," 317.

11 King, Jr., "Where Do We Go From Here?," In *A Testament of Hope: The
Essential Writing and Speeches of Martin Luther King, Jr.* Edited by
James W. Washington (San Francisco: Harper 1986), 246.

12 King, Jr. "A Testament of Hope," 323.

13 See, for instance, Will Kymlicka, *Multicultural Citizenship: A Liberal Theory
of Minority Rights* (Oxford: Clarendon Press, 1995); Charles Taylor,
Multiculturalism. Edited by Amy Gutmann (Princeton, NJ: Princeton
University Press, 1994).

14 Amy Gutmann, *Identity in Democracy* (Princeton: Princeton University
Press, 2003).

15 See Rachel Sieder, *Multiculturalism in Latin America: Indigenous Rights,
Diversity, and Democracy* (London: Palgrave Macmillan, 2002); Will
Kymlicka and Baogang He, *Multiculturalism in Asia* (Oxford: Oxford
University Press, 2005); Will Kymlicka and Eva Pfosti, *Multiculturalism and
Minority Rights in the Arab World* (Oxford: Oxford University Press, 2014).

16 Marc Cushman with Susan Osborn, *These Are the Voyages: TOS: Season Three* (San Diego: Jacobs/Brown Press, 2015), 229.

17 Marc Cushman with Susan Osborn, *These Are the Voyages: TOS: Season Three*, 229.

18 Sharon DeGrew, *The Subject of Race in American Science Fiction* (New York: Routledge, 2007), 16; Isiah Lavender III, *Race in American Science Fiction* (Bloomington, IN: Indiana University Press, 2011), 26.

19 See Amy Sturgis, "If This is the (Final) Frontier, Where Are the Natives?" In *Star Trek and History*. Edited by Nancy R. Reagin (Hoboken, NJ: Wiley, 2013), 138–41; and Kanzler, Katja, "A Cuchi Moya!—Star Trek's Native Americans." *American Studies Journal*, Vol. 49 (2007). http://www.asjournal.org/49-2007/star-treks-native-americans/#

20 Amanda Barroso, "Most Black Adults Say Race Is Central to Their Identity and Feel Connected to a Broader Black Community." *Pew Research Center Fact Tank* (February 5, 2020). https://www.pewresearch.org/fact-tank/2020/02/05/most-black-adults-say-race-is-central-to-their-identity-and-feel-connected-to-a-broader-black-community/

21 See Yair Bar-Haim et al., "Nature and Nurture in Own-Race Face Processing." *Psychological Science*, Vol. 17, No. 2 (2006), 159–63; Tiffany A. Ito and Geoffrey Urland, "Race and Gender on the Brain: Electrocortical Measures of Attention to the Race and Gender of Multiply Categorizable Individuals." *Journal of Personality and Social Psychology*, Vol. 85, No. 4 (2003); Cheryl Dicker and Bruce Bartholow, "Racial Ingroup and Outgroup Attention Biases Revealed by Event Related Brain Potentials." *Social Cognitive and Affective Neuroscience*, Vol. 2, No. 3 (September 2007), 189–98.

22 See Evan P. Apfelbaum et. al., "In Pursuit of Racial Equality?" *Psychological Science*, Vol. 21 (2011), 1587–92. "Learning (Not) to Talk about Race: When Older Children Underperform in Social Categorization." *Developmental Psychology*, Vol. 44, No. 5 (2008), 1513–18.

23 Evan P. Apfelbaum et al., "Racial Color Blindness: Emergence, Practice, Implications." *Current Directions in Psychological Science*, Vol. 21, No. 3 (2012), 205–9.

24 Eduardo Bonilla Silva, *Racism without Racists: Color-Blind Racism and the Persistence of Racial Inequality in the United States*, 5th edn (Lanham, MD: Rowman and Littlefield, 2017): Ian Haney Lopez, "Intentional Blindness." *New York University Law Review*, Vol. 87, No. 6 (December 2012), 1779–1877.

25 Helen Neville et al., "Construction and Initial Validation of the Color Blind Racial Attitudes Scale (CoBRAS)." *Journal of Counseling Psychology*, Vol. 47, No. 1 (2000), 59–70.

26   Rita Chin, *The Crisis of Multiculturalism in Europe: A History* (Princeton, NJ: Princeton University Press, 2017).

27   Steven Vertovec and Susanne Wessendorf, "Introduction: Assessing the Backlash against Multiculturalism in Europe." In *The Multicultural Backlash: European Discourses, Policies, and Practices*. Edited by Steven Vertovec and Susanne Wessendorf (New York: Routledge, 2010).

28   Ashley Jardina, *White Identity Politics* (Cambridge: Cambridge University Press, 2019), 1–20.

29   Maria Abascal and Delia Baldassarri, "Love Thy Neighbor? Ethnoracial Diversity and Trust Reexamined." *American Journal of Sociology*, Vol. 121, No. 3 (November 2015), 722–82.

30   Maureen A. Craig and Jennifer A. Richeson, "More Diverse Yet Less Tolerant? How the Increasingly Diverse Racial Landscape Affects White Americans' Racial Attitudes." *Personality and Social Psychology Bulletin*, Vol. 40, No. 6 (June 2014), 750–61.

31   Maureen A. Craig and Jennifer A. Richeson, "On the Precipice of a 'Majority-Minority' America: Perceived Status Threat From the Racial Demographic Shift Affects White Americans' Political Ideology." *Psychological Science.*

32   Larry M. Bartels, "Ethnic Antagonism Erodes Republicans' Commitment to Democracy." *Proceedings of the National Academy of Sciences (PNAS)*, Vol. 117, No. 37 (August 31, 2020), 22752–9.

33   Ibram X. Kendi, *How to Be an Anti-Racist* (New York: One World, 2019), 23.

34   King, Jr. "Testament of Hope," 317.

35   Rick Webb, *The Economics of Star Trek: The Proto Post Scarcity Economy* (Las Vegas: Rick Webb, 2018), 46–7.

36   Peter Frase, *Four Futures: Life after Capitalism* (London: Verso, 2016), 48.

37   Martin Luther King, Jr., "A Time to Break the Silence." In *A Testament of Hope: The Essential Writing and Speeches of Martin Luther King, Jr.* Edited by James W. Washington (San Francisco: Harper 1986), 240.

38   Kendi, *How to Be an Anti-Racist*, 162–3.

39   W. E. B. Du Bois, *Black Reconstruction: An Essay Toward a History of the Part Which Black Folk Played in the Attempt to Reconstruct Democracy in America 1860-1880* (New York: Harcourt, Brace, and Co., 1935), 700–1.

40   W. E. B. Du Bois, "A Negro Nation within the Nation" (1935). In *W.E.B. Du Bois: A Reader*. Edited by David Levering Lewis (New York: Henry Holt, 1995), 566.

41   W. E. B. Du Bois, "Marxism and the Negro Problem" (1933). In *W.E.B. Du Bois: A Reader*. Edited by David Levering Lewis (New York: Henry Holt, 1995), 542.

42   See David Roediger, *The Wages of Whiteness: Race and the Making of the American Working Class* (London: Verso, 1999) and also David Roediger, *Working toward Whiteness: How America's Immigrants Became White* (New York: Basic Books, 2005).

43   Derrick Bell, "Who's Afraid of Critical Race Theory?" *University of Illinois Law Review*, Vol. 1995, No. 833 (1995), 906.

44   Keenanga Yamatta-Taylor, *From #BlackLivesMatter to Black Liberation* (London: Haymarket Books, 2016), 206.

45   Terrance MacMullen, *Habits of Whiteness: A Pragmatist Reconstruction* (Indianapolis: Indiana University Press, 2009).

46   George Yancy, *Black Bodies, White Gazes: The Continuing Significance of Race in America* (Landham, MD: Rowman and Littlefield, 2017), 255.

47   Keeanga Yamatta Taylor, *From #BlackLivesMatter to Black Liberation*, 216.

48   Walidah Imarisha, "Rewriting the Future: Using Science Fiction to Re-Envision Justice." *Bitch Magazine*, bitchmedia.org (February 11, 2015), https://www.bitchmedia.org/article/rewriting-the-future-prison-abolition -science-fiction.

Chapter 5

1   Marc Cushman and Susan Osborn, *These Are the Voyages: TOS: Season One* (San Diego: Jacobs/Brown Press, 2013), 325.

2   Martin Luther King, Jr., "Nonviolence and Racial Justice." In *A Testament of Hope: The Essential Writings and Speeches of Martin Luther King, Jr*. Edited by James M. Washington (San Francisco, Harper, 1991), 8.

3   Gandhi, *Selected Political Writings*. Edited by Dennis Dalton (Indianapolis: Hackett, 1996), 56.

4   Martha Nussbaum, *Anger and Forgiveness: Resentment, Generosity, Justice* (Oxford: Oxford University Press, 2016), 1–5.

5   Kit R. Christensen, *Nonviolence, Peace, and Justice: A Philosophical Introduction* (Ontario: Broadview Press, 2010), 155.

6   Micheline R. Ishay, *The History of Human Rights: From Ancient Texts to the Globalization Era* (Berkeley: University of California, Press, 2008), 28–9.

7 Kit R. Christensen, *Revenge and Social Conflict* (Cambridge: Cambridge University Press, 2016), 123–4.

8 Martin Luther King, Jr., "An Experiment in Love." In *A Testament of Hope: The Essential Writings and Speeches of Martin Luther King, Jr.* Edited by James M. Washington (San Francisco, Harper, 1991), 18–19.

9 Gandhi, *All Men Are Brothers: Life and Thoughts of Mahatma Gandhi as Told in His Own Words.* Edited by Krishna Kripalani (Ahmedabad: Jitendra T. Desai, 1960), 102–3.

10 Gandhi, *Selected Political Writings*, 41.

11 Nussbaum, *Anger and Forgiveness*, 206.

12 Quoted in Micheline R. Ishay, *The Human Rights Reader: Major Political Essays, Speeches, and Documents from Ancient Times to the Present*, 2nd edn (New York: Routledge, 2007), 35.

13 Quoted in Ishay, *The Human Rights Reader*, 91.

14 Terry J. Ermann and Paula M. Block, *Star Trek: Deep Space Nine Companion* (New York: Pocket Books, 2000), 308.

15 Peter King "Introduction." In Augustine, *On the Free Choice of the Will, On Grace and Free Choice, and Other Writings.* Edited and Translated by Peter King (Cambridge: Cambridge University Press, 2010), xxiv.

16 Reinhold Niebuhr, *Moral Man and Immoral Society* (New York: Charles Schribner's Sons, 1932), 127.

17 Reinhold Niebuhr, *Moral Man and Immoral Society* (New York: Charles Schribner's Sons, 1932), 253.

18 Paul Vallely, "How Philanthropy Benefits the Super Rich." *The Guardian* (September 8, 2020), https://www.theguardian.com/society/2020/sep/08/how-philanthropy-benefits-the-super-rich.

19 Desmond Tutu, *No Future without Forgiveness* (New York: Doubleday, 1999), 13–30.

20 Tutu, *No Future without Forgiveness*, 270.

21 Quoted in Gail M. Presby, "Philosophy of Nonviolence in Africa." In *The Routledge Handbook of Pacifism and Nonviolence.* Edited by Andrew Fiala (New York: Routledge, 2018), 74.

22 Tutu, *No Future without Forgiveness*, 271.

23 Tutu, *No Future without Forgiveness*, 271.

24 Tutu, *No Future without Forgiveness*, 272.

25 Tutu, *No Future without Forgiveness*, 273.

26 Quoted in Cheryl de la Rey, "Reconciliation in Divided Societies." In *Peace, Conflict, and Violence: Peace Psychology for the 21st Century.*

Edited by Daniel J. Christie, Richard V. Wagner, and Deborah Dunann Winter (Upper Saddle River: Prentice Hall, 2001), 258.

27 For an excellent overview, see Colleen Murphy, *The Conceptual Foundations of Transitional Justice* (Cambridge: Cambridge University Press, 2017).

28 James L. Gibson and Amanda Gouws, "Truth and Reconciliation in South Africa: Attributions of Blame and the Struggle over Apartheid." *The American Political Science Review*, Vol. 93, No. 3 (September 1999), 501–17.

29 Audrey R. Chapman, "Truth Commissions and Intergroup Forgiveness: The Case of the South African Truth and Reconciliation Commission." *Peace and Conflict: Journal of Peace Psychology*, Vol. 13, No. 1, 51–69.

30 Terry Bell, *Unfinished Business: South Africa, Apartheid, and Truth* (New York: Verso, 2003), 4.

31 Angela D. Nichols, *Impact, Legitimacy, and Limitations of Truth Commissions* (London: Palgrave Macmillan, 2019); Colleen Murphy, "How Nations Heal." *Boston Review* (January 21, 2021), http://bostonreview.net/politics-law-justice/colleen-murphy-how-nations-heal.

32 Bhiku Parekh, *Gandhi: A Very Short Introduction* (Oxford: Oxford University Press, 1997), 64–7.

33 Gandhi, *Selected Political Writings*, 50–1; See also Tara Sethia, *Gandhi: Pioneer of Nonviolent Social Change* (Upper Saddle Ridge, NJ: Pearson, 2012), for an excellent introduction to the ways in which Gandhi incorporated satyagraha into his various nonviolent campaigns.

34 Mary Burton, "Custodians of Memory: South Africa's Truth and Reconciliation Commission." *International Journal of Legal Information*, Vol. 32, No. 2 (2004), 417–25.

35 Nussbaum, *Anger and Forgiveness*, 241–6.

36 Martha Minow, *Between Vengeance and Forgiveness: Facing History after Genocide and Mass Violence* (Boston: Beacon Press, 1998), 52–90.

Chapter 6

1 Rob Nixon, *Slow Violence and the Environmentalism of the Poor* (Cambridge, MA: Harvard University Press, 2011), 2.

2 Nixon, *Slow Violence and the Environmentalism of the Poor*, 2.

3 Brian Merchant, "Behold the Rise of Dystopian 'Cli-Fi.'" *Vice* (May 31, 2013), https://www.vice.com/en/article/ypp7nj/behold-the-rise-of-cli-fi.

4 Derrick O'Keefe, "Imagining the End of Capitalism with Kim Stanley Robinson." *Jacobin* (October 22, 2020), Jacobin.com. https://www.jac obinmag.com/2020/10/kim-stanley-robinson-ministry-future-science-ficti on.

5 William J. Ripple, Christopher Wolf, Thomas M. Newsome, Mauro Galetti, Mohammed Alamgir, Eileen Crist, Mahmoud I. Mahmoud, William F. Laurance, 15,364 scientist signatories from 184 countries, "World Scientists' Warning to Humanity: A Second Notice." *BioScience*, Vol. 67, No. 12 (December 2017), 1026, 1026–8.

6 William J. Ripple, Christopher Wolf, Thomas M. Newsome, Phoebe Barnard, William R. Moomaw, "World Scientists' Warning of a Climate Emergency." *BioScience*, Vol. 70, No. 1 (January 2020), 11 (8–12).

7 Bradshaw Corey J. A., Ehrlich Paul R., Beattie Andrew, Ceballos Gerardo, Crist Eileen, Diamond Joan, Dirzo Rodolfo, Ehrlich Anne H., Harte John, Harte Mary Ellen, Pyke Graham, Raven Peter H., Ripple William J., Saltré Frédérik, Turnbull Christine, Wackernagel Mathis, Blumstein Daniel T., "Underestimating the Challenges of Avoiding a Ghastly Future." *Frontiers in Conservation Science*, Vol. 1 (January 2021), 6 (1–10).

8 The humpback almost did go extinct in the mid-twentieth century, but a ban on whaling in the 1970s has allowed the whales to rebound; Elizabeth Weise, "For Once, Good Environment News: A Humpback Whale Population Has Come Back From the Brink." *USA Today* (October, 16, 2019). https://www.usatoday.com/story/news/nation/2019/10/16/g ood-news-humpback-whale-population-back-after-near-extinction/399 7894002/.

9 Dolly Jorgensen, "Who's the Devil: Species Extinction and Environmentalist Thought in *Star Trek*." In *Star Trek and History*. Edited by Nancy R. Reagin (Hoboken, NJ: Wiley, 2013), 246.

10 Rashid Hassan, Robert Scholes, Nevile Ash, *Ecosystems and Human Well-Being: Current State and Trends, Vol. 1.* (Washington, DC: Island Press, 2005), vii.

11 Rashid Hassan, Robert Scholes, Nevile Ash, *Ecosystems and Human Well-Being: Current State and Trends, Vol. 1.*, x.

12 Morgan M. Robertson, "The Nature That Capital Can See: Science, State, and Market in the Commodification of Ecosystem Services." *Environment and Planning D: Society and Space*, Vol. 24 (2006), 367–87.

13 Roldan Muradian, "The Ecosystem Services Paradigm: Rise, Scope, and Limits." In *Rethinking Nature: Challenging Disciplinary Boundaries*. Edited by Aurelie Chone, Isabelle Hajek, and Phillipe Hamman (New York: Routledge, 2017), 195–208.

14 Dolly Jorgensen, "Who's the Devil? Species Extinction and Environmentalist Thought in *Star Trek*," 246.

15 See Kenneth M. Murchison, *The Snail Darter Case: TVA versus the Endangered Species Act* (Lawrence, KS: University Press of Kansas, 2007).

16 Aldo Leopold, *A Sand County Almanac: And Sketches Here and There* (Oxford: Oxford University Press, 1949), viii.

17 Quoted in Michelle Nijhuis, "Can Aldo Leopold's Land Ethics Tackle Our Toughest Problems?" High Country News (January 19, 2015) https://www.hcn.org/issues/47.1/can-aldo-leopolds-land-ethic-tackle-our-toughest-problems.

18 Leopold, *A Sand County Almanac: And Sketches Here and There,* 221.

19 Leopold, *A Sand County Almanac: And Sketches Here and There,* 220.

20 Leopold, *A Sand County Almanac: And Sketches Here and There,* 204.

21 Leopold, *A Sand County Almanac: And Sketches Here and There,* 214.

22 J. Baird Callicot surveys these philosophical criticisms in his *In Defense of the Land Ethic: Essays in Environmental Philosophy* (Albany, NY: State University of New York Press, 1989).

23 Wanjiku Gatheru, "It's Time for Environmental Studies to Own Up to Erasing Black People." *Vice* (June 11, 2020). https://www.vice.com/en/article/889qxx/its-time-for-environmental-studies-to-own-up-to-erasing-black-people.

24 Nick Ottens, "Where Do I Find the Dolphins." *Forgotten Trek* (May 8, 2006), https://forgottentrek.com/where-do-i-find-the-dolphins/.

25 Vandana Shiva, *Earth Democracy: Justice, Sustainability, and Peace* (Berkeley: North Atlantic Books, 2015), 6.

26 Shiva, *Earth Democracy: Justice, Sustainability, and Peace,* 20.

27 Shiva, *Earth Democracy: Justice, Sustainability, and Peace,* 20–5.

28 Shiva, *Oneness vs. the 1%: Shattering Illusions, Seeding Freedom* (White River Junction, VT: Chelsea Green Publishing, 2020), 17.

29 Shiva, *Earth Democracy: Justice, Sustainability, and Peace,* 60.

30 Shiva, *Oneness vs. the 1%: Shattering Illusions, Seeding Freedom, 171;* See also Vandana Shiva, "Everything I Need to Know I Learned in the Forest." *Yes Magazine* (May 3, 2019). https://www.yesmagazine.org/issue/nature/2019/05/03/vandana-shiva-seed-saving-forest-biodiversity/.

31 Timothy Williams, "Legal Rights for Lake Erie? Voters in Ohio City Will Decide." *New York Times* (February 17, 2019). https://www.nytimes.com/2019/02/17/us/lake-erie-legal-rights.html. The ballot measure was invalidated a year later by a district judge but is significant for being one of the first attempts in the United States, apart from Native American tribal governments to grant legal personhood to nature. See Tom Henry, "Lake Erie Bill of Rights Ruled Invalid by Judge Zouhary." *The Blade* (February,

27, 2020). http://www4.toledoblade.com/local/environment/2020/02/27/lake-erie-bill-of-rights-ruled-invalid-judge-jack-zouhary-toledo-lucas-county/stories/20200227155. Anna V. Smith, "The Klamath River Now Has the Legal Rights of a Person." *High Country News* (September 24, 2019). https://www.hcn.org/issues/51.18/tribal-affairs-the-klamath-river-now-has-the-legal-rights-of-a-person.

32 Villavicencio Calzadilla, Paola, and Louis J. Kotzé. "Living in Harmony with Nature? A Critical Appraisal of the Rights of Mother Earth in Bolivia." *Transnational Environmental Law*, Vol. 7, No. 3 (2018), 423 (397–424).

33 Rick Sternback and Michael Okuda, *Star Trek: The Next Generation: Technical Manual* (New York: Pocket Books, 1991).

34 Shiva, *Oneness vs. the 1%: Shattering Illusions, Seeding Freedom,* 11–12.

Conclusion

1 Josh Weiss, "William Shatner Says Star Trek Is as Popular as Ever Because Humanity's on the 'Verge of Extinction.'" *SyFy Wire* (March 29, 2021), https://www.syfy.com/syfywire/william-shatner-star-trek-popularity-extinction?fbclid=IwAR2ienni1UUBEKlcDFncfV3Sb7SkKK0ppNC6CqD-4imZiZXlUMgsHGH-Wpl.

2 Frederick Jameson, "An American Utopia." In *An American Utopia: Dual Power and the Universal Army*. Edited by Slavoj Zizek (London: Verso, 2016), 1.

3 To get a sense of how much this episode is reviled, see Marc Cushman and Susan Osborn, *These Are the Voyages: TOS: Season Three* (San Diego: Jacobs/Brown Press, 2014), 542–68.

4 Karl Popper, "Utopia and Violence." *World Affairs*, Vol. 149, No. 1 (1986), 3–9.

5 Ruth Levitas, *Utopia as Method: The Imaginary Reconstitution of Society* (London: Palgrave Macmillan, 2013), 7.

6 Russel Jacoby, *Picture Imperfect: Utopian Thought for an Anti-Utopian Age* (New York: Columbia University Press, 2005), xv.

7 Tom Moylan, *Demand the Impossible: Science Fiction and the Utopian Imagination* (New York and London: Methuen, 1986), 10.

8 Sigal Samuel, "Why Cornel West Is Hopeful (But Not Optimistic)." *Vox* (July 29, 2020), https://www.vox.com/future-perfect/2020/7/29/21340730/cornel-west-coronavirus-racism-way-through-podcast.

References

Abascal, Maria and Delia Baldassarri. "Love Thy Neighbor? Ethnoracial Diversity and Trust Reexamined." *American Journal of Sociology*, Vol. 121, No. 3 (November 2015), 722–82.

Adams, David. "The Seville Statement on Violence: A Progress Report." *Journal of Peace Research*, Vol. 26, No. 2 (1989).

Addams, Jane. *Democracy and Social Ethics* (New York: Macmillan, 1902).

Addams, Jane. *Newer Ideals of Peace*. Introduction by Berenice A. Carroll and Clinton F. Fink (Urbana and Chicago: University of Illinois Press 2007).

Addams, Jane. *Twenty Years at Hull House* (New York: Macmillan, 1911).

Adejunmobi, Moradewun. "Introduction: African Science Fiction." *The Cambridge Journal of Postcolonial Literary Inquiry*, Vol. 3, No. 3 (2016), 265–72.

Altman, Mark A. and Edward Gross. *The Fifty Year Mission: The Complete, Uncensored, Unauthorized Oral History of Star Trek; The Next 25 Years from The Next Generation to J.J. Abrams* (New York: St. Martin's Press, 2016).

Annan, Kofi. "Two Concepts of Sovereignty." *The Economist* (September 16, 1999). https://www.economist.com/international/1999/09/16/two-conce pts-of-sovereignty.

Apfelbaum, Evan P. "In Pursuit of Racial Equality?" *Psychological Science*, Vol. 21 (2011), 1587–92.

Apfelbaum, Evan P. "Learning (Not) to Talk About Race: When Older Children Underperform in Social Categorization." *Developmental Psychology*, Vol. 44, No. 5. (2008), 1513–18.

Apfelbaum, Evan P. "Racial Color Blindness: Emergence, Practice, and Implications." *Current Directions in Psychological Science*, Vol. 21, No. 3. (2012), 205–9.

Atchison, Amy L. and Shauna L. Shames. *Survive and Resist: The Definitive Guide to Dystopian Politics* (New York: Columbia University Press, 2019).

Barad, Judith and Ed Robertson. *The Ethics of Star Trek* (New York: HarperCollins, 2000).

Barash, David P. and Charles P. Webel. *Peace and Conflict Studies*, 3rd edn (Los Angeles: Sage, 2014).

Bar-Haim, Yair. "Nature and Nurture in Own-Race Face Processing." *Psychological Science*, Vol. 17, No. 2 (2006), 159–63.

Barroso, Amanda. "Most Black Adults Say Race Is Central to Their Identity and Feel Connected to a Broader Black Community." *Pew Research Center Fact Tank* (February 5, 2020). https://www.pewresearch.org/fact-tank/2020/02/05/most-black-adults-say-race-is-central-to-their-identity-and-feel-connected-to-a-broader-black-community/.

Bartels, Larry M. "Ethnic Antagonism Erodes Republicans' Commitment to Democracy." *Proceedings of the National Academy of Sciences (PNAS)*, Vol. 117, No. 37 (August 31, 2020), 22752–9.

Basu, Blaka and Katherine Broad, and Carrie Hintz. *Contemporary Dystopian Fiction for Young Adults: Brave New Teenagers* (New York: Routledge, 2013).

Bauer-Wolf, Jeremy. "Activists, but Not for Political Parties." *Inside Higher Education* (October 29, 2018). https://www.insidehighered.com/news/2018/10/29/report-students-prefer-issue-based-groups-rather-political-parties.

Bell, Derrick. "Who's Afraid of Critical Race Theory?" *University of Illinois Law Review*, Vol. 1995, No. 833 (1995).

Bell, Terry. *Unfinished Business: South Africa, Apartheid, and Truth* (New York: Verso, 2003).

Bellamy, Alex J. *Just Wars* (Cambridge: Polity Books 2006).

Bellamy, Alex J. *World Peace: And How We Can Achieve It* (Oxford: Oxford University Press, 2019).

Bernardi, Daniel L. *Star Trek and History: Race-ing Toward a White Future* (New Brunswick, NJ: Rutgers University Press, 1998).

Block, Melissa. "The Racially Charged Meaning Behind the Word 'Thug,'" *All Things Considered*. (April 20, 2015). https://www.npr.org/2015/04/30/403362626/the-racially-charged-meaning-behind-the-word-thug.

Boersma, David. "'We Are Not Going to Kill Today?': Star Trek and the Philosophy of Peace." In *The Ultimate Star Trek and Philosophy: The Search for Socrates*. Edited by Kevin S. Decker and Jason T. Eberl (Malden, MA: Wiley Blackwell, 2016).

Boulding, Elise. *Cultures of Peace; The Hidden Side of History* (Syracuse: Syracuse University Press, 2000).

Bradshaw Corey J. A., Ehrlich Paul R., Beattie Andrew, Ceballos Gerardo, Crist Eileen, Diamond Joan, Dirzo Rodolfo, Ehrlich Anne H., Harte John, Harte Mary Ellen, Pyke Graham, Raven Peter H., Ripple William J., Saltré Frédérik, Turnbull Christine, Wackernagel Mathis, Blumstein Daniel T. "Underestimating the Challenges of Avoiding a Ghastly Future." *Frontiers in Conservation Science*, Vol. 1 (January 2021), 1–10.

Burton, Mary. "Custodians of Memory: South Africa's Truth and Reconciliation Commission." *International Journal of Legal Information*, Vol. 32, No. 2 (2004), 417–25.

Bush, George H. W. "Address to the Nation on the Civil Disturbances in Los Angeles, California." *George H.W. Bush Presidential Library and Museum* (May 1, 1992). https://bush41library.tamu.edu/archives/public-papers/4 252.

Calamur, Krishnadev, Ayesha Rascoe, Alana Wise. "Trump Says He Spoke with Floyd's Family, Understands Hurt and Pain of Community." *National Public Radio* (May 29, 2020). https://www.npr.org/2020/05/29/864722348 /twitter-hides-trumps-tweet-on-minneapolis-saying-it-glorifies-violence.

Callicot, J. Baird. *In Defense of the Land Ethic: Essays in Environmental Philosophy* (Albany, NY: State University of New York Press, 1989).

Campbell, Majorie S., et al. "Postdeployment PTSD and Addictive Combat Attachment Behaviors in U.S. Military Service Members." *American Journal of Psychiatry*, Vol. 173, No. 12 (December 2016), 1171–6.

Chaires, Robert H. and Bradley Chilton. "Law, Justice, and Star Trek." In *Star Trek Visions of Law and Justice*. Edited by Robert Chaires and Bradley Chilton (Dallas: Adios Press, 2003).

Chaires, Robert H. and Bradley Chilton. *Star Trek Visions of Law and Justice* (Dallas: Adios Press, 2003).

Chapman, Audrey R. "Truth Commissions and Intergroup Forgiveness: The Case of the South African Truth and Reconciliation Commission." *Peace and Conflict: Journal of Peace Psychology*, Vol. 13, No. 1, (December 2007), 51–69.

Chavez, Cesar. "At Exposition Park." In *Cesar Chavez: An Organizer's Tale*. Edited by Ilan Stavans (New York: Penguin, 2008).

Chin, Rita. *The Crisis of Multiculturalism in Europe: A History* (Princeton, NJ: Princeton University Press, 2017).

Chone, Aurelie, Isabelle Hajek, and Phillipe Hamman. *Rethinking Nature: Challenging Disciplinary Boundaries* (New York: Routledge, 2017).

Christensen, Kit R. *Nonviolence, Peace, and Justice: A Philosophical Introduction* (Ontario: Broadview Press, 2010).

Christensen, Kit R. *Revenge and Social Conflict* (Cambridge: Cambridge University Press, 2016).

Christie, Daniel, J Richard V. Wagner, and Deborah Dunann Winter. *Peace, Conflict, and Violence: Peace Psychology for the 21st Century* (Upper Saddle River: Prentice Hall, 2001).

CIRCLE: The Center for Information Research on Civic Learning and Engagement. "Absentee and Early Voting by Youth in the 2020 Election" (October 30, 2020). https://circle.tufts.edu/latest-research/absentee-and-e arly-voting-youth-2020-election.

CIRCLE: The Center for Information Research on Civic Learning and Engagement. "Youth Voting Rose in 2018 Despite Concerns about American Democracy" (April 17, 2019). https://circle.tufts.edu/latest-research/youth -voting-rose-2018-despite-concerns-about-american-democracy

Claeys, Gregory. *Dystopia: A Natural History* (Oxford: Oxford U Press, 2017).

Claeys, Gregory and Lyman Tower Sargent. *The Utopia Reader*, 2nd edn (New York: New York University Press, 2017).

Craig, Maureen A., and Jennifer A. Richeson. "More Diverse Yet Less Tolerant? How the Increasingly Diverse Racial Landscape Affects White Americans' Racial Attitudes." *Personality and Social Psychology Bulletin*, Vol. 40, No. 6 (June 2014), 750–61.

Craig, Maureen A., and Jennifer A. Richeson. "On the Precipice of a 'Majority-Minority' America: Perceived Status Threat From the Racial Demographic Shift Affects White Americans' Political Ideology." *Psychological Science*, Vol. 25, No. 6 (June 2014), 1189–97.

Crews, Robin J. "A Modest Proposal for Peace Studies." *Peace Review: A Journal of Social Justice*, Vol. 14. No. 1 (2002), 73–80.

Cushman, Marc and Susan Osborn. *These Are the Voyages: TOS Season One* (San Diego: Jacobs/Brown Press, 2013).

Cushman, Marc and Susan Osborn. *These Are the Voyages: TOS Season Three* (San Diego: Jacobs/Brown Press, 2014).

Cushman, Marc and Susan Osborn. *These Are the Voyages TOS: Season Two* (Los Angeles: Jacobs/Brown, 2014).

Dawkins, Richard. *The Selfish Gene* (Oxford: Oxford University Press, 1989).

Decker, Kevin S., and Jason T. Eberl. *The Ultimate Star Trek and Philosophy: The Search for Socrates* (Malden, MA: Wiley Blackwell 2016).

De Cruz, Helen, Johan De Smedt, and Eric Schwitzgebel. *Philosophy through Science Fiction Stories: Exploring the Boundaries of the Possible* (London: Bloomsbury, 2021).

DeGrew, Sharon. *The Subject of Race in American Science Fiction* (New York: Routledge, 2007).

Devlin, Hannah. "Earliest Known Cave Art by Modern Humans Found in Indonesia." *The Guardian* (December 11, 2019). https://www.theguardian.com/science/2019/dec/11/earliest-known-cave-art-by-modern-humans-found-in-indonesia.

Dicker, Cheryl and Bruce Bartholow. "Racial Ingroup and Outgroup Attention Biases Revealed by Event Related Brain Potentials." *Social Cognitive and Affective Neuroscience*, Vol. 2, No. 3 (September 2007), 189–98.

Du Bois, W. E. B. *Black Reconstruction: An Essay Toward a History of the Part Which Black Folk Played in the Attempt to Reconstruct Democracy in America 1860–1880* (New York: Harcourt, Brace, and Co., 1935).

Du Bois, W. E. B. "Marxism and the Negro Problem" (1933). In *W.E.B. Du Bois: A Reader*. Edited by David Levering Lewis (New York: Henry Holt, 1995).

Du Bois, W. E. B. "A Negro Nation Within the Nation" (1935). In *W.E.B. Du Bois: A Reader*. Edited by David Levering Lewis (New York: Henry Holt, 1995).

Duca, Lauren. *How to Start a Revolution: Young People and the Future of American Politics* (New York: Simon and Schuster, 2019).

Einstein, Albert. "Why War?" In *The Standard Edition of the Complete Psychological Works of Sigmund Freud*. Volume XXII. Edited by Sigmund Freud (1932–1936) (London: The Hogarth Press and the Institute of Psycho-Analysis, 1964), 198–201.

Ermann Terry J. and Paula M. Block. *Star Trek: Deep Space Nine Companion* (New York: Pocket Books, 2000).

Falk, Richard. *On Humane Governance: Toward a Global Politics* (Oxford: Polity Press, 1995).

Fern, Yvonne. *Gene Roddenberry: The Last Conversation* (New York: Pocket Books, 1996).

Fiala, Andrew. *Nonviolence: A Quick Immersion* (New York: Tibidabo, 2020).

Fiala, Andrew. *The Routledge Handbook of Pacifism and Nonviolence* (New York and London 2014).

Fitz-Gibbon, Andrew. "Becoming Nonviolent: Sociobiological, Neurophysiological, and Spiritual Perspectives." In *The Routledge Handbook of Pacifism and Nonviolence*. Edited by Andrew Fiala (New York and London: Routledge, 2018).

Fox, Michael Allen. "Nonviolence and Pacifism in the Long Nineteenth Century." In *The Routledge Handbook of Pacifism and Nonviolence*. Edited by Andrew Fiala (New York and London 2014).

Frase, Peter. *Four Futures: Life after Capitalism* (New York: Verso, 2016).

de Freytas-Tamura, Kimiko. "George Orwell's '1984' Is Suddenly a Best Seller." *The New York Times* (January 25, 2017). https://www.nytimes.com/2017/0 1/25/books/1984-george-orwell-donald-trump.html.

Fry, Douglas P. "Life without War?" *Science*, Vol. 336, No. 6083 (May 18, 2012), 879–84.

Fry, Douglas P. *War, Peace, and Human Nature: The Convergence of Evolutionary and Cultural Views* (Oxford: Oxford University Press, 2013).

Freud, Sigmund. "Why War to 'Why War?'" In *The Standard Edition of the Complete Psychological Works of Sigmund Freud*. Volume XXII (1932–1936), 208–14.

Galtung, Johan. "Cultural Violence." *Journal of Peace Research*. Vol. 27, No. 3 (August 1990), 291-305.

Galtung, Johan. "Twenty-Five Years of Peace Research: Ten Challenges and Responses." *Journal of Peace Research*, Vol. 22, No. 2 (1985), 141–58.

Galtung, Johan. "Violence, Peace, and Peace Research." *Journal of Peace Research*, Vol. 6, No. 3 (1969), 167–91.

Gandhi, Mohandas. *All Men Are Brothers: Life and Thoughts of Mahatma Gandhi as Told in His Own Words*. Edited by Krishna Kripalani (Ahmedabad: Jitendra T. Desai, 1960).

Gandhi, Mohandas. *Selected Political Writings*. Edited by Dennis Dalton (Indianapolis: Hackett, 1996).

Gatheru, Wanjiku. "It's Time for Environmental Studies to Own Up to Erasing Black People." *Vice* (June 11, 2020). https://www.vice.com/en/article

/889qxx/its-time-for-environmental-studies-to-own-up-to-erasing-black
-people.

Geraughty, Lincoln. *Living with Star Trek: American Culture and the Star Trek
Universe* (London: I. B. Tauris, 2007).

Gerrold, David, and Robert J. Sawyer. *Boarding the Enterprise: Transporters,
Tribbles, and the Vulcan Death Grip in Gene Roddenberry's Star Trek*
(Dallas: Smart Pop, 2016).

Gerrold, David, and Robert J. "Foreword: Still Trekkin' after All These Years." In
*Boarding the Enterprise: Transporters, Tribbles, and the Vulcan Death Grip
in Gene Roddenberry's Star Trek*. Edited by David Gerrold and Robert J.
Sawyer (Dallas: Ben Bella Books, 2016).

Gibson James L. and Amanda Gouws. "Truth and Reconciliation in South
Africa: Attributions of Blame and the Struggle over Apartheid." *The
American Political Science Review*, Vol. 93, No. 3 (September 1999),
501–17.

Eric Greene. "The Prime Question." In *Boarding the Enterprise: Transporters,
Tribbles, and the Vulcan Death Grip in Gene Roddenberry's Star Trek*.
Edited by David Gerrold and Robert J. Sawyer (Dallas: Smart Pop, 2016),
55–80.

Gonzalez, George. *Justice and Popular Culture: Star Trek as Philosophical Text*
(Lanham: Rowman and Littlefield, 2019).

Gonzalez, George. *Star Trek and the Politics of Globalism* (New York: Palgrave
Macmillan, 2018).

Gutmann Amy. *Identity in Democracy* (Princeton: Princeton University Press,
2003).

Hanley, Rick. *The Metaphysics of Star Trek* (New York: Basic Books, 1997).

Hansen, Drew D. *The Dream: Martin Luther King, Jr. and the Speech that
Inspired a Nation* (New York: HarperCollins, 2003).

Harari, Yuval Noah. *Sapiens: A Brief History of Humankind* (New York: Harper
Perennial, 2018).

Haas, Jonathan and Matthew Piscitelli. "The Prehistory of Warfare: Misled by
Ethnography." In *War, Peace, and Human Nature: The Convergence of
Evolutionary and Cultural Views*. Edited by Douglas P. Fry (Oxford: Oxford
University Press, 2013).

Hassan, Rashid, Robert Scholes, and Nevile Ash. *Ecosystems and Human
Well-Being: Current State and Trends, Vol. 1* (Washington, DC: Island
Press, 2005).

Havel, Vaclav. "The Politics of Responsibility." *World Policy Forum*, Vol. 12, No.
3 (1995), 81–7.

Hay, Carol. "Justice and Objectivity for Pragmatists: Cosmopolitanism in the
Work of Marth Nussbaum and Jane Addams." *The Pluralist*, Vol. 7, No. 3
(Fall 2012), 86–95.

Hedges, Chris. *War Is a Force That Gives Us Meaning* (New York: Anchor,
2003).

Henry, Tom. "Lake Erie Bill of Rights Ruled Invalid by Judge Zouhary." *The Blade* (February 27, 2020). http://www4.toledoblade.com/local/enviro nment/2020/02/27/lake-erie-bill-of-rights-ruled-invalid-judge-jack-zouhary-toledo-lucas-county/stories/20200227155.

Hoagland, Ericka and Reema Sarwal. *Science Fiction, Imperialism, and the Third World: Essays on Postcolonial Literature and Film* (Jefferson, NC: McFarland and Co., 2010).

Horgan, John. *The End of War* (New York: McSweeneys, 2014).

Horton, Adrian. "John Oliver: When Trump 'Uses the Word Thugs, You Know What It's Code for.'" *The Guardian* (June 1, 2020). https://www.theguardian.com/culture/2020/jun/01/john-oliver-when-trump-uses-thugs-code-racism-george-floyd-protests.

Ishay, Micheline. *The History of Human Rights: From Ancient Texts to the Globalization Era* (Berkeley: University of California, Press, 2008).

Ishay, Micheline. *The Human Rights Reader*, 2nd edn (New York: Routledge, 2007).

Ito, Tiffany A. and Geoffrey Urland. "Race and Gender on the Brain: Electrocortical Measures of Attention to the Race and Gender of Multiply Categorizable Individuals." *Journal of Personality and Social Psychology*, Vol. 85, No. 4. (2003), 616–26.

Jackson, David. "Obama Stands by the Term 'Thugs,' White House Says." *USA Today* (April 29, 2015). https://www.usatoday.com/story/theoval/2015/04/29/obama-white-house-baltimore-stephanie-rawlings-blake/26585143/.

Jacoby, Russell. *Picture Imperfect: Utopian Thought for an Anti-Utopian Age* (New York: Columbia University Press, 2005).

Jaffe, Ina. "After the L.A. Riots, A Failed Effort for a Broken City." *National Public Radio* (April 29, 2012), https://www.npr.org/2012/04/29/151608071/after-l-a-riots-an-effort-to-rebuild-a-broken-city.

James, Edward and Farah Mendelsohn. *The Cambridge Companion to Science Fiction* (Cambridge: Cambridge University Press, 2003).

James, William. "The Moral Equivalent of War." In *The Works of William James: Essays in Religion and Morality.* Introduction by John J. McDermott. (Cambridge, MA: Harvard University Press, 1982), 162–73.

Jameson, Frederck. "An American Utopia." In *An American Utopia: Dual Power and the Universal Army.* Edited by Slavoj Zizek (London: Verso, 2016), 1–96.

Janfranza, Rachel. "'Tired of Waiting': Gen Z Is Ready for a Revolution." CNN (June 22, 2020). https://edition.cnn.com/2020/06/16/politics/genz-voters-2020-election/index.html :.

Jardina, Ashley. *White Identity Politics* (Cambridge: Cambridge University Press, 2019).

Johnson, David Kyle. "Destroying Utopias: Why Kirk Is a Jerk." In *The Ultimate Star Trek and Philosophy: The Search for Socrates*. Edited by Kevin S. Decker and Jason T. Eberl (Malden, MA: Wiley Blackwell 2016), 47–58.

Johnson, David Kyle. "What Sci Phi Is All About: Treating Science Fiction as Philosophy." *Sci Phi Journal* (2019). https://www.sciphijournal.org/index.php/2019/02/14/sci-phi-journal-2019-1-for-printing/.

Johnson, Mark. *Moral Imagination: Implications of Cognitive Science for Ethics* (Chicago: University of Chicago Press, 1993).

Jones, Calvert and Celia Paris. "How Dystopian Narratives Can Incite Real World Radicalism." *Aeon* (April 15, 2020). https://aeon.co/ideas/how-dystopian-narratives-can-incite-real-world-radicalism.

Jones, Calvert and Celia Paris. "It's the End of the World and They Know It: How Dystopian Fiction Shapes Political Attitudes." *Perspectives on Politics*, Vol. 16, No. 4 (December 2018), 969–89.

Jones, Esther. "Science Fiction Builds Mental Resiliency in Young Minds." *The Conversation* (May 11, 2020). https://theconversation.com/science-fiction-builds-mental-resiliency-in-young-readers-135513.

Jorgensen, Dolly. "Who's the Devil: Species Extinction and Environmentalist Thought in *Star Trek*." In *Star Trek and History*. Edited by Nancy R. Reagin (Hoboken, NJ: Wiley, 2013), 242–59.

Keely, Lawrence. *War before Civilization: The Myth of the Peaceful Savage* (New York: Oxford University Press, 1997).

Kelly, Raymond C. "The Evolution of Lethal Intergroup Violence." *Proceedings of the National Academy of Sciences of the United States*, Vol. 102, No. 43 (October 25, 2005), 15294–8.

Kendi, Ibram X. *How to Be an Anti-Racist* (New York: One World, 2019).

Kilgo, Danielle. "Riot or Resistance? The Way the Media Frames the Unrest in Minneapolis Will Share the Public's View of Protest." *Nieman Lab* (May 30, 2020). https://www.niemanlab.org/2020/05/riot-or-resistance-the-way-the-media-frames-the-unrest-in-minneapolis-will-shape-the-publics-view-of-protest/.

King, Jr., Martin Luther. "An Experiment in Love." In *A Testament of Hope: The Essential Writings and Speeches of Martin Luther King, Jr*. Edited by James M. Washington (San Francisco, Harper, 1991), 16–20.

King, Jr., Martin Luther. "I Have a Dream." In *A Testament of Hope: The Essential Writing and Speeches of Martin Luther King, Jr*. Edited by James W. Washington (San Francisco: Harper 1986), 217–20.

King, Jr., Martin Luther. "Letter from a Birmingham City Jail." In *A Testament of Hope: The Essential Writing and Speeches of Martin Luther King, Jr*. Edited by James W. Washington (San Francisco: Harper 1986), 289–302.

King, Jr., Martin Luther. *Letter to Coretta Scott* (July 18, 1952). https://kingsinstitute.stanford.edu/king-papers/documents/coretta-scott.

King, Jr., Martin Luther. "Nonviolence and Racial Justice." In *A Testament of Hope: The Essential Writings and Speeches of Martin Luther King, Jr*. Edited by James M. Washington (San Francisco, Harper, 1991), 5–9.

King, Jr., Martin Luther. "Nonviolence and Social Change." In *The Radical King*. Edited by Cornel West (Boston: Beacon Press, 2015), 147–54.

King, Jr., Martin Luther. "The Other America." Speech Delivered at Gross Pointe High School, March 14, 1968. https://www.gphistorical.org/mlk/ml kspeech/mlk-gp-speech.pdf.

King, Jr., Martin Luther. "A Testament of Hope." In *A Testament of Hope: The Essential Writing and Speeches of Martin Luther King, Jr.* Edited by James W. Washington (San Francisco: Harper 1986), 313–28.

King, Jr., Martin Luther. "A Time to Break the Silence." In *A Testament of Hope: The Essential Writing and Speeches of Martin Luther King, Jr.* Edited by James W. Washington (San Francisco: Harper 1986), 231–44.

King, Jr., Martin Luther. "Where Do We Go From Here?," In *A Testament of Hope: The Essential Writing and Speeches of Martin Luther King, Jr.* Edited by James W. Washington (San Francisco: Harper 1986), 555–633.

King, Peter. "Introduction." In Augustine, *On the Free Choice of the Will, On Grace and Free Choice, and Other Writings*. Edited and Translated by Peter King (Cambridge: Cambridge University Press, 2010), lx–xxxii.

Kant, Immanuel. *Perpetual Peace, and Other Essays on Politics, History, and Morals*. Translated with Introduction by T. Humphrey (Indianapolis: Hackett Publishing, 1983).

Kanzler, Katja. "A Cuchi Moya!—Star Trek's Native Americans." *American Studies Journal*, Vol. 49 (2007). http://www.asjournal.org/49-2007/star-tr eks-native-americans/#

Kinkley, Jeffrey C. *Visions of Dystopia in China's New Historical Novels* (New York: Columbia University Press, 2014).

Kitanova, Magdelina. "Youth Political Participation in the EU: Evidence from a Cross-National Analysis." *Journal of Youth Studies*, Vol. 23, No. 7 (2020), 819–36.

Krauss, Lawrence. *The Physics of Star Trek* (New York: Basic Books, 2007).

Kropotkin, Peter. *Mutual Aid: A Factor of Evolution* (London: Heinemann, 1902).

Kymlicka, Will. *Multicultural Citizenship: A Liberal Theory of Minority Rights* (Oxford: Clarendon Press, 1995).

Kymlicka, Will, and Baogang He. *Multiculturalism in Asia* (Oxford: Oxford University Press, 2005).

Kymlicka, Will, and Eva Pfosti. *Multiculturalism and Minority Rights in the Arab World* (Oxford: Oxford University Press, 2014).

Lagon, Mark P. "'We Owe It to Them Not to Interfere': *Star Trek* and U.S. Statecraft in the 1960s and 1990s." *Extrapolation*, Vol. 34, No. 3 (1993), 254–61.

Landon, Brookes. *Science Fiction after 1900: From the Steam Man to the Stars* (New York; Twayne, 1997).

Lavender III, Isiah. *Race in American Science Fiction* (Bloomington, IN: Indiana University Press, 2011).

Lawson, Jr. James M. "Nonviolence and the Non-Existent County." In *The Routledge Handbook of Pacifism and Nonviolence*. Edited by Andrew Fiala (New York and London: Routledge, 2018), 384–92.

Le Guin, Ursula K. "A War without End." In *Utopia by Thomas More*. Edited and Introduction by China Mieville (New York: Verso, 2016), 199–210.

Le Guin, Ursula K. "Science Fiction and the Future." In *Dancing at the Edge of the World: Thoughts on Words, Women, Places* Edited by Ursula K. Le Guin (New York: Harper & Row, 1989), 142–3.

Le Guin, Ursula K. "The Carrier Bag Theory of Fiction." In *Dancing at the Edge of the World: Thoughts on Words, Woman, and Places* (New York: Grove Press, 1989), 165–70.

Leon, Cristian, Antonella Perini, and Matthias Bianchi. "Transforming Political Participation in Latin America." *Open Democracy* (July 5, 2017). https://www.opendemocracy.net/en/democraciaabierta/transforming-political-partic ipation/.

Leonard, Elisabeth Anne. "Race and Ethnicity in Science Fiction." In *The Cambridge Companion to Science Fiction*. Edited by Edward James and Farah Mendelsohn (Cambridge: Cambridge University Press, 2003), 253–63.

Leopold, Aldo. *A Sand County Almanac: And Sketches Here and There* (Oxford: Oxford University Press, 1949).

LeVine, Steve. "The Coming Reckoning for Capitalism." *Axios* (December 20, 2018) https://www.axios.com/coming-reckoning-capitalism-2020-presi dential-election-7f55e9f7-ab90-45a9-9cc1-47e1a102f4bb.html.

Levitas, Ruth. *Utopia as Method: The Imaginary Reconstitution of Society* (London: Palgrave Macmillan, 2013).

Levitt, Lauren. "The Hunger Games and the Dystopian Imagination." In *Popular Culture and the Civic Imagination*. Edited by Henry Jenkins, Gabriel Peters-Lazaro, and Sangita Shresthova (New York: New York University, 2020), 43–50.

Lopez, Ian Haney. "Intentional Blindness." *New York University Law Review*, Vol. 87, No. 6 (December 2012), 1779–1877.

McGorrery Paul and Marilyn McMahon. *Criminalising Coercive Control: Family Violence and Criminal Law* (Singapore: Springer, 2020).

MacMullen, Terrance. *Habits of Whiteness: A Pragmatist Reconstruction* (Indianapolis: Indiana University Press, 2009).

Maganga, Tafadzwa. "Youth Demonstrations and Their Impact on Political Change and Development in Africa." *Accord.org.za* (2020), https://www.accord.org.za/conflict-trends/youth-demonstrations-and-their-impact-on -political-change-and-development-in-africa/.

Maguire, Edward. "New Directions in Protest Policing." *Saint Louis University Public Law Review*, Vol. 35, No. 1, Article 6. (2015). https://scholarship.law.slu.edu/plr/vol35/iss1/6

Maritain, Jacques. "The Grounds for an International Declaration of Human Rights (1947)." In *The Human Rights Reader*, 2nd edn. Edited by Micheline R. Ishay (New York: Routledge, 2007), 2–6.

Martinez, Elizabeth. "Don't Call This Country 'America.'" *Z Magazine* (August 1, 2003), https://zcomm.org/zmagazine/dont-call-this-country-and-quot-america-and-quot-by-elizabeth-martinez/.

Maas, Jennifer. "'Outbreak' Is Netflix's 9th Most Popular Overall Title in the US Right Now." *The Wrap.com* (March 14, 2020). https://www.thewrap.com/o utbreak-movie-top-10-netflix-titles-movies-pandemic-tv-series-coronavirus/.

Mendizabal, Ivan Fernando Rodrigo. "Andean Dystopias: When the Future Clashes with Desire." *Latin American Literature Today*, Vol. 1, No. 7. (August 2018). http://www.latinamericanliteraturetoday.org/en/2018/august /andean-dystopias-when-future-clashes-desire-iv%C3%A1n-rodrigo-mend iz%C3%A1bal.

Merchant, Brian. "Behold the Rise of Dystopian 'Cli-Fi.'" *Vice* (May 31, 2013). https://www.vice.com/en/article/ypp7nj/behold-the-rise-of-cli-fi.

Minow, Martha. *Between Vengeance and Forgiveness: Facing History after Genocide and Mass Violence* (Boston: Beacon Press, 1998).

Morris, Brian. *Kropotkin: The Politics of Community* (Oakland, CA: PM Press, 2018).

Morrison Aaron, and Kat Stafford. "AP-NORC Poll: Support for Racial Injustice Protests Declines." *AP News* (September 24, 2020). https://apnews.com /article/breonna-taylor-race-and-ethnicity-shootings-police-new-york-24a f876f135f529d95c9c857ad9aaa0e.

Moylan, Tom. *Demand the Impossible: Science Fiction and the Utopian Imagination* (New York and London: Methuen, 1986).

Muradian, Roldan. "The Ecosystem Services Paradigm: Rise, Scope, and Limits." In *Rethinking Nature: Challenging Disciplinary Boundaries*. Edited by Aurelie Chone, Isabelle Hajek, and Phillipe Hamman (New York: Routledge, 2017), 195–208.

Murchison, Kenneth M. *The Snail Darter Case: TVA versus the Endangered Species Act* (Lawrence, KS: University Press of Kansas, 2007).

Murphy, Colleen. *The Conceptual Foundations of Transitional Justice* (Cambridge: Cambridge University Press, 2017).

Murphy, Colleen. "How Nations Heal." *Boston Review* (January 21, 2021). http://bostonreview.net/politics-law-justice/colleen-murphy-how-nations-heal.

Nichols, Angela D. *Impact, Legitimacy, and Limitations of Truth Commissions* (New York: Palgrave Macmillan, 2019).

Niebuhr, Reinhold. *Moral Man and Immoral Society* (New York: Charles Schribner's Sons, 1932).

Nijhuis, Michelle. "Can Aldo Leopold's Land Ethics Tackle Our Toughest Problems?" *High Country News* (January 19, 2015). https://www.hcn.org/ issues/47.1/can-aldo-leopolds-land-ethic-tackle-our-toughest-problems.

Nixon, Rob. *Slow Violence and the Environmentalism of the Poor* (Cambridge, MA: Harvard University Press, 2011).

Neville, Helen, et al. "Construction and Initial Validation of the Color Blind Racial Attitudes Scale (CoBRAS)." *Journal of Counseling Psychology*, Vol. 47, No. 1. (2000), 59–70.

Nichols, Nichelle. *Beyond Uhura: Star Trek and other Memories* (London: Boxtree, 1994).

Noor, Mohammed A.F. *Live Long and Evolve: What Star Trek Can Teach Us about Evolution, Genetics, and Life on Other Worlds* (Princeton: Princeton University Press, 2018).

Nussbaum, Martha. *Anger and Forgiveness: Resentment, Generosity, Justice* (Oxford: Oxford University Press, 2016).

Nussbaum, Martha. *Creating Capabilities: The Human Development Approach* (Cambridge, MA: Harvard University Press, 2011).

O'Keefe, Derrick. "Imagining the End of Capitalism with Kim Stanley Robinson." *Jacobin* (October 22, 2020). https://www.jacobinmag.com/2020/10/kim-stanley-robinson-ministry-future-science-fiction.

Osterweil, Vickey. *In Defense of Looting: A Riotous History of Uncivil Action* (New York: Bold Type Books, 2020).

Parekh, Bhiku. *Gandhi: A Very Short Introduction* (Oxford: Oxford University Press, 1997).

Presby, Gail M. "Philosophy of Nonviolence in Africa." In *The Routledge Handbook of Pacifism and Nonviolence*. Edited by Andrew Fiala (New York: Routledge, 2018), 64–79.

Popper, Karl. "Utopia and Violence." *World Affairs*, Vol. 149, No. 1. (1986), 3–9.

Porter, Jennifer. *Star Trek and Sacred Ground: Explorations of Star Trek, Religion and American Culture* (Albany: State University of New York Press, 1999).

Pounds, Michael. *Race in Space: The Representation of Ethnicity in Star Trek and Star Trek: The Next Generation* (Lanham, MD: Scarecrow Press, 1999).

Reagin, Nancy R. *Star Trek and History*. Edited by Nancy R. Reagin (Hoboken, NJ: Wiley, 2013).

Rennix, Brianna. "The Regrettable Decline of Space Utopias." *Current Affairs* (June 14, 2017). https://www.currentaffairs.org/2017/03/the-regrettable-decline-of-space-utopias.

Resnick, Danielle and Daniela Casale. "Political Participation of Africa's Youth: Turnout, Partisanship And Protest." *Afrobarometer*. Afrobarometer Working Paper/136 (2011). https://afrobarometer.org/publications/political-participation-africa%E2%80%99s-youth-turnout-partisanship-and-protest.

de la Rey, Cheryl. "Reconciliation in Divided Societies." In *Peace, Conflict, and Violence: Peace Psychology for the 21st Century*. Edited by Daniel J. Christie, Richard V. Wagner, and Deborah Dunann Winter (Upper Saddle River: Prenctice Hall, 2001).

Richmond, Oliver P. *Peace: A Very Short Introduction* (Oxford: Oxford University Press, 2014).

Ripple, William J., Christopher Wolf, Thomas M Newsome, Phoebe Barnard, William R Moomaw. "World Scientists' Warning of a Climate Emergency." *BioScience*, Vol. 70, No. 1. (January 2020), 8–12.

Ripple, William J., Christopher Wolf, Thomas M. Newsome, Mauro Galetti, Mohammed Alamgir, Eileen Crist, Mahmoud I. Mahmoud, William F.

Laurance, 15, 364 scientist signatories from 184 countries. "World Scientists' Warning to Humanity: A Second Notice." *BioScience*, Vol. 67, No. 12 (December 2017), 1026–8.

Robertson, Morgan M. "The Nature That Capital Can See: Science, State, and Market in the Commodification of Ecosystem Services." *Environment and Planning D: Society and Space*, Vol. 24 (2006), 367–87.

Roediger, David. *The Wages of Whiteness: Race and the Making of the American Working Class* (London: Verso, 1999).

Roediger, David. *Working toward Whiteness: How America's Immigrants Became White* (New York: Basic Books, 2005).

Saadia, Manu. *Trekonomics: The Economics of Star Trek* (San Francisco: Pipertexts, 2016).

Saadia, Manu. "The Seville Statement on Violence." *American Psychologist*, Vol. 45, No. 10 (1990), 1167–8.

Samuel, Sigal. "Why Cornel West Is Hopeful (But Not Optimistic)." *Vox* (July 29, 2020). https://www.vox.com/future-perfect/2020/7/29/21340730/cornel-west-coronavirus-racism-way-through-podcast.

Scott, James C. *Against the Grain: A Deep History of the Earliest States* (New Haven and London: Yale University Press, 2017).

Sethia, Tara. *Gandhi: Pioneer of Nonviolent Social Change* (Upper Saddle Ridge, NJ: Pearson, 2012).

Shiva, Vandana. *Earth Democracy: Justice, Sustainability, and Peace* (Berkeley: North Atlantic Books, 2015).

Shiva, Vandana. "Everything I Need to Know I Learned in the Forest." *Yes Magazine* (May 3, 2019) https://www.yesmagazine.org/issue/nature/2019/05/03/vandana-shiva-seed-saving-forest-biodiversity/.

Shiva, Vandana. *Oneness vs. the 1%: Shattering Illusions, Seeding Freedom* (White River Junction, Vermont: Chelsea Green Publishing, 2020).

Sieder, Rachel. *Multiculturalism in Latin America: Indigenous Rights, Diversity, and Democracy* (London: Palgrave Macmillan, 2002).

Silva, Eduardo Bonilla. *Racism without Racists: Color-Blind Racism and the Persistence of Racial Inequality in the United States*, 5th edn (Lanham, MD: Rowman and Littlefield, 2017).

Sen, Amartya. "Human Rights and Capabilities." *Journal of Human Development*, Vol. 6, No. 2 (July 2005), 151–66.

Shiffern, Kent D. *From War to Peace: A Guide to the Next One Hundred Years* (Jefferson, NC: McFarland, 2011).

Sloam, James. "'Voice and Equality': Young People's Politics in the European Union." *West European Politics*, Vol. 36, No. 4 (March 2013), 836–58.

Smith, Anna V. "The Klamath River Now Has the Legal Rights of a Person." *High Country News* (September 24, 2019). https://www.hcn.org/issues/51.18/tribal-affairs-the-klamath-river-now-has-the-legal-rights-of-a-person.

Solis, Marie. "Why Gen Z Is Turning to Socialism." *Vice* (May 4, 2020). https://www.vice.com/en/article/g5xz7j/gen-z-socialism-ydsa.

Stavans Ilan. *Cesar Chavez: An Organizer's Tale* (New York: Penguin, 2008).

Sturgis, Amy. "If This Is the (Final) Frontier, Where Are the Natives?" In *Star Trek and History*. Edited by Nancy R. Reagin (Hoboken, NJ: Wiley, 2013), 138–41.

Suvin, Darko. *Positions and Presuppositions in Science Fiction* (Kent, OH: Kent State University, 1988).

Star Trek.com Staff. "Poll Says Captain with the Most Respect for the Prime Directive is . . . " *Startrek.com* (September 29, 2013). https://www.startrek.com/article/poll-says-captain-with-the-most-respect-for-the-prime-directive-is.

Sternback, Rick and Michael Okuda. *Star Trek: The Next Generation: Technical Manual* (New York: Pocket Books, 1991).

Streeby, Shelley. *Imagining the Future of Climate Change: World Making Through Science Fiction and Activism* (Berkeley and Los Angeles: University of California Press, 2018).

Taylor, Charles. *Multiculturalism*. Edited by Amy Gutmann (Princeton, NJ: Princeton University Press, 1994).

Tutu, Desmond. *No Future without Forgiveness* (New York: Doubleday, 1999).

Vallely, Paul. "How Philanthropy Benefits the Super Rich." *The Guardian* (September 8, 2020). https://www.theguardian.com/society/2020/sep/08/how-philanthropy-benefits-the-super-rich.

Villavicencio Calzadilla, Paola, and Louis J. Kotzé. "Living in Harmony with Nature? A Critical Appraisal of the Rights of Mother Earth in Bolivia." *Transnational Environmental Law*, Vol. 7, No. 3. (2018), 397–424.

Vertovec, Steven, and Susanne Wessendorf. "Introduction: Assessing the Backlash against Multiculturalism in Europe." In *The Multicultural Backlash: European Discourses, Policies, and Practices*. Edited by Steven Vertovec and Susanne Wessendorf (New York: Routledge, 2010), 1–31.

Vertovec, Steven, and Susanne Wessendorf. *The Multicultural Backlash: European Discourses, Policies, and Practices* (New York: Routledge, 2010).

Vint, Sherryl. *Science Fiction* (Cambridge and London: MIT Press, 2021).

Walzer, Michael. *Just and Unjust Wars*, 4th edn (New York: Basic Books, 1977).

Weise, Elizabeth. "For Once, Good Environment News: A Humpback Whale Population Has Come Back From the Brink." *USA Today* (October 16, 2019). https://www.usatoday.com/story/news/nation/2019/10/16/good-news-humpback-whale-population-back-after-near-extinction/3997894002/.

Weiss, Josh. "William Shatner Says Star Trek Is as Popular as Ever Because Humanity's on the 'Verge of Extinction.' " *SyFy Wire* (March 29, 2021). https://www.syfy.com/syfywire/william-shatner-star-trek-popularity-extinction?fbclid=IwAR2ienni1UUBEKIcDFncfV3Sb7SkKK0ppNC6CqD-4imZiZXIUMgsHGH-WpI.

Weitekamp, Margaret A. "More than 'Just Uhura': Understanding *Star Trek*'s Lt. Uhura, Civil Rights, and Space History." In *Star Trek and History*. Edited by Nancy R. Reagin (Hoboken, NJ: Wiley, 2013), 22–38.

West, Cornel. *The Radical King* (Boston: Beacon Press, 2015).

Wike, Richard and Shannon Schumacher. "Democratic Rights Popular Globally but Commitment to Them Not Always Strong." Pew Research Center (February 27, 2020) https://www.pewresearch.org/global/2020/02/27/democratic-rights-popular-globally-but-commitment-to-them-not-always-strong/#many-are-frustrated-with-how-democracy-is-functioning.

Williams, Timothy. "Legal Rights for Lake Erie? Voters in Ohio City Will Decide." *The New York Times* (February 17, 2019). https://www.nytimes.com/2019/02/17/us/lake-erie-legal-rights.html.

Wilson, E. O. *The Meaning of Human Existence* (New York: W. W. Norton, 2015).

Wilson, E. O. *The Social Conquest of Earth* (New York: W. W. Norton, 2012).

Wood, Houston. *Current Debates in Peace and Conflict Studies* (New York: Oxford University Press, 2018).

Wood, Houston. *Invitation to Peace Studies* (Oxford: Oxford University Press, 2016).

Yamatta-Taylor, Keeanga. *From #BlackLivesMatter to Black Liberation* (London: Haymarket Books, 2016).

Yancy, George. *Black Bodies, White Gazes: The Continuing Significance of Race in America* (Landham, MD: Rowman and Littlefield, 2017).

Young, Lauren. "Gen Z Is the Most Progressive—and Least Partisan—Generation." *Teen Vogue* (October 2, 2019). https://www.teenvogue.com/story/how-will-gen-z-vote.

Zimbardo, Phillip. *The Lucifer Effect: Understanding How Good People Turn Evil* (New York: Random House, 2008).

Index

196   Index

nonviolence, theory of   8
Nozick, Robert   13
nuclear war   16
Nussbaum, Martha   20, 65, 71–3,
     75–7, 80, 99, 109, 113
  human capabilities approach   20

Obama, Barack   51
ocean acidification   129
oppression   7, 9, 14–15, 20–2, 42,
     47, 54, 57, 70, 79, 83, 92,
     99, 117, 124
Oresteia (Aeschylus)   109
Original Position, Rawl's   13
ozone depletion   129

pacifists   31–2
Paris, Celia   15
peace
  agreement   70
  antiwar activism   69
  capabilities with specific human
     rights   72
  core capabilities   72
  duty of the government   70
  dynamic peace   71
  global peace by Kant   72–3
  and human flourishing, nature
     of   63–80
  human rights violations   72
  and justice studies   3–9, 43, 47,
     52, 62
  liberal philosophies   70
  moral conscience of
     humanity   73
  negative and positive   65
     distinction   80
  negative peace   69, 72
  in polarized world   9–11
  positive peace   71–2
  use of military force   65
Peace and Justice Studies
     Association   5
peace philosophers   105

peace studies   2–9, 18–20, 22,
     27, 29–43, 47, 50–2, 62,
     69–75, 125, 146, 154
personal violence   19–20, 100
Piller, Michael   45, 46, 58
police attack on the San Francisco
     Sanctuary District   59
political attitudes of young
     people   10
political imagination   8, 12–15
political violence   86, 128
Popper, Karl   23, 151
popularity of *Star Trek*   153
portrayal of humanity   1
positive peace   20–1, 65, 69–78,
     80, 83, 123
"post-racial" society   87
Prophet Muhammad   22, 113, 125
protests in Minneapolis,
     Minnesota   50
"proto post scarcity society"   96
pyramid of violence   19, 47, 57

racial capitalism   96–7
racial identity   82, 87, 92, 101
racial justice   8, 83, 88, 101
racism   2, 52, 55, 82, 86, 96–100
Ramose, Mogobe   121
Rawls, John   13
Rennix, Brianna   15
reproductive justice   10
Responsibility to Protect doctrine
     (R2P)   74
retribution/retributive justice   104–5,
     108–11, 114, 120, 125
retributive punishment   22, 110, 126
revenge   104–5, 108–11
Richmond, Oliver P.   70
Riordan, Richard   59
Robinson, Kim Stanley   128
Roddenberry, Gene   4, 16–18, 25,
     26, 45, 82, 89, 93
Roediger, David   98
Rwandan genocide of 1994   74